RESTRUCTURING THE LABOUR MARKET

CAMBRIDGE STUDIES IN SOCIOLOGY

Editors: R.M. Blackburn and K. Prandy

This series presents research findings of theoretical significance on subjects of social importance. It allows a wide variety of topics and approaches, though central themes are provided by economic life and social stratification. The format ranges from monographs reporting specific research to sets of original research papers on a common theme. The series is edited in Cambridge and contains books arising mainly from work carried out there. However, suitable books, wherever they originate, are included.

David Ashton, Malcolm Maguire and Mark Spilsbury
RESTRUCTURING THE LABOUR MARKET: THE IMPLICATIONS FOR YOUTH

Huw Beynon and R.M. Blackburn
PERCEPTIONS OF WORK

R.M. Blackburn and Michael Mann
THE WORKING CLASS IN THE LABOUR MARKET

K. Prandy, A. Stewart and R.M. Blackburn
WHITE-COLLAR UNIONISM
WHITE-COLLAR WORK

Janet Siltanen
LOCATING GENDER: THE STRUCTURING OF EMPLOYMENT AND DOMESTIC RESPONSIBILITIES

A. Stewart, K. Prandy and R.M. Blackburn
SOCIAL STRATIFICATION AND OCCUPATIONS

Peter Whalley
THE SOCIAL PRODUCTION OF TECHNICAL WORK

Restructuring the Labour Market

The Implications for Youth

David Ashton, Malcolm Maguire and Mark Spilsbury

MACMILLAN

First published 1990

Published by
THE MACMILLAN PRESS LTD
Houndmills, Basingstoke, Hampshire RG21 2XS
and London
Companies and representatives
throughout the world

Printed in Hong Kong

British Library Cataloguing in Publication Data
Ashton, D.N. (David Norman), *1942–*
Restructuring the Labour Market: Implications for Youth. (Cambridge Studies in Sociology).
1. Great Britain. Labour market. Participation of young persons
I. Title II. Maguire, Malcolm III. Spilsbury, Mark
IV. Series
331.3′4′0941

ISBN 0–333–45170–8
ISBN 0–333–45171–6 pbk

For Betty Jennings, whose commitment to our research group helped make this book possible

For Betty Jennings, whose commitment to our research group helped make this book possible

Contents

List of Figures

List of Tables

Acknowledgements

Our foremost debt in producing this book is to the hundreds of respondents, the managers, young employed and unemployed, who gave up their time to be interviewed by us. In this task we were fortunate to have the services of Diana Bowden, Pauline Dellow, Sue Kennedy, Geoff Stanley and Geoff Woodhead as researchers responsible for interviewing the young adults. Johnny Sung provided invaluable help with the computing of the work history data. As ever Betty Jennings provided our administrative back-up, typed the manuscript and maintained order in the research team. Many thanks are also due to Bob Blackburn, whose incisive comments helped sharpen up the presentation of our ideas.

We are grateful to the Economic and Social Research Council which funded the analysis of the Labour Force Survey data and the interviews with the large corporations, under grant number F00232118, and the Department of Employment and the MSC which funded the young adults study. The Department of Employment also funded the further analysis of the work histories data reported in Chapter 7. None of these organisations are responsible for the views expressed here.

David Ashton, Malcolm Maguire and Mark Spilsbury

Introduction

THE PROBLEM

The election of a Conservative Government in 1979 heralded a new era in the political and economic management of the United Kingdom. In response to an accelerating inflation rate, and a developing world recession, the new Government adopted radical monetarist policies. The resulting unemployment levels were on a scale not seen since the 1930s, with the impact on young people being especially severe. More recently, a greater economic buoyancy, coupled with demographic trends which have significantly decreased the numbers of young people entering the labour market, have seen youth unemployment fade from view as a topical issue. This book addresses the question of whether the effects of the recession were merely cyclical and epiphenomenal or whether they masked other underlying trends which were transforming the British economy and the labour market. It draws on the results of a series of research projects undertaken by the Labour Market Studies Group at the University of Leicester. Our findings indicate that not only has the demand for labour been fundamentally reshaped during the 1980s, but also that the part played by the policies of the Thatcher administration in generating change has not been as important as is widely believed. In sociological terms the role of the political process has been constrained by more deep-seated and fundamental social and economic processes. The book focuses especially on the examination of these longer-term processes of change as they were manifested in the transformation of the youth labour market.

One of our central concerns has been to establish what determines the overall demand for labour and the demand for the labour of youths in particular. In so doing, we have been able to differentiate between the effect of cyclical changes and those of more long-term processes of change. We have also been able to identify the source of these longer-term trends and their impact on the demand for the labour of adults and young people. This has led us to examine the emergence of global product markets, the relocation of capital, increasing industrial concentration and the effects of new technology. These broad structural changes are affecting all advanced industrial societies and are profoundly influencing the demand for labour. The impact of political changes will be assessed against the weight of these economic and social forces. In a British context this means evaluating the attempts by the Thatcher administration to introduce change in the field of education and youth training in its attempts to facilitate the process of industrial adjustment and to combat the problem of youth unemployment.

The results of our research suggest that we are currently witnessing a radical restructuring of the labour market in general and the youth labour market in particular. The immediate political concerns with youth unemployment and the measures introduced to combat it have directed attention away from the more fundamental underlying structural changes which have produced a mismatch between the supply flow of young people entering the labour market and the demands of employers for a highly educated labour force.

In focusing on these issues our research has involved detailed studies of the relationship between the youth and adult labour markets, and of the structure of the youth labour market. The linkages between the general demand for labour and the demand for youth labour, and how they generate pressures to segment the labour market have been investigated. In addition, the way in which the structure of the youth labour market is affected by the educational and training institutions has been considered. We believe that the ensuing analysis represents a significant contribution to our understanding of the segmentation of the labour market. It does this by furthering our understanding of the relationships between the various segments, as well as by showing how the composition of the segments and the relationships between them have developed in response to the broader economic and political changes. These processes are transforming the labour market and, through that, the British class structure.

The issues of labour demand and the structure and functioning of labour markets, which are addressed in this book, are conventionally approached from a number of academic disciplines. However, we argue that if we are to further our understanding of these issues an interdisciplinary approach is required. We have attempted to develop such an approach drawing predominantly on sociology and economics, with recent developments in labour market segmentation theory being used as the vehicle for integrating the contributions from the two disciplines.

Sources of Data

The analysis of the British labour market, and the arguments and policy recommendations which form the main focus of the book, are derived from the results of a number of research projects undertaken by the Labour Market Studies Group since 1977. Those which are of most relevance for the book are:

i) The 'Youth in the Labour Market' project (1977–80) involved interviews with a representative sample of 360 employers in three contrasting local labour markets; Leicester, Sunderland and St Albans. The interviews covered topics such as the recruitment and selection of young people, and opportunities for promotion and training.
ii) The 'Young Adults in the Labour Market' project (1982–84) involved structured interviews with a sample of 1786 18–24-year-olds in four local labour markets; Leicester, Stafford, Sunderland and St Albans. The sample excluded those who were in higher education at the time of interviewing, or had been educated to degree level. The four local labour markets were chosen to represent localities with contrasting industrial and occupational structures and levels of unemployment. Sunderland was representative of areas with a declining manufacturing base and high levels of unemployment. St Albans typified the more affluent South East with a high-tech manufacturing industry, a strong service sector and a low level of unemployment. Leicester was chosen for its fairly diverse industrial base and a level of unemployment that was close to the national average, while Stafford, which also had an average level of unemployment, was selected for its high proportion of non-manual workers. The samples from each individual area were representative of the locality, but when combined, also had the advantage of approximating the national distribution of the youth labour force in terms of age, sex and type of work entered. Throughout the book 'youth' refers to 16- and 17-year-olds and 'young adults' to 18-24-year-olds.
iii) The 'Changing Structure of the Youth Labour Market' project (1984–86) provides the main source of data for this book. The project had two distinct components. In the first, interviews were carried out in 40 major employing organisations, covering a wide range of industrial orders. Information was sought, through a series of semi-structured interviews with different levels of man-

agement, about the factors which determine the general demand for labour, the sources of structural change in the labour market and the reasons why employers prefer one type of labour to another. Large employers were chosen because of the power they exercise in determining the conditions upon which labour is recruited. Data on small and medium-sized firms, which employ the majority of 16- and 17-year-olds, had already been obtained from the 'Youth in the Labour Market' project, and was supplemented by other secondary sources to maintain a balance in our analysis.

The second component of the project was an analysis of the Labour Force Survey (LFS), a national data set. The aim of this analysis was to examine the effects of structural and cyclical changes in the demand for (youth) labour. The LFS data, which are collected by a household survey, are one of the few sources of information based on a national sample with a sufficiently disaggregated age breakdown to allow precise identification of changes in the occupational distribution of young people. Our analysis covered the years 1979–84, thereby enabling us to analyse the impact of the recession on the demand for youth labour. In bringing together the results of the two components our objective has been to use the findings from the interviews with employers to explain the changes revealed by the analysis of the LFS.

OUTLINE OF THE BOOK

Chapter 1 contains a discussion of some of the conceptual issues which informed our research. It also examines the implications which some of the findings have for the way in which we approach the study of the labour market in general and the youth labour market in particular. The findings from our research begin in Chapter 2. This contains the main results of the analysis of the LFS, which aimed to establish the location of youths within the labour market and to explore the adequacy of cyclical theories as explanations of the changes which took place during the recession. The results of that analysis suggest that 'structural' factors were of equal, if not greater significance than cyclical factors.

Chapter 3 examines the factors which impinge upon employers to determine the general demand for labour. Conventional, neo-classical economics postulates that the level of wages is the most important of these factors. However, we argue that other factors, notably changes induced in the product market, the actions of the state, the employment-output relationship and patterns of ownership are more important than wage levels in determining variations in the general level of employment.

Chapter 4 begins the analysis of the factors which determine the type of labour recruited by employers. It is argued that institutional structures, especially those of the educational and training systems, play a leading role in shaping both employers' recruitment decisions and the workers' subsequent experience of the labour market. Yet employers remain powerful agents in differentiating labour supply, especially through their ability to incorporate into their selection process their attitude towards what they perceive to be the personal characteristics of different types of labour. Chapter 5 explores further the power of employers to structure the labour market, but concentrates on youths, and explains why they are concentrated in some parts of the labour market and excluded from others.

In Chapter 6 we identify four major processes which are responsible for some of the structural changes noted in Chapter 2. These are: (i) the growth of global product markets; (ii) increasing industrial concentration; (iii) the introduction of new technology; and (iv) political changes, especially those in the institutional structure of the youth labour market. One effect of these processes is to induce employers to switch their recruitment from one type of labour to another. We argue that these four processes, together with the relocation of capital to low labour-cost countries, are responsible for the restructuring of the labour market. The chapter concludes with a discussion of the implications of this restructuring for the demand for youth labour, while acknowledging that the effects of the current restructuring of the labour market extend well beyond the youth labour market.

The effects of labour market segmentation on the young adults' experience of the labour market are identified in Chapter 7. This chapter examines the pattern of movement of young people both within and between segments and assesses the impact of the recession on the different segments. It also demonstrates some of the distinctive features of the youth labour market and its relationship with the labour market for adults. Chapter 8 develops these themes in the context of the local labour market, by showing how the broader processes of change which are transforming the national labour market have a differential impact on its constituent segments. It is this process which is so significant in creating the local labour market effect, that is the independent influence which local labour markets exert on life chances. We argue that these broader processes of change are radically transforming the terms and conditions of employment of a large section of the working class. In some localities this is leading to the exclusion of sections of the working class from effective participation in the labour market.

A further theme developed in the book concerns the relationship between the institutional structures which influence the supply of labour and the underlying processes of change at work in transforming the labour market. The final chapter explores the policy implications of what is argued to be a growing mismatch between the two. It proposes that the existing institutional structures are helping to produce a large pool of relatively unskilled youth labour for which there is a declining demand. At the same time these institutional structures are hindering the creation of a more highly educated labour force for which there is an increasing demand. As existing policy measures are failing to address these questions, alternative measures are suggested to resolve the problem.

1 Conceptualising the Youth Labour Market

INTRODUCTION

> People engaged in empirical research often put forward propositions or theories whose merit is that they are truer than others, or, to use a less hallowed term, that they are more adequate, more consistent, both with observations and in themselves. In general terms, one might say it is characteristic of these scientific, as distinct from non-scientific forms of solving problems, that in the acquisition of knowledge, questions emerge and are solved as a result of an uninterrupted two-way traffic between two layers of knowledge: that of general ideas, theories or models and that of observations and perceptions of specific events . . . It is the objective of scientists, one might say, to develop a steadily expanding body of theories or models and an equally expanding body of observations about specific events by means of a continuous, critical confrontation to greater and greater congruity with each other. (Elias, 1956)

Throughout the course of the research reported in this volume we have attempted to explore a number of such general ideas about the structure of the youth labour market, which are prevalent in the literature and assess their adequacy in the light of our research findings. Cyclical and structural theories provide radically different ways of conceptualising change in the labour market. Similarly, neo-classical economics and segmentation theory provide different interpretations of the structure of the labour market. In engaging in the two-way traffic of which Elias speaks, our primary task has been to establish the general applicability or otherwise of the various models and to modify them, where necessary, in accordance with our observations of specific events.

The present debates about these theories can be viewed as being informed by three broad paradigms, the first of which is rooted in neo-classical economic theory and systems theory in sociology. Here, the fundamental assumption is that society and the economy are part of a social system which is guided by self-regulating mechanisms. Any disturbance to the system, such as the emergence of mass unemployment which occurred in Britain during the period 1979 to 1981, initiates mechanisms which restore the equilibrium of the system. Thus, with regard to rising levels of unemployment, neo-classical economics posits that market mechanisms, if left free from intervention, will restore a natural level of unemployment to the economy.

The second paradigm emerges from the Keynesian school, which used the concept of equilibrium but does not imply that the equilibrium position would be a position of 'full employment'.

In contrast to these ideas, sociologists following the tradition of Comte, Marx and, more recently, Elias, and economists following Marx and Schumpeter, believe that society, rather than having any 'natural' or 'normal' equilibrium state, evolves in a process of continuous change. The concept of equilibrium, and its assumption of a fundamentally static society, is discarded in favour of a belief that change is endemic in society, and is itself structured.[1] Also, as societies are interdependent, they can only be understood in terms of their relationship with each other. Segmentation and long wave theories, which have particular relevance to the labour market, have emerged from this tradition.

Without in any way claiming to be able to resolve disputes over the validity or respectability of these opposing paradigms, we will seek to provide evidence, arguments and hypotheses which will inform them. The focus of this chapter will be on an issue over which these different opinions clearly conflict and will set out the approach we have adopted in this book.

The study of the youth labour market in Britain exemplifies these diverging theoretical standpoints. Explanations of recent developments in the demand for youth labour, and, especially, of the dramatic upsurge in youth unemployment in the early 1980s, may be placed in two opposing camps. On the one hand are those who subscribe to the notion that changes in the demand for youth labour are attributable to variations in the economic cycle. On the other hand are the structuralists, who believe that the post-1979 recession merely exacerbated long-term trends in industrial and occupational structures. It hardly needs saying that this dichotomy represents a gross over-simplification of the complexity of approaches to this issue. Nevertheless, this division between the cyclicalists and the structuralists provides an appropriate starting point for the ensuing discussion.

THEORETICAL APPROACHES

Cyclical Theories

Most economists, in both Britain and the USA, have for many years assumed that the youth labour market is subject to the same economic forces, and reacts to them in the same way, as the adult labour market. British evidence shows that the employment of young people is particularly sensitive to shifts in the general level of demand (Makeham, 1980; Layard, 1982; Raffe, 1984). By analysing fluctuations in the level of youth unemployment, compared to that of adult unemployment, for the period 1959–77, Makeham estimated that for every 1 per cent increase in overall male unemployment, male youth unemployment rose by 1.7 per cent (Makeham, 1980, p. 42). For female youth unemployment the sensitivity was even more pronounced, increasing by 3 per cent for every 1 per cent rise in overall female unemployment. In the same way, when an economic upturn occurred, young people were recruited in disproportionately greater numbers than adults, thereby generating a faster reduction in their level of unemployment. Freeman and Wise (1982) reached the same conclusion when studying youth unemployment in the USA.

Drawing on this, and other evidence, Raffe has argued strongly that the youth and adult labour markets are undifferentiated. Using a quasi shift-share analysis, he showed that adverse industrial or structural shifts could only account for 1.3 per cent of the increase in the level of youth unemployment between 1979 and 1983, during which time the number of jobs taken by school-leavers fell by 45 per cent. He therefore discounted the validity of structural explanations of youth unemployment, and subsequently commented:

> Most of the arguments which attribute the recent rise of youth unemployment to structural economic changes refer to shifts in either the industrial or occupational structure of the demand for labour. It has been shown above that changes in industrial structure have had very little effect on recent levels of youth unemployment. The evidence for an effect of changes in occupational structure is more substantial but nevertheless equivocal. The impact of both types of change is in any case likely to have been substantially cushioned by the flexibility of the labour market in switching recruitment between age groups. Moreover, the different industrial and occupational changes have had different and often

> opposing effects on the demand for youth labour. Had aggregate levels of unemployment remained constant since 1970, there is little reason to believe that youth unemployment would have been significantly affected by these changes. The *net* explanation is therefore small. (Raffe, 1986, p. 57)

Structural Theories

Briefly stated, the structuralists believe that the disadvantaged position of young people in the labour market is due to the concentration of the jobs available to them in a limited number of occupational and industrial orders. As, generally, employers do not regard different types of labour as being easily substitutable, then any modifications in these entry points will have important implications for the demand for youth labour. School-leavers will face a reduced number of job opportunities if young people's employment is disproportionately located in declining industries or occupations, or if there is a displacement of young workers by other types of labour, such as older part-time workers. In general, structural explanations attribute rising youth unemployment to factors over and above the declining aggregate demand for labour generated by the recession.

The writers we group together under the 'structuralist' banner would not necessarily agree on a common interpretation of what was meant by the term 'structural'. Indeed, a number of different positions have emerged, of which four are identified below.[2]

(i) In the earlier work of two of the authors (Ashton and Maguire, 1983) the term 'structural' was used to refer to long-term changes, such as the decline of manufacturing industries and the growth of service industries, the process of qualification inflation, with its associated upgrading of occupations, and employers' internal reorganisation, resulting in the displacement of youth labour by adult female part-time workers, which were all claimed to have adversely affected the employment opportunities for 16-year-old school-leavers.

(ii) Taking up Braverman's deskilling thesis, Frith (1980) and Finn (1983 and 1987) have argued that changes in the division of labour are divesting many of the jobs done by young people of their skill content. This is particularly true in the service sector, which increasingly demands a disciplined but unskilled young workforce.

(iii) Others argue that skill levels in the economy have risen, thereby reducing the number of jobs available to unqualified young people. A more sophisticated version of this idea appears in Roberts *et al.* (1986):

> The evidence from all official sources, and from our employers' surveys suggests that, while trends in the 1980s have varied between firms and occupations, the net change is more consistent with the upgrading than degrading thesis. Between 1971 and 1981 in Britain the numbers employed in all white-collar grades increased and decreased in all manual strata. Our survey findings suggest that these trends will continue.

They also distinguish between the contribution of sector and occupational shifts and show how each is making an independent contribution to reshaping Britain's occupational structure. Overall, they argue that occupation rather than sector-shifts is likely to become the main source of future upgrading. Among the factors put forward to explain this upgrading are the introduction of new technology and the political context of the firm, when managers are encouraged to use the technology to enhance their status and control.

(iv) Changes in the relationship between employment and output, often as a consequence of the introduction of new technology, have led to what Roberts has called 'jobless growth' (Roberts *et al.*, 1986a). Referring to manufacturing industries in the early 1980s Roberts says:

> employment trends in, and forecasts by our companies indicate that general unemployment may well have become structural by virtue of its capacity to persist, despite economic growth, and that young people are bearing a disproportionate share of the burden. (p. 9)

Firms were reporting an increase in business but not in employment as new technology was enabling them to produce more with a smaller workforce. A similar trend was identified in the financial sector in the late 1970s (Ashton, Maguire and Garland, 1982).

In exploring these ideas in Chapter 2, the results of our analysis do not provide unequivocal support for either school of thought. Cyclical theory provides a partial explanation of some of the changes which have occurred in the demand for youth labour over the recession, but as a general explanation it is shown to have many inadequacies. Similarly, some of the hypotheses we identified as structuralist proved to be adequate as explanations of specific changes, but totally inadequate as general propositions. The displacement of youths by adults is taking place, but only in limited parts of the labour market. There is evidence of deskilling, particularly in retailing, but this does not preclude a process of upgrading of skills in other areas such as engineering, and, while technological change may appear in the short-term to produce jobless growth, this is not necessarily the case, providing the firms can expand their product markets. What our results have enabled us to do is to specify the conditions under which the various structural changes operate. However, these are not the only processes of change which are affecting the youth labour market. In Chapter 6 we identify a number of changes, operating at different levels, which incorporate aspects of these structural processes, but which extend beyond them to account for the restructuring of the labour market. Among these trends are the relocation of capital, the impact of global markets, changes in technology and employers' labour management strategies, the increasing industrial concentration in parts of the service sector, the impact of political changes, and new forms of government intervention. All of these processes operate in the context of an ongoing struggle between capital and labour.

In our research, the attempt to extend the analysis of these sources of change beyond those currently considered in the sociological literature on labour markets was influenced by the work of the Labour Studies Group at the University of Cambridge (Rubery *et al.*, 1984, and Wilkinson, 1981). Questions stemming from their development of labour market segmentation theory were used to structure the interviews with employers. For sociologists, unaccustomed to exploring the significance of product markets and wage levels on the demand for labour, this opened up a fertile field of enquiry, and, importantly, led to a more systematic exploration of what were discovered to be some of the most powerful sources of change. In addition, their incorporation of power relations between management and labour, and the recognition of the ways in which social, political and institutional factors shape both the demand and supply of labour has opened up an important dialogue between sociologists and economists. Hopefully, this book will contribute towards that dialogue.[3]

Competition between Youths and Adults

Any attempt to examine neo-classical and segmentation theories immediately raises questions about the nature of competition and the labour market. Neo-classical economics conceptualises the labour market as relatively undifferentiated and regulated by the laws of supply and demand.[4] From this perspective, youths represent just one form of labour which competes with adults for the various jobs that are available. In its more refined versions, some youths are seen to be at a disadvantage in this situation as they lack the human capital, which is seen as essential in order to reap the higher rewards to be obtained in the exchange of labour for income.

Labour market segmentation provides a very different conceptualisation of the labour market. Its proponents argue that pressures of supply and demand do influence the purchase and sale of labour and the conditions under which labour is utilised. However, these pressures and the social and economic forces they generate are seen to operate in different ways in each of the various segments. For example, neo-classical theory would predict that an increase in the level of unemployment would lead to a condition of surplus labour which in turn would create pressure to reduce the level of wages. A fall in the price of labour would then induce employers to hire more, so raising the general level of employment back to the original equilibrium position at which full employment is obtained. In contrast, labour market segmentation theory suggests that because economic and social forces operate differentially between segments, an increase in the level of unemployment in one segment will not necessarily affect either wages or employment levels in another. Indeed, what our evidence suggests very strongly is that in certain segments an increase in the level of unemployment will have little or no effect on the behaviour of employers and workers in other segments. This is especially so in the higher segments where the conditions and level of wages are determined primarily by the institutional arrangements which govern internal labour markets, such as those typically found in the professions and large corporations. Precisely because these forces operate differentially across segments, it is difficult for workers to move between them. Thus, one of the consequences of labour market segmentation is that once workers enter a given segment they tend to remain in them.

The early versions of labour market segmentation theory postulated a two-fold division between primary and secondary labour markets, with different processes determining the allocation of income in each of the segments. In this version of the theory, youths were seen as competing with adults only in the secondary sector (Osterman, 1980), as they were excluded from the primary sector. As dual labour market theory evolved into segmentation theory, the simple dichotomy between primary and secondary markets was abandoned in favour of a more complex set of divisions (Rubery *et al.*, 1984). The primary market was divided into independent and subordinate sectors. Youths and females were no longer lumped together as being confined to the secondary labour market. However, while it was recognised that the labour market was most appropriately conceptualised as consisting of a variety of segments, the precise number and composition of these segments continues to be a focus of dispute (Sengenberger, 1988).

In the 'Youth in the Labour Market' research project, Ashton, Maguire and Garland (1982) attempted to refine this conceptualisation of the relationship between the youth and adult labour markets by making a distinction between the different levels at which competition takes place in the labour market. These were as follows:

(a) at the *individual* level, competition takes place between any two or more people who seek access to the same jobs.

(b) at the *group* level, competition takes place between specific categories or groups of people (for example, youths/adults, full-timers/part-timers, males/females, blacks/whites), whose labour is perceived by employers as having certain qualities in common. The employer makes the decision about whether to recruit from any one specific group in the light of the company's demand for labour and what are seen as the shared characteristics of the various groups that compete in the labour market. These decisions are often made at the higher levels of the employing organisation, and the outcome determines the mode of competition that operates at the point of entry to the employing organisation.

With regard to the competition between young people and adults, these decisions give rise to three possible modes of competition:

(i) where competition is restricted to young people. As adults are excluded from competing this provides young people with a *sheltered* point of entry. For example, apprenticeships have age restrictions on entry. In 1985 these accounted for approximately 20 per cent of the jobs entered by young people, although these are not the only jobs with age restrictions on entry.

(ii) where competition is restricted to adults. At the point of entry to the organisation such jobs are *closed* to young people. This is often the case with respect to semi-skilled and unskilled jobs in manufacturing industry where employers seek to recruit married adults with family responsibilities. Our own estimates suggest that over 50 per cent of such jobs are closed to young people.

(iii) where young people compete directly with adults. This creates *exposed* points of entry to the labour market for young people.

By determining the kinds of job to which young people have access and the extent to which they compete with adults at the point of entry, we argue that these modes of competition help give the youth labour market its distinctive characteristics.

This conceptual distinction sensitises us to the fact that substitution at the individual level is likely to be restricted to those jobs where youths are exposed to competition from adults. Substitution at group level is only likely to take place following upheavals in the labour market, in the form of changing skill requirements, the emergence of skill shortages, or excess supply of labour. At other times employers are content to continue recruiting from those groups which have traditionally provided workers for particular occupations. They have no reason to consider alternative policies.

These distinctions also have important implications for our understanding of the relationship between the youth and adult labour markets. While youths and adults do compete in parts of the labour market it is a mistake to regard this as evidence of competition throughout the labour market. A number of neo-classical economists in both Britain (Makeham, 1980; Wells, 1983) and the USA (Freeman and Wise, 1982) have made this mistake. It has been most clearly articulated in the work of a sociologist, David Raffe (1987, p. 241). He argues that young people are broadly in the same labour market(s) as adults. Age discrimination is seen as being far less significant than sex discrimination and where employers do discriminate in terms of age they do so flexibly. Raffe specifies three factors which affect employers' decisions in this respect. These are:

i) the training costs associated with recruiting inexperienced young people;
ii) young people's personal and behavioural characteristics, which are often regarded as undesirable in comparison with those of adults;
iii) the relative wage costs of young people.

For these reasons, young workers are regarded as less employable than adults and hence occupy the rear of the job queue.

The main reason why such a view is inadequate is that it is based on a fundamental misunderstanding of the forces of age discrimination.

Age discrimination is crucial in determining the jobs for which competition is restricted to young people, those from which young people are excluded, and those for which young people can compete with adults. Chapter 5 will detail our research findings which show the range of jobs for which employers would not consider recruiting 16-year-old school-leavers, and their reasons for this policy. Even the introduction of free youth labour, through the Youth Opportunities Programme (YOP) and later the Youth Training Scheme (YTS) has had little effect in opening up a greater range of jobs to 16-year-olds. This discrimination does not result from the personal whims and idiosyncracies of recruiters, but from sources such as the organisation of the production process, the firm's position in the product market, its technology, and the relationship between management and workers. In addition, powerful institutional factors, such as the apprenticeship system, and the organisation of YTS, have the effect of imposing age discrimination on employers' practices.[5]

In some instances, positive discrimination in favour of employing young people rather than adults works to the advantage of young people. Employers may take group level decisions to exclude adults from consideration. Two factors may encourage such decisions. One is the institutional regulation of training, which encourages, or even enforces, the recruitment of school or college leavers for positions as trainees. The other is the pressure on some employers, operating in competitive product markets, to recruit youths because of the low cost of their labour relative to adults. These issues are dealt with in more detail in Chapter 5.[6]

In terms of the distinctions made above, it is clear that the only area where youths and adults compete at the individual level is for those jobs about which employers had not made prior decisions to either exclude or positively discriminate in favour of youths. There can be no doubt that such jobs constitute a majority of positions actually entered by youths, but they are unlikely to constitute a majority of all jobs that are available on the labour market at any one point in time, given that some jobs are exclusively for youths while many more are closed to them. It is in this limited part of the labour market that the flexibility of which Raffe speaks comes into operation. It is here that in times of high unemployment employers may discriminate against youths, possibly because of their personal and behavioural characteristics, as a plentiful supply of experienced adults is available. Indeed, Roberts *et al.* (1986) found that during the recession, in those jobs where youths and adults competed, employers opted for the experienced adults. However, at group level, the underlying sources of age segmentation continue to operate, leading employers to exclude youths from many jobs and preferring them for others. The mistake is to generalise from the changes which take place in one area of the labour market to the labour market as a whole.

We are not arguing that the outcome of these group level decisions are immutable. In fact, the results presented in Chapter 6 suggest that there are a number of changes under way at that level. Perhaps the most significant is the substitution of youths for married females taking place in jobs in the retail and hotel and catering sector. This practice has been encouraged by the introduction of YTS. In view of this it would be misleading to regard the existing parameters which determine areas where youths and adults do and do not compete at group level, as in any sense fixed. The history of labour in retail and administration already bears witness to the ability of employers to switch between sources of labour as they seek to reduce costs. These have been shifts from the employment of males to females in clerical work and from skilled males to unskilled females in retail. Although these are, in general, long-term trends, the impact of YTS shows how they can be accelerated by political intervention in the short term.

THE SEGMENTATION OF THE YOUTH LABOUR MARKET

Our concern to identify the outcomes of group-level decisions led us to view the youth labour market as segmented. However, it did not resolve the problem about the number of segments to be identified. To address this problem we drew on three separate sources of information.

Within British sociology there are a number of studies of the transition from school to work (Ashton and Field, 1976; Jenkins, 1983; Brown, 1987) which emphasised the cultural divisions which youths and their parents make between different types of working-class and middle-class jobs. These studies pointed towards clear divisions between unskilled and semi-skilled jobs as one category, skilled manual and clerical jobs as a second, and professional, managerial, technical and administrative jobs as the third. Each of these categories was characterised by different conditions of work, levels of income and career chances, all of which were recognised by both youths and parents. Unfortunately, these studies were almost exclusively concerned with males and, until recently, little attention was paid to understanding the distinctive experience of females.[7]

A second source of information derived from our discussions with representatives of employers. These suggested that employers also operated with clear distinctions between the characteristics of males and females, unskilled and semi-skilled labour as opposed to skilled manual labour and of clerical as opposed to professional and managerial employees. The criteria for the distinctions is explained later in this Chapter. These categories frequently formed the parameters within which they discussed and answered questions on the recruitment, employment and training of labour. They also corresponded to major divisions within employing organisations' internal labour markets. The only difference between these and the categories used by youths and their parents was the recognition of clerical and junior white-collar work as a distinctive category. From a theoretical perspective, employers' definitions are important because of the employer's role as a powerful occupational gatekeeper. They play a major part in controlling entry to labour market segments. In addition, through their influence over the structure of internal labour markets, they are able to determine the pattern of movement available to youths once they enter a particular segment.

Finally, the results of our study of young adults who had had up to eight years' experience of the labour market provided the opportunity to see how far these categories, and those drawn from the literature, corresponded to the actual pattern of job movement found among those who entered the labour market. To operationalise them a modified version of the Hope/Goldthorpe scale was used. The Hope/Goldthorpe scale was employed as a heuristic device as we were not primarily concerned with the ranking of occupations. The aim was to find a set of categories which most closely approximated the distinctive patterns of movement over time that were observed in our sample.

A qualification should be made about the categorisation of sales workers. Should they be classified with clerical, rather than semi-skilled or unskilled manual workers? Analysis of recruitment criteria, the learning time of the jobs, the characteristics of those entering the occupation, their chances of unemployment and the direction of job movement, suggest that the majority are more appropriately conceptualised as part of the lower segment of less-skilled workers. Exceptions to this are those workers (usually males) who are recruited as potential managers.

Taken together, these three sources of information suggested that the youth labour market is most appropriately conceptualised as having eight major labour market segments. These are:

i) the higher segments consisting of professionals, administrators, managers and technicians;
ii) the clerical segment consisting of junior office workers, secretaries, clerks, etc;
iii) the skilled manual segment of apprentice engineers and craft workers, hairdressers, etc.,
iv) the lower segment consisting of operatives in manufacturing industry, labourers and service sector operatives such as cleaners, traditional shop sales jobs, check-out operators, shelf-fillers, waiters and waitresses, etc.

Each of these segments is further divided by gender to create the eight divisions which our results suggest are the main ones.

The gender division is important because the four horizontal dimensions which reflect underlying skill differences are not simple mirror images of each other. As noted above, the number of male skilled manual jobs is much higher than in the corresponding female segment, which is indicative of the overall differences in the structure of opportunities available for males and females. Similarly, the level of income of females entering skilled jobs is much lower than that of males in the corresponding segment. In the higher segments, the jobs to which females have access such as in nursing, tend to be of a lower status and less well paid than those to which males have access. Even in the lower segment, female jobs are characterised by far fewer chances of promotion than are available to males. In this sense the overall configuration of the male and female segments creates a very different opportunity structure for the two sexes.

The situation is further complicated by the fact that at certain points, the male and female segments overlap. Respondents were asked whether there was any member of the opposite sex employed in the same job they did. In the highest segment almost three-quarters of the females reported that there was, whereas only two-fifths of males reported this to be the case. This implies that males faced much less competition from the opposite sex than females did. By contrast, in skilled manual work only approximately one-quarter of males and females gave a positive response. Here, quite clearly, gender segregation was at its greatest. In the lower segment segregation was still evident in that the majority of both sexes were working in single-sex work groups, although the degree of segregation did vary considerably from one local labour market to another. The results suggest that in most segments there is relatively little competition at group level between males and females. This may be because employers restrict recruitment to one of the sexes, or the other, or because the majority of applicants are of one sex. The overlap tends to take place in certain professional and clerical jobs especially in the public sector, or in the lower segments where the labour required is unskilled and interchangeable as in the case of shelf-fillers, cashiers, fast food operatives, and so on.

Entry to the Labour Market Segments

Finally, if parents and youths and employers recognised major divisions in the labour market which were in turn reflected in the pattern of job movement of young adults, we would expect entry to each of these segments to be determined on the basis of different criteria. This is exactly what we have found. Our earlier research on employers' recruitment practices had revealed that when recruiting for the higher segments most employers, or the professional bodies which control entry, regard '0'-level and 'A'-level educational qualifications as essential. These qualifications perform a screening function which helps reduce the potential number of applicants to those who are thought to possess the appropriate level of ability. Beyond that, selection decisions are made on the basis of evidence about the personality and attitudes of the applicants, often with special attention paid to their ambition and future potential. In the middle segments, lower level educational qualifications ('0'-level or CSE) may be required, although they are sometimes dispensed with. They enable employers to focus their recruitment drive on a particular ability level. In the case of craft skills, independent evidence of such practical skills is often sought, but in all cases the final decision is made on the basis of evidence of suitable personality and attitudinal characteristics deemed necessary to ensure that they persevere with the training. In the lower segments, educational qualifications are often ignored, as employers seek only the requisite personality and attitudes. The personal characteristics required may be very different to those deemed appropriate in the higher segments. Here employers require a positive commitment to work, reliability and an ability to accept discipline. Indeed, at this level the possession of educational qualifications may prevent an individual from getting a job as they may be perceived to be evidence of a degree of ambition which would not be appropriate to such a routine or 'dead-end' job. It is on the basis of these criteria that recruitment decisions are made.

Taken together, these findings provide powerful evidence for the existence of distinct labour market segments. In Chapters 2 and 6 we argue that there are important changes taking place in the relative size and composition of the various segments. In Chapter 7 we argue that once entered each of these segments exerts an independent influence on the pattern of job movement and other aspects of the young adult's experience of the labour market. In Chapter 8 we shift our focus to the local level and show how the relative size and composition of the various labour market segments determine the life chances of young people.

THE INSTITUTIONAL REGULATION OF THE LABOUR MARKET

Group level decisions, and hence the structure of labour market segments, are also influenced by the prevailing institutional structures which regulate the labour market. Foremost among these are the regulations governing training. Yet while these regulations play a powerful role in shaping employers' decisions about which type of labour to recruit, they have not, until recently, formed a significant focus of academic enquiry. On a theoretical level Marsden (1986) has argued that the competitive markets of neo-classical economic theory are only found to operate for casual and unskilled labour. For skilled labour the markets are institutionally regulated either in the form of occupational labour markets or firm internal labour markets.

Occupational labour markets distribute transferable skills and rely for their effective operation on considerable institutional underpinning. Institutional underpinning provides the basis for the establishment of standards of skill performance, training and job descriptions which can be recognised by all employers and workers alike. It operates through employer/union agreements and/or state licensing and ensures that the costs of producing such transferable skills are shared. However, these labour markets are inherently unstable and in the absence of strong institutional support the tendency is for firms to establish company internal labour markets. Where these occur the firms use their own internal labour markets to design pay and progression structures to discourage internally trained staff from moving. Where institutionally occupational labour markets exist the range of discretion available to employers in determining not just whom to recruit and when to recruit but also in the internal organisation and design of their own firms is reduced. Thus, these institutional pressures provide another important source of labour market segmentation, for in socialising workers into either occupational or firm internal labour markets they simultaneously create barriers to movement by closing jobs within the occupations or firms to outsiders.

Labour market segments also exert a powerful influence on the educational system, while the educational system structures the flow of young people into them. Thus, Maurice, Sellier and Silvestre (1986) have argued that this institutional regulation of labour markets generates a distinctive set of relations which link the education, training and industrial relations systems of each society. By comparing education training and employing organisations in France and Germany, Maurice *et al.* (1986) have demonstrated at the empirical level the significance of differences in the educational and vocational systems for the internal organisation of the firm and vice versa. Their work suggests that while the French system tends to be organised around the principle of firm internal labour markets, the German system is organised around that of institutionally regulated occupational labour markets.

Our results suggest that in Britain, large parts of the manufacturing sector, together with the construction industry, approximate the institutionally regulated occupational labour markets, while in most of the service sector training is provided through firm internal labour markets. In this respect the British system of training is an uneasy compromise between the two alternative forms of provision. Thus, the institutional regulation of occupational labour markets through the apprenticeship system, distinguishes it from the French and Canadian systems which rely more extensively on internal labour markets to provide training. This has important consequences for the age at which young people leave school and start training in the three societies. However, when compared with the German apprenticeship system, which is more comprehensive and trains to higher standards, the British occupational labour markets appear less well regulated and confined to a restricted number of industries such as engineering, printing, hairdressing, and the motor trades.

While the model advocated by the Aix school represents an important advance in our thinking, its main shortfall is the failure to incorporate the family as one of the crucial institutions regulating the supply of labour. As most of the extended training that is currently available is provided for males, models which incorporate educational and training institutions without also incorporating the family tend to focus only on the experience of males. In Chapter 4 we explore this question in greater depth showing how the position of a person in the family is important in determining why males are recruited into the more prestigious training positions and why females are excluded.

Our results also suggest that the institutional structures which currently regulate the British labour market may now be anachronistic. They were developed in the course of attempts to regulate the supply of labour for what were previously labour intensive methods of production. We argue that given the underlying direction of change identified in Chapters 2 and 6, these institutional structures are rapidly becoming inappropriate. The policy implications of this mismatch are discussed in Chapter 9.

CONCLUSION

Our attempt to engage in this two-way traffic between general ideas, theories or models and the observation of specific events, of which Elias speaks, has, we hope, provided a more adequate basis for conceptualising the youth labour market and its relationship with the adult labour market. In particular, we hope to have improved our understanding of the relationship between patterns of labour market segmentation and the educational and training institutions.

Our objectives are to take a number of theories and models from sociology and economics and explore their adequacy in providing explanations of the contemporary labour market. We find that as individual theories they ultimately fail. Whilst they offer ideas and hypotheses, which are useful in their own right, as general theoretical explanations they are all flawed. However, if we were to stop our intellectual activity at that point we would produce nothing more than a set of disparate hypotheses. In an attempt to move beyond that and so contribute towards the expansion of the general theories or models which exhibit a greater congruity with observations of specific events, we have focused on those general ideas which form the basis of segmentation theory.

We have used segmentation theory as the basis for integrating the results of this two-way traffic. In this respect another of our aims has been to expand the range of observations which segmentation theory can help us understand. Thus, one outcome of our research has been to show the utility of conceptualising the youth labour market as segmented. Once that is accepted one can, using the analytical framework provided by segmentation theory, ask more precise questions about the impact of the various components of cyclical and structural change on the size and compositon of the youth and adult labour market and the relationship between its various segments. We can start to explore, in a more systematic manner, the relationship between labour market structures and the provision of education and training. We believe that the measure of the adequacy of these ideas is not just that they provide a more comprehensive explanation of what is happening to the youth and adult labour markets, but also that they help refine our understanding of social policy. It is for this reason that we conclude our analysis with a discussion of the policy implication in Chapter 9.

NOTES

1. In Neo-classical economics, the concept of an equilibrium is only used as an analytic tool to show in which direction the economy would move if a variable changes, *ceteris paribus*. The fact that the economy is in a constant state of flux is accepted. Our argument is that such a conceptual appratus leads the observer to perceive change as a movement back to the equilibrium. In the case of those social scientists who focus on development or change, their conceptual apparatus leads them to perceive change as structured, as containing its own dynamic.
2. Raffe (1986) identified five: industrial shifts, occupational shifts, upskilling, deskilling and competition from married women.
3. There is now a developing literature on this theme, see for example Ashton, 1986; Marsden, 1986; Dale, 1987.
4. Although the idea of non-competing groups was first developed by Cairnes (1874) and is still used in theoretical discussions (Sapsford, 1981), it has not been developed in empirical studies of the youth labour market.
5. These sources of age discrimination do not figure prominently in neo-classical accounts of the labour market, because of the assumption of an open market in which all groups compete.
6. Although the idea of positive discrimination at group level in favour of new entrants is a simple one, it is very difficult to operationalise in practice. The reason for this is that while some jobs have occupational titles, such as 'apprentice', which enable them to be identified as youth jobs, many do not. Many of those who enter the professions start as trainees, in positions which are only filled by young people, but the

occupational titles we conventionally use to categorise them do not enable us to distinguish them as part of the youth labour market. They are usually categorised just as members of professions. Yet other occupational titles may contain both starting positions for young people and final career destinations for adults. The work of Stewart *et al.* (1980) has shown how this is the case for male clerks. Young people enter these jobs as a means of gaining experience with the probability that they will lead to higher positions in a different occupational category. Our results suggest that this is also the case for many of the sales jobs entered by males. Similarly, dead-end jobs for which employers only recruit youths are not always easily identifiable from occupational titles. However, in spite of these operational difficulties, it is clear in practice that there are a large number of occupations for which employers only consider youths as potential recruits.

7. For recent studies of females see Griffin (1985) and Cockburn (1987).

2 The Impact of the Recession

LABOUR MARKET TRENDS

Any attempt to assess the impact of structural or cyclical change over a given time period has to be set in the context of the longer-term changes which have been occurring in the general labour market. One of the most significant in Great Britain has been the decline of the manufacturing sector as a source of employment and the continued growth of the service sector. The decline in employment in manufacturing, which was evident throughout the 1970s, was accelerated by the subsequent recession.[1] In 1979 approximately seven million people were employed in the manufacturing industry, whereas by 1983 that figure had fallen to five and a half million.[2] Even after the recession, the fall in employment in manufacturing continued until 1987, since when it has stabilised at around five million.

In Britain, as in other advanced industrial societies, employment in the service sector has continued to increase, rising from just over thirteen million in 1979 to almost fifteen million in 1989, although there was a small decrease over the period 1980–83. While the fall in employment levels in manufacturing has been fairly general throughout the various industries, this has not been the case in the service sector. Growth since 1979 has been uneven and has been most significant in Financial Services, with a 39.5 per cent increase, and, to a lesser extent, in Hotels and Catering (a 9.7 per cent increase), and Other Services (7.3 per cent increase). By contrast, employment in Transport and Communication has fallen, while Distribution has shown a small growth.

This shift in the sectoral location of employment is associated with two other structural changes in the labour market which are also common to other advanced industrial societies, namely the growth of part-time employment and the increasing participation of females. In 1971, 15 per cent of all employees were working part-time. This figure had risen to 24 per cent by 1989. The decline of manufacturing industry has had a disproportionate impact on male full-time employees, whose jobs were lost in large numbers during the height of the recession, and continue to be reduced. The new part-time jobs which have emerged in the service sector have largely been filled by women. Growth in the availability of part-time jobs accounted for all the increase in the number of employees in employment during 1986, with females taking 80 per cent of the additional part-time jobs. These trends in the types of job becoming available have led to the participation rate of females in the labour force increasing from 38 per cent in 1971 to 45 per cent in 1987.

Another fundamental change in the structure of the labour force which has occurred in all industrial societies has been the growth in the number and proportion of workers in managerial, professional and technical occupations. This tendency has long been noted in the literature (Bendix, 1963). Our own analysis of the Labour Force Survey data shows that during the period of the recession, this trend continued. In a period when there was a major contraction in the overall size of the labour force, the three orders of Professional, Administrative and Scientific workers increased by some 16.6 per cent. In addition, the number of Managerial and Selling workers increased by 11.6 per cent, although some of this may have been due to reclassification and the shift to self-employment (Spilsbury, Maguire and Ashton, 1986). Other studies have documented this trend and predicted its continuation into the 1990s (Goldthorpe and Payne, 1986; Rajan and Pearson, 1986).

At the other end of the occupational hierarchy, unskilled manual jobs, especially those of operatives in manufacturing, have been in long-term decline. Again this is a trend common to all industrial societies. Whereas in 1971 operatives and labourers accounted for 29 per cent of total employment, by 1986 this figure had fallen to 20 per cent and is projected to decline further to 16 per cent in 1995.[3] The loss of less skilled jobs in manufacturing was particularly pronounced in Britain during the recession when the three main manual occupations, the two Processing and the Miscellaneous orders, were each reduced in number by over 25 per cent. Rajan and Pearson (1986) identified a decrease in the less skilled occupations in production industries as one of the major trends currently affecting the labour force in the 1980s. They saw this trend as a net effect of a combination of larger employers' technological innovations which demand a more highly skilled labour force and smaller employers' growing demand for the less skilled employees.

This decline in the demand for unskilled labour in manufacturing is sometimes seen as evidence for a general upgrading of the skills of the labour force. However, the net reduction in unskilled jobs does not mean that all the remaining jobs have been upgraded. As we show, parts of the service sector have produced an increase in the demand for less skilled or low skill-intensive occupations.[4] Analysis of the LFS data revealed that between 1979 and 1984 the number of workers in occupational orders such as Security and Protective Services and Catering, Cleaning, Hairdressing, etc., continued to grow against the background of a general fall in employment.

The other major trend which has been affecting the labour market has been the growth of self-employment and the decline in the number of employees. It is common for self-employment to increase during recession. However, it does appear that the increase in self-employment in Britain since 1979 has been greater than that experienced by comparable industrial societies. The proportion of the labour force who were self-employed increased from 8 per cent in 1981 to 12 per cent in 1988. During the recession, the number of self-employed people increased by 48.6 per cent (Spilsbury, Maguire and Ashton, 1986). These figures have to be viewed with some caution owing to the problems of defining and measuring self-employment, but the Department of Employment estimates that since 1983, 40 per cent of the increase in overall employment has been in self-employment.

While important changes have been taking place, a number of features of the labour market have remained relatively constant. Sex segregation is still widespread, for although there has been a shift in the relative sizes of the male and female labour forces, the gender stereotyping of jobs shows little change. This was suggested by our analysis of the LFS, but has been demonstrated more convincingly by the OECD (1985) study.[5]

Age segmentation has also remained relatively unaffected. While the type of jobs available to 16-year-olds has changed, young people remain confined to a limited part of the labour market, and are excluded from areas such as the Other Services, Energy and Transport industries and the Professional, Managerial and Security occupations. As one moves up the age range, the distribution of each age group across the industrial and occupational categories increasingly approximates that of the all-age labour force, so that the distribution of 24-year-olds is almost identical to that of all-ages. The process of age segmentation gives the youth labour market its distinctive character.

Other advanced industrial societies are experiencing similar changes in their patterns of employment. Indeed, there is already considerable debate in North America on the 'declining middle' thesis which addresses the issue of the growth of professional and scientific jobs and part-time unskilled jobs, and the decline in skilled manual and lower white-collar jobs (Harvey and Blakely, 1985). All this suggests that the sources of these changes lie in major structural transformations that are common to all contemporary capitalist societies. Chapters 2 and 3 will take up this theme and examine the nature and consequence of the processes involved.

TRENDS IN THE YOUTH LABOUR MARKET

These long-term changes inevitably affect the number and type of jobs available to school-leavers as they seek entry to the labour market.

Industrial Concentration

In Britain, young people entering the labour market at the minimum school-leaving age have traditionally possessed relatively few marketable skills or recognised qualifications. This has resulted in their points of entry to the labour market being concentrated in a limited number of industries. In 1971, when the minimum school-leaving age was 15 years, half of the employed 15-year-old males were in just six of the 27 industrial orders (Agriculture, Metal Goods, Timber and Furniture, Construction, Distributive Trades, and Miscellaneous Services). These same industrial orders accounted for 41.7 per cent of employed 16-year-old males and 25.6 per cent of employed all-age males. The concentration of points of entry for females was even greater, with just four industrial orders (Textiles, Clothing and Footwear, Paper and Print, and Distributive Trades) accounting for 56.0 per cent of 15-year-olds, 46.2 per cent of 16-year-olds and 27.5 per cent of all-age females in employment. By the end of the decade the age at which young people could leave school had been raised to 16 but the concentration of employment in a limited number of industrial orders remained broadly similar.

Comparisons between these figures and the period of the recession, 1979–84, are difficult because of the change which took place in the definition of industrial orders.[6] However, when analysing the figures available since the revision of the categories, it is clear that during the recession there occurred a far more radical change in the distribution of points of entry available to 16-year-olds than was the case in the whole of the preceding decade.

In 1979, 81 per cent of employed 16-year-old males were concentrated in five of the nine industrial orders. These were Metal Goods (15 per cent), Other Manufacturing (15 per cent), Distribution (31 per cent), Other Services (9 per cent), and Construction (11 per cent). By 1984 the proportion entering Manufacturing industries had fallen so that opportunities became more highly concentrated in Distribution, which took 42 per cent, and Other Services which took 12 per cent. By the end of the five-year period just four categories accounted for 77 per cent of 16-year-old males in employment.

Pressures of sex segmentation meant that a different set of entry ports existed for females, although again there was a higher degree of industrial concentration than among males. In 1979 just three categories, Other Manufacturing (21 per cent), Distribution (41 per cent) and Financial Services (17 per cent) accounted for 79 per cent of all 16-year-old females in employment. By 1984 just two categories, Distribution (57 per cent) and Financial Services (22 per cent) accounted for 79 per cent.

Occupational Concentration

There has been a similar restructuring of the occupations entered by school-leavers. We examined this using the 16 occupational categories of the LFS. These are detailed in Table 2.3. For 16-year-old males the percentage employed in the two main manual occupations fell from 24 per cent in Metal and Electrical Processing and Machining, and 17 per cent in Other Processing and Machining in 1979 to 12 and 8 per cent respectively in 1984. By contrast, the percentage entering Selling and Clerical occupations increased from 10 and 7 per cent respectively in 1979 to 18 and 17 per cent in 1984. For females the changes were no less radical. In 1979 four occupational orders, Clerical (28 per cent), Selling (25 per cent), Catering (16 per cent) and Other Processing and Making (14 per cent), accounted for 83 per cent of 16-year-olds. By 1984 Other Processing and Making, at 4 per cent, was much less significant, leaving just three orders, Selling (36 per cent), Catering (28 per cent) and Clerical (21 per cent) to account for 85 per cent of female school-leavers in employment. Overall, the redistribution was away from the manual occupations and towards Selling and Catering.

As these changes in both the industrial and occupational distributions were taking place within a relatively static labour force in terms of size, this represented a major restructuring of opportunities for school-leavers. Also of note is the direction of that restructuring, for 16-year-old school-leavers are unable to enter a number of professional and technical jobs and with the disappearance of many skilled manual and lower-level clerical jobs, find themselves concentrated in the growing number of unskilled and semi-skilled service sector jobs.

The Youth Training Scheme

The Youth Training Scheme was introduced in 1983 as a one-year scheme and extended in 1986 to two years. This was a major policy innovation with the declared aim of providing a bridge to work for every 16-year-old school-leaver. The scheme provides work experience and a minimum period of off-the-job training. Trainees receive a grant of a fixed amount which may be 'topped up' by the employer if desired. In its first year it catered for 24 per cent of 16-year-olds and a similar proportion (27 per cent) in 1987.

Intervention on such a massive scale has important implications for the structure of the youth labour market. However, Britain was not alone in introducing such measures. Other industrial societies either already had them, as in West Germany, or introduced them in response to the problem of youth unemployment, as in France.

Analysis of the impact of YTS on the labour market, using official LFS data, is complicated because of a change of status of those on the sceme. Initially they were not defined as being in employment, but this decision was subsequently reversed, and they were included in the official count of employees. In order to establish the impact of YTS on the youth labour market, we were able to adjust the LFS data and establish reliable estimates of the effect of the scheme on the distribution of opportunities facing 16-year-olds as they enter the labour market (details of these adjustments are presented in the annex).

It has often been argued that many of those on Government schemes are not in 'real' jobs, and that their inclusion in the analysis will distort the results. For this reason the data was analysed firstly by including all those on schemes and secondly, by removing those on schemes from the data. This involved estimating the numbers on YTS at the time of the LFS survey. This is not without problems in that, as the LFS was conducted in May 1984, those on schemes would have started in September of the preceding year. Many of those who were 16 at the start of the scheme, would be 17 by the time of the LFS. The distribution of 16-year-olds would, therefore, have been inadequate, so the distribution of 16–19-year-olds in the LFS was used. The results of the analyses of both the adjusted and unadjusted, data were then compared.

In 1984 almost a half of 16-year-old school-leavers but only 14.9 per cent of 16–19-year-olds in employment were on YTS. The overall effect of YTS can be seen in Table 2.1 which shows the results of subtracting those on YTS on the direction of change since 1979. In general YTS exaggerated existing trends rather than changed their direction. Thus, if the underlying trend was for an increase in the numbers of young people within a given order, the inclusion of those on YTS served to increase the magnitude of the trend. Only in three industrial sectors did it create a change in direction: Construction changed from a 3.9 thousand job increase to a 6.8 thousand decrease; Banking and Finance changed from a 2.5 thousand increase to a 13.6 thousand decrease; and Other Services changed from a 3.3 thousand increase to a 55.8 thousand decrease. In these industries we suspect that YTS placements were used to replace traditional trainees, whereas in other industries they were more likely to be used as cheap production workers. Overall the particular skew of YTS placements appears to have accelerated developments that were already under way. It has further concentrated opportunities in the less skilled jobs in the service sector. However, there are some noticeable exceptions to this which will be discussed later.

These findings have received support from more recent cohort studies which show that the occupations of those on YTS broadly reflect the distribution of those of the same age group who are in full-time employment (*Labour Market Quarterly Report* (LMQ), September 1987). The only exception to this was that females on YTS were over-represented in Catering, Cleaning and Hairdressing, and so on, and Processing (not metal and electrical). All this suggests that Government intervention in the youth labour market has not made any radical change in the underlying trends which are concentrating the ports of entry of school-leavers in relatively unskilled jobs in a narrow range of industries and occupations.

TABLE 2.1: *The effect of removing YTS placements from the total numbers employed in each industrial classification*

SIC	Unadjusted 1979–1984 Change in No. Empl.	% Change	Adjusted 1979–1984 Change in No. Empl.	% Change
Agriculture	7.90	19.55	2.50	6.19
Energy & Water	–20.02	–47.42	–20.02	–47.42
Ex. of Minerals	–47.17	–51.18	–57.87	–62.79
Metal Goods Manu.	–106.25	–38.94	–138.45	–50.74
Other Manu.	–77.57	–26.09	–93.67	–31.51
Construction	3.90	2.67	–6.80	–4.65
Dist. Hotels	131.63	25.79	21.63	4.24
Trans. & Comm.	–20.33	–24.14	–23.03	–27.34
Banking & Finance	2.45	1.79	–13.65	–9.94
Other Services	3.33	1.08	–55.77	–18.09
No Reply	0.60	No Val	0.60	Mis. Val
Workforce outside UK	–16.40	–54.49	–24.40	–81.06
Not Applicable	–137.65	–7.02	–408.85	–20.84

THE IMPACT OF CYCLICAL AND STRUCTURAL CHANGE

The increasing concentration of young people's ports of entry in a limited range of jobs is not in itself evidence of a major structural change having a disproportionate impact on the youth labour market. One could hypothesise that the increasing concentration of the ports of entry available to youth merely reflects the shift which occurred in all-age employment between manufacturing and the service sector. From the perspective of cyclical theory, it could be hypothesised that these changes were a consequence of the differential effect of the recession on youth employment. From the point of view of structural theory an alternative hypothesis is that changes in the structure of industry were disproportionately affecting the opportunities for young people (16–19-year-olds). In order to provide a more rigorous test of these hypotheses we used a quasi-shift-share analysis of the type employed by Raffe to measure the impact of cyclical change. Details of this technique are documented in Raffe (1984a). It provides an estimate of the extent to which the decline in youth employment which occurred in the period 1979–84 was due to each one of three components: changes in all-age employment, changes in the industrial or occupational structure and changes in the proportion of youth to all-age employment. The first component, the change in all-age employment, provides an estimate of the impact of changes in the general level of demand (cyclical change) on the demand for youth labour; the second provides an estimate of the extent to which change is due to shifts in the industrial or occupational structure (structural change).

The LFS data were used to test these hypotheses. This is the only national data set which covered the relevant period and provided an age breakdown of employees. It is a household survey but its use is not without problems (Raffe, 1987, p. 226). Of particular concern is the unreliability of the data on the 16-year-olds' employment status for 1983, due to the change in the status of those on Government schemes. The way in which we dealt with this is discussed in the annex. In addition, given the problem of small numbers of 16-year-olds in some categories, it was felt that the 16–19 category provided a firmer base on which to conduct the analysis.

The analysis looks at the number of 16–19-year-olds demanded by employers and the changes therein. The fact that the numbers of 16–19-year-olds entering the labour market started to decline during this period does not affect the nature of the analysis, especially as there was an excess supply of youths throughout the period 1979–84. Similarly, the fall in the numbers of youths entering the labour market, which continues until 1995, may contribute towards a decline of levels of youth unemployment, but it does not alter the fundamental restructuring of the labour market which has taken place.

Industrial Shifts

On the basis of his analysis of Scottish data, Raffe argues that 'any disproportionate tendency for young people to work in declining industries was very slight, and very little of the reduction in youth employment can be accounted for in this way' Raffe (1986, p. 47). He attributes the increase in youth unemployment almost totally to the change in the general level of demand. When we used the combined data for 16–19-year-old males and females and measured this against the combined male and female all-age data, the results were similar to those of Raffe. It appeared that the loss of jobs in the labour-intensive industries was counteracted by the growth of new jobs in the service sector. In fact, over the period 1979–84 industrial shifts actually favoured the employment of 16–19-year-olds which, other things being equal, would have increased employment by 9.65 thousand jobs.

However, combining the data for males and females assumes a certain homogeneity in the labour market and an associated openness in the competition for jobs between males and females which our own, and a great deal of other research, suggested did not exist (Ashton and Maguire, 1983; OECD, 1985; Martin and Roberts, 1984). For this reason separate analyses for males and females were conducted, thereby assuming that the two groups were in totally separate markets. This assumption is not completely accurate in that there are areas where the two groups do compete at the individual level, but it represents a closer approximation to the realities of the segregated labour market which we know exists (Ashton and Maguire, 1986). The results show a very different pattern of change.

When changes in employment among 16–19-year-old males are compared with those of the total all-age employment, and separately with male all-age employment, both analyses show that for young male adults the industrial shifts did produce a loss of jobs over and above those due to the falling all-age employment. When 16–19-year-old males were estimated against male all-age employment there was a loss of 100 thousand jobs, of which industrial shifts accounted for 42.9 thousand (Table 2.2). The same analysis for females produced a smaller loss of 18 thousand jobs. It is clear from these results that changes taking place in the industrial structure are reducing the opportunities for young males and to a lesser extent, those for young females.

The change in the level of all-age employment, which cyclical theory would predict as being the most significant cause of the reduction in employment opportunities, operated in different directions in the male and female labour markets. For males it was by far the most important contributory factor to the reduction in employment opportunities, accounting for about twice the number of jobs lost through adverse industry shifts. With regard to females, for whom all-age employment grew during this period, the change was in the other direction. There was a small increase in opportunities, almost equal to that lost due to adverse industry shifts. The importance of this finding is that it casts doubts on some of the cruder interpretations of cyclical theory, for the change in the aggregate level of employment was concealing counter trends in the male and female labour markets.

The third component of the shift-share analysis is the changing

TABLE 2.2: *Changes in youths' (16–19) share of employment within industries, 1979–84*

SIC	No. due to change in all-age employment		No. due to structural change		No. due to proportional change		Actual change	
	M	F	M	F	M	F	M	F
Agri/Forest/Fishing	–2.68	0.07	13.71	1.07	–5.53	1.26	5.50	2.40
Energy/Water Supply	–2.37	0.19	–14.44	0.45	0.93	–4.78	–15.88	–4.14
Ext. of Minerals, Ores Manu of Metals, etc	–4.36	0.62	–36.41	–12.03	10.17	–5.17	–30.59	–16.58
Metal Goods, Eng. & Vehicles	–13.92	1.58	–94.28	–28.85	34.84	–5.62	–73.36	–32.8
Other Manu. Indus.	–9.89	3.10	–17.34	–38.53	10.54	–25.46	–16.69	–60.8
Construction	–9.98	0.19	15.62	2.08	–3.67	–0.35	1.98	1.9
Dist., Hotels & Catering, Repairs	–16.55	5.45	108.75	28.76	–21.47	26.69	70.74	60.8
Trans. & Commun.	–4.21	0.51	–20.64	0.08	5.14	–1.04	–19.72	–0.6
Bank/Finance, etc	–3.50	1.72	13.18	22.91	–11.65	20.21	1.97	
Other Services	–8.24	3.75	–0.53	15.29	–4.0			16.3
Work Place Outside UK	0.00	0.00	–	0.00	–	0.30	0.30	0.3
Not Applicable/No Reply/ Inadequately described	–1.10	0.29	–10.48	–9.09	3.99	0.00	–7.60	–8.8
TOTAL	–76.79	17.4	–42.9	–18.02	18.99	–37.03	–100.35	–37.5

Source: LFS, author's analysis.

proportion of youths *vis-à-vis* all-age employment. In quantitative terms this proved to be the most significant element of change in the female labour market, accounting for the greater part of the reduction in female youth unemployment. The displacement of 16–19-year-old females by all-age females was largely responsible for the reduction in opportunities for young females. For males this was the smallest of the three components of change and moved in the opposite direction, with 16–19-year-old males displacing all-age males. When the data was adjusted for YTS, the direction of the three components of the shift-share analysis stayed the same, the only difference being the magnitude of the changes.

These results reveal very different processes of change operating in the male and female labour markets. During this period the all-age female labour market grew and job losses among young females were primarily due to their displacement by all-age females, although adverse industrial shifts did play a part. In the male market the main cause of job losses among 16–19-year-olds was the cyclical effect, with the decline in male all-age employment, but losses due to adverse industrial shifts were substantial. These losses were partially offset by the displacement of all-age males by youths.

Occupational Shifts

Occupational changes were seen as a further source of change within the general labour market and their impact on the youth labour market was analysed (Table 2.3). When we examine 16–19-year-old males against male all-age employment, the two Professional and Related and Literary and Sports orders showed a small growth in employment due to the favourable occupational shifts. The only other major areas of growth for males resulting from occupational shifts were in Selling, Catering, Cleaning, Hairdressing, and so on, Farming, Fishing and Related, and Construction, Mining and Related. However, there were losses due to reductions in the proportions of 16–19-year-olds, *vis-à-vis* all-age employees in the higher occupational orders of Professional and Related, Literary and Sport, and in some of the other expanding orders such as Selling and Catering, Cleaning, Hairdressing, and so on. It is interesting that the main areas where there was a growth in proportions were in Clerical and Related, Processing (Excluding Metal), Processing (Metal), Printing, Packing and Assembling, and Transport and Miscellaneous, all of which were declining occupations. The overall picture is one of

TABLE 2.3: *Changes in youths' (16–19) share of employment within occupations, 1979–84*

Occupations	No. due to change in all-age employment M	F	No. due to structural change M	F	No. due to proportional change M	F	Actual change M	F
Prof. Man/Admin	–0.75	0.14	3.73	1.91	–2.18	–6.15	0.80	–4.10
Prof. Educ/Welfare/ Health	–0.30	0.60	0.59	5.22	–0.29	–5.42	0.00	0.40
Lit/Art/Sports	–0.58	0.12	0.20	3.35	–0.82	–3.27	–1.20	0.20
Prof/Sci/Eng	–3.22	0.12	–12.05	0.88	–3.84	–1.70	–19.10	–0.70
Managerial	–2.11	0.17	–1.69	3.28	–2.50	–3.56	–6.30	–0.10
Clerical & Related	–6.86	7.39	–10.17	–17.68	19.33	–66.71	2.30	–77.00
Selling	–5.02	2.74	47.68	6.15	–3.16	39.61	39.50	48.50
Security/Prot. Serv.	–0.55	0.02	–1.76	0.05	–0.19	0.33	–2.50	0.40
Catering/Cleaning Hairdressing etc	–3.35	2.09	32.00	5.75	–9.35	64.36	19.30	72.20
Farming/Fish & Rel.	–2.95	0.07	22.60	1.60	–6.85	5.24	12.80	6.90
Proc., Making, etc (excl. Metal & Elec)	–9.70	1.88	–12.65	–23.19	11.35	–20.09	–11.00	–41.40
Proc., Making, etc (metal & elec)	–22.16	0.31	–138.45	–6.73	49.41	2.82	–111.20	–3.60
Print/Assem/Pack. etc	–4.18	1.34	–17.50	–24.60	9.58	–3.13	–12.10	–26.40
Construction, Mining & Rel. NIE	–4.44	0.02	21.37	0.35	–1.42	0.43	15.50	0.80
Trans/Moving & Stor	–5.80	0.13	–19.76	–1.60	13.15	–0.43	–12.40	–1.90
Misc.	–4.16	0.14	–17.91	–2.63	11.87	–1.21	–10.20	–3.70
No Reply/N.A./Not Stated	–0.69	0.20	–6.60	–6.35	2.49	–1.45	–4.80	–7.60
TOTAL	–76.81	17.46	–110.37	–54.24	86.58	–0.33	–100.50	–37.40

Source: LFS, author's analysis.

declining opportunities for 16–19-year-olds in the higher occupational orders, a reduction in their proportions in the occupations which are expanding and an increase in the proportion of young males, *vis-à-vis* all males in those occupations which are declining most rapidly. This suggests that changes in the occupational structure are working against young males, especially in closing off opportunities in the higher segments, comprising the professions, management and administration.

For the 16–19-year-old females the occupational shifts showed little movement either way, with the exception of Clerical and Related, Processing (Excluding Metal), and Printing, Packing and Assembling which produced substantial falls resulting in a net loss of 54.2 thousand jobs. Like the males the higher orders were characterised by a fall in proportions but unlike the males the females recorded substantial gains due to increasing proportions in some of the lower orders such as Selling and Catering, Cleaning, Hairdressing, and so on, although these were largely offset by a substantial fall in proportions in Clerical and Related. The resultant picture is one of decreasing opportunities in the higher orders with some compensatory expansion of opportunities, albeit of a semi-skilled and unskilled nature, in the lower orders.

Our analysis implies that occupational changes are having a differential impact in the male and female youth labour markets. Males were failing to maintain access to the expanding higher occupational orders and becoming increasingly concentrated in the declining manual occupations. A limited number of new opportunities in the expanding service occupations offset some of these losses. Females were increasingly being displaced from clerical occupations but were gaining opportunities in service occupations to offset the loss of opportunities in clerical and manual occupations.

Changes in the Female Labour Market

Given the considerable shifts in the patterns of employment for young people, it could be expected that there must be compensating movements in the pattern of employment for other groups. After all, the increasing proportions of all-age females provided the most significant factor in accounting for female youth unemployment. One of the most striking features of the labour market in the early 1980s has been the rise in the participation of women in employment.

There has also been an even sharper rise in women's share of all employment. In view of this, we sought to establish which occupations were responsible for the growth in employment opportunities for females and, within the female labour market, whether there were any significant changes in the proportions of single, widowed and divorced women (this category accounts for most younger females) in relation to married women.

Within the all-age female labour market the main occupational shifts responsible for the increase in female jobs was in the Professions and Related in Education, Welfare and Health, which produced an increase of 205.5 thousand jobs. There was a similar increase of some 255.7 thousand jobs in the Catering and Cleaning order. This growth took place among both the more highly skilled and the unskilled jobs. The main sources of job losses were in the Clerical and Related Order and the Printing, Assembling and Packing Order, where females were concentrated, as well as in the two Processing Orders where they were under-represented. This growth in the demand for female labour represents a major structural change.

In this context the relative position of single, widowed and divorced (SWD) females, *vis-à-vis* married females, also underwent significant changes. Although two-thirds of all female employees were married, the single, widowed and divorced category accounted for most (60.2 per cent) of the overall increase in employment. At first sight this appeared to contradict the earlier finding that youths were displaced by all-age females. However, more analysis by occupational order (Table 2.4) revealed that married women had displaced SWD females in the Professional and Related occupational orders, whereas in Selling occupations, and Catering, Cleaning and Hairdressing, where young females are concentrated, the opposite was the case and SWD females were displacing married women.

These results are tentative, and there was no breakdown of full-time and part-time employment by age. However, they suggest, as did our interviews with employers, that contradictory trends are at work. In the higher segments of the labour market, in the Professions, Banking and Clerical work, married women returning to the labour market are preferred for the new jobs. They are also displacing SWD females as firms reorganise their internal labour markets and replace younger full-time employees by older married women on a part-time basis. However, at the bottom of the labour market, in Selling and in Catering, Cleaning and Hairdressing, where YTS is having a significant effect, SWD females are displacing married

TABLE 2.4: *Changes in married females' and single, widowed and divorced females' share of employment within occupations, 1979–84*

Occupation	No. due to change in all-age employment		No. due to structural change		No. due to proportional change		Actual change	
	Married	SWD	Married	SWD	Married	SWD	Married	SWD
Prof./Man/Admin	–4.35	–3.10	30.09	21.44	15.36	–1.44	41.10	16.89
Prof. Educ/Welfare/Health	–28.65	–13.15	140.86	64.63	67.97	–20.29	180.20	31.20
Lit/Art/Sports	–1.35	–1.05	11.12	8.65	18.03	1.30	27.80	8.90
Prof/Sci/Eng	–1.82	–1.16	9.56	6.07	–4.74	5.49	3.00	10.40
Managerial	–11.21	–3.63	62.11	20.10	64.90	22.13	115.80	38.59
Clerical & Related	–65.17	–42.07	–68.31	–44.10	111.49	29.76	–22.00	–56.40
Selling	–22.37	–10.60	52.40	24.83	–51.73	63.57	–21.70	77.79
Security/Prot.Serv.	–0.83	–0.56	1.77	1.18	4.07	–2.92	5.00	–2.30
Catering/Cleaning/ Hairdressing etc	–59.31	–17.53	197.35	58.32	–105.04	77.81	33.00	118.60
Farming/Fish & Rel.	–1.23	–0.52	7.11	2.98	3.82	10.54	9.70	13.00
Proc., Making, etc. (excl. metal & elec)	–14.54	–8.35	–39.29	–22.56	–37.47	–14.09	–91.30	–45.00
Proc., Making, etc (metal & elec)	–3.94	–1.98	–24.58	–12.34	–15.17	–5.88	–43.70	–20.20
Print/Assem/ Pack. etc	–13.07	–6.50	–82.86	–41.21	–26.07	–9.19	–122.00	–56.90
Construction, Mining & Rel. NIE	–0.06	–0.07	0.09	0.11	–0.53	2.06	–0.50	2.10
Trans/Moving & Stor.	–2.10	–1.19	–9.28	–5.24	2.28	–4.27	–9.10	–10.70
Misc	–0.87	–0.50	–5.34	–3.06	–2.60	–0.74	–8.80	–4.30
No Reply/N.A./Not Stated	–1.43	–0.84	–20.48	–12.10	–2.29	–0.34	–24.20	–12.60
TOTAL	–232.30	–112.77	262.40	67.5	42.00	154.20	72.3	109.08

Source: LFS, author's analysis.

women. This is counteracting the earlier trend in Selling whereby young females were being displaced by adult part-timers (Ashton, Maguire and Garland, 1982; Trinder, 1986). These results suggest a significant shift in the compositon of the respective segments as employers, either in response to political or market pressures, switch from one type of labour to another. It is part of a longer term process, discussed in Chapter 7, whereby the relative size and composition of the segments change over time.

The results confirm that the general demand for labour plays a major part in determining the overall demand for youth labour. Yet the youth labour market still retains distinctive characteristics which mean that the demand for youth labour is in important respects independent of that for adults. One consequence of this is that there has been a contraction of the demand for youth labour over and above that brought about by the fall in demand associated with the recession. Yet, these broad changes conceal a major restructuring of the demand for youth labour, with very different and sometimes contradictory trends operating in different parts of the labour market. Some of these are discussed in the next section while the factors responsible for them are discussed in Chapter 6.

THE SCHOOL-LEAVER HYPOTHESIS

The validity of cyclical theory was also examined through a test of the 'school-leaver hypothesis', which is used by proponents of that theory to explain the cyclical sensitivity of youth unemployment. There are a number of variants of the school-leaver hypothesis but in general terms the argument is that school-leavers have relatively little choice about when they can enter the labour market. They have to enter in the summer of each year irrespective of the general state of demand. Moreover, as new entrants with relatively few skills, they occupy the rear of the 'job queue' and are only hired when the aggregate demand for labour is sufficient. This sensitivity to cyclical fluctuation is aggravated by the relative concentration of young people in occupations which are themselves vulnerable to recession. The main reason for this sensitivity is the behaviour of employers who, when faced with a falling demand for their products cut back on recruitment, and in the case of redundancies, impose a 'last in, first out' policy. This has an immediate impact on new entrants in general and youths in particular. However, with the onset of recovery, youths are the first to be taken on as employers seek to rebuild their labour forces.

The Relative Concentration Ratio was used to measure changes in the proportion of youths employed in a particular industry or occupation over the period 1979–84. The RCR is the proportion of a demographic group employed in a particular industry, sector or occupational order relative to the proportion of all employed persons in that sector. A value of one indicates that the sector or order employs the same proportion of the demographic group as it does of all persons in general; a value of greater than one indicates over-representation.[7] In doing this, it also provides an index of changes in employers' recruitment practices which can be used to examine the adequacy of cyclical theory. If the school-leaver hypothesis is supported, we would expect to see a fall in the proportion of youths *vis-à-vis* all-age adults in employment as the recession starts, followed by a rise in the proportion of youths as the industry sectors recover.[8]

Industrial Trends

The school-leaver hypothesis found support for both sexes in only one of the six non-service sector categories, which was the Other Manufacturing category (Table 2.5). When recession first hit (1979–81) employers stopped recruiting school-leavers, thus driving down the RCR of 16–19-year-olds. Following a recovery in 1983–84, school-leavers were again taken on, thus increasing the level of the RCR. This could be expected in the more labour-intensive industries encompassed by this category, where the relationship between employment and output is a smooth curve and where youths are over-represented. Confirmation came from interviews with employers in industries such as textiles and footwear.

The only other non-service sector categories which provided support for the school-leaver hypothesis were males in Agriculture and females in Metal Goods Manufacture.

There was no support for the school-leaver hypothesis in the case of males in the Metal Goods, Engineering and Vehicle category. A fall in the RCR for males in 1981 was then followed by a further fall in 1984. Interviews with employers suggest that this pattern is a result of two separate but related processes of change. One was the collapse of demand in 1981 and the subsequent loss of markets which has led employers to restrict the recruitment of manual workers, especially

TABLE 2.5: *Industrial relative concentration ratios for 16–19-year olds, 1979–84 – unadjusted data*

SIC	1979	1981	1983	1984
Males:				
Agriculture	1.28	1.17	1.41	1.33
Energy & Water	0.72	0.71	0.64	0.40
Ex. of Minerals	0.87	0.68	0.56	0.67
Metal Goods Manu.	0.93	0.88	0.90	0.84
Other Manu	1.21	1.01	1.05	1.19
Construction	1.21	1.30	1.29	1.23
Dist. Hotels	1.58	1.96	2.01	1.98
Trans & Comm	0.60	0.53	0.52	0.47
Banking & Finance	0.81	0.66	0.63	0.63
Other Servs	0.67	0.68	0.50	0.58
No Reply	0.00	0.49	0.22	0.30
Workforce outside UK	1.21	0.96	1.37	1.32
Not Applic	1.00	1.01	1.00	1.00
Females:				
Agriculture	0.42	0.58	0.62	0.56
Energy & Water	1.04	0.70	0.78	0.60
Ex. of Minerals	1.18	1.01	1.01	0.95
Metal Goods Manu.	1.07	0.91	0.98	1.02
Other Manu	1.43	1.11	1.22	1.21
Construction	0.83	0.76	1.15	0.86
Dist. Hotels	1.29	1.54	1.49	1.49
Trans & Comm	1.00	1.14	0.87	1.03
Banking & Finance	1.28	1.48	1.30	1.12
Other Servs	0.58	0.56	0.56	0.61
No Reply	0.00	0.00	0.65	1.84
Workforce outside UK	1.20	0.80	1.46	1.28
Not Applic	1.00	1.00	1.00	1.00

Source: LFS, author's own analysis.

apprentices, and to continue to reduce the size of their labour forces. The school-leaver hypothesis fails to account for this pattern of change because it assumes a constant relationship between employment and output. In fact this relationship altered during the recession with the introduction of new technology. CNC machines, robots and other innovations have enabled firms to make dramatic improvements in productivity and increase output without taking on additional labour. Consequently the recruitment of male youths continued to fall in 1984.

In two of the remaining non-service sector categories, namely Energy and Water and Extraction of Minerals and Manufacture of Metals, the RCRs of both sexes declined over the recession. The reduction in Energy and Water was partly attributable to the constant political pressure on the relevant authorities to reduce their labour costs. This resulted in cuts in recruitment so that voluntary redundancies and retirements reduced the size of the labour force. In the case of the Extraction of Minerals and Manufacture of Metals, the shrinking of the product market, combined with pressure to reduce labour costs, created the same result.

In Construction, an industry which is traditionally a major employer of young males, the movement of the male RCRs was counter-cyclical. It increased in the period 1979–81 and fell during the recovery of 1983–84. Recruitment was sustained during a period when output was falling and the school-leaver hypothesis would predict a decline. This is surprising in an industry which has traditionally been noted for its sensitivity to cyclical fluctuations in the product market. We suspect that the increase in the RCR was due to the extensive use made of Government schemes during the recession.[9] In this industry, the Construction Industry Training Board developed a centrally organised system of recruitment through the use of Government schemes. In the case of YTS trainees they were recruited into the first year of the apprenticeship.

There was even less support for the school-leaver hypothesis in the service sector. In Transport and Communications, the RCR for males declined throughout the recession while that for females moved erratically. Similarly, in Other Services, the male RCR showed a slight fall while the female RCR remained stable. This was not the case in Distribution Hotels and Catering. The movement of the RCRs shows that throughout the period, youths expanded their share of this market at the expense of adults. Discussions with employers suggest that one reason for this was the employers' response to the introduction of the Youth Opportunities Programme, and later YTS, which provided the labour of youths either free or in the case of the Young Worker Scheme (YWS) heavily subsidised, thereby encouraging them to switch recruitment from adults (usually females) to youths.

Amongst the other major employers of youths in the service sector, Banking, Finance etc., the male RCR on both the adjusted and unadjusted data sets declined throughout the period, in spite of a growth of output. This we believe is a result of the increasing professionalisation of banking and finance which now require higher levels of educational qualifications before entry to the career jobs. For females the pattern was very different. Their RCR increased in the period 1979–81 but then fell between 1981 and 1984. The movement of the RCR on the adjusted data reflected the same pattern. We suspect that the increase to 1981 was a result of increasing business volume creating more jobs, with the subsequent fall being a consequence of the introduction of new information technology changing the relationship between employment and output and reducing the demand for clerks and typists.

Occupational Trends

The findings from the occupational analysis provide further clarification of the main trends (Table 2.6). The RCRs of both sexes in the Professional and Managerial occupations declined steadily throughout the period. This was a result of the need for young people to stay on in education and enhance their educational qualifications before entry. In clerical work, there are marked differences in the movement of the RCR between the sexes. The female RCR continued to fall throughout the period whereas that for males increased.

Information from interviews suggested that it was the rationalisation of the use of labour, namely the replacement of full-timers by part-timers which would explain the fall in the RCR of young females, as employers recruited older married women for part-time jobs. In the case of males, the growth in the number of senior clerical jobs with responsibility for computer systems was leading to increased recruitment.

The RCRs of both sexes continued to increase throughout the period in the main service occupations of Selling and Catering. As stated earlier, this was partly attributable to employers' responses to the introduction of government schemes.

The movement of the RCRs in the manual occupations differed considerably from one occupation to another. In the Processing (excluding metal) occupations, such as operatives in Textiles and Footwear, the RCR followed the pattern predicted by the school-leaver hypothesis. This was also the case for 16–19-year-old females in both of the Process and Making occupations and for both sexes in Printing, Assembling and Packing, where a recovery in output from the low of 1981 led to an increased recruitment of youths. For males the RCR in the category covering the engineering industry (Process-

TABLE 2.6: *Occupational relative concentration ratios for 16–19-year-olds, 1979–84 – unadjusted data*

SECTOR	1979	1981	1983	1984
MALES:				
Prof & Rel:				
Man & Admin	0.18	0.19	0.11	0.17
Education	0.09	0.09	0.09	0.08
Lit, Arts & Sports	0.81	0.57	0.65	0.63
Prof & Rel:				
Science etc	0.75	0.56	0.44	0.38
Managerial	0.26	0.23	0.22	0.19
Cler. & Rel.	1.18	1.42	1.51	1.54
Selling	1.62	2.17	2.26	2.53
Security Etc	0.30	0.60	0.22	0.20
Catering, Cleaning etc	1.38	1.69	1.77	1.76
Farm, Fish & Rel.	1.81	1.94	2.30	2.16
Processing etc				
(exc metal & elec)	1.51	1.40	1.46	1.57
(metals & elec)	1.37	1.41	1.23	1.20
Printing, Assembling, etc	1.26	1.19	1.26	1.30
Construction, Mining etc	1.03	1.07	1.36	1.30
Transport Operating	0.71	0.65	0.69	0.76
Misc	1.77	1.52	2.10	2.00
No Reply	1.34	1.42	2.15	1.46
Not Applic	1.00	1.01	1.00	1.00
FEMALES:				
Prof & Rel:				
Man & Admin	0.37	0.26	0.28	0.13
Education	0.29	0.27	0.27	0.26
Lit, Arts & Sports	0.98	0.87	0.60	0.69
Prof & Rel:				
Science etc	0.78	0.92	0.24	0.63
Managerial	0.23	0.18	0.23	0.18
Cler. & Rel.	1.36	1.28	1.21	1.19
Selling	1.64	2.18	2.17	2.20
Security Etc	0.27	0.49	0.13	0.38
Catering,				
Cleaning etc	0.54	0.68	0.82	0.88
Farm, Fish & Rel.	0.76	1.68	1.55	1.63
Processing etc				
(exc metal & elec)	1.62	1.25	1.42	1.27
(metals & elec)	1.04	0.89	1.25	1.42
Printing,				
Assembling, etc	1.35	1.15	1.20	1.34
Construction, Mining etc	2.37	1.91	0.92	3.46
Transport Operating	0.77	0.94	0.70	0.75
Misc	1.97	1.35	1.81	1.55
No Reply	1.73	1.26	1.94	1.21
Not Applic	1.00	1.00	1.00	1.00

Source: LFS, author's analysis.

ing etc; metal and electrical) rose slightly between 1979 and 1981 but thereafter fell to a level below that of 1979. This reflects both the radical change in the employment output relationship mentioned earlier which is reducing the need for skilled (male) labour and apprenticeships and the continuous cut in the recruitment which took place over the period 1981–84.

In Construction, Mining and Related occupations the RCR for females followed the pattern predicted by the school-leaver hypothesis, as did that of males in Transport and for both males and females in Miscellaneous Services.

BEYOND THE SCHOOL-LEAVER HYPOTHESIS

As a general explanation of what happened to the recruitment of youths during the recession, the school-leaver hypothesis is inadequate. It did explain changes in the recruitment of youths, *vis-à-vis* adults in many of the manual occupations and those manufacturing industries which relied on labour-intensive methods of manufacture. These were among the industries hardest hit by the recession, but there remained other industries which were equally badly affected where it did not apply; for example, males in the engineering industry and manual occupations within that industry. The reason for its failure there is that the explanation does not take into account the possibility of changes in the employment-output relationship, which has had a major impact on recruitment practices.

In the service sector, the dominant trend was an increase in the RCR in the major industries employing youths. Banking was one exception where this was not the case. There, in spite of the continued growth in employment which took place during this period, the movement of the RCR suggested that the new technology was starting to reduce the recruitment of youths relative to adults. In the other industries employers continued to recruit youths throughout the recession. This, we would argue, is the result of a major structural change in demand for labour associated with the growth of the service sector. This was an underlying trend which was only marginally affected by the impact of the recession.

Yet it could still be argued, according to the school-leaver hypothesis, that as these employers were recruiting in a market characterised by mass unemployment they would move up-market and recruit the more experienced and qualified adults, leaving the youths at the rear of the queue. This would have produced a fall in the RCR in 1981, perhaps followed by a small recovery later. In fact there was a continuous growth in the RCR. Moreover, the proportion of youths relative to adults increased at the very point when employers, according to the theory, should have been seeking to recruit adults. This implies that these employers had a strong preference for recruiting youth as opposed to adult labour. This, we have suggested, was linked to the introduction of YOP, YTS and associated schemes which lowered the cost of youth labour and encouraged the substitution of youths for adults. We discuss this process in greater depth in Chapter 6.

The occupational analysis also highlighted parts of the labour market where the school-leaver hypothesis lacked support. In the higher segments (Profession, Management etc), where the occupations were expanding, the fall in the RCRs was a product of other factors which are not taken into account by the school-leaver hypothesis such as the process of qualification inflation. Similarly, in the lower segments, especially in Construction and the service occupations, the introduction of subsidised labour provided yet another factor affecting recruitment practices.

While the school-leaver hypothesis was found to have validity in some industries and occupations these results suggest that a number of other factors were operating on the pattern of demand for youth labour. These factors are not taken into account by the hypothesis and the theory from which it is derived.

CONCLUSIONS

The results of both the shift-share and RCR analyses have highlighted parts of the labour market where hypotheses derived from cyclical theory have contributed towards an explanation of the changes which occurred during the recession. However, in both analyses these hypotheses proved to be inadequate as a general explanation. On the other hand, structural theories fared little better. Hypotheses derived from them were found to have a degree of applicability, but, like those derived from cyclical theory, were inadequate as a total explanation of the changes taking place. Our analysis has shown that it is vital to move beyond the level of generality at which these explanations are pitched if we are to further our understanding of the (youth) labour market.

The first step in this direction is to recognise that just as the male and female labour markets are segregated so too are the markets for youths and adults. This is important because the forces of change which our analysis identified are having a differential impact on the male and female labour markets. The major impact of the recession, with the fall in the general level of demand, was largely confined in its effects to the all-age male labour market. While this labour market shrank, that for all-age female labour continued to grow. It was this factor which was primarily responsible for the increase in male youth unemployment. For young females, however, their unemployment was primarily attributable to shifts in employers' preferences and their subsequent displacement by older women.

While the size of the male labour market shrank, professional, scientific and technical jobs continued to expand in accordance with the upgrading thesis and the long-term trend identified above. This was of little benefit to 16-year-old school-leavers who are progressively excluded from such jobs, as entry to them becomes increasingly restricted to graduates. With the adverse industry shifts causing the loss of many middle-level jobs, such as apprenticeships, this left the 16-year-old males crowding into the remaining less skilled jobs in manufacturing and the service sector where they displaced all-age males. In this the young males were seriously affected by the process of technological change which is eradicating many of the skilled and semi-skilled manual jobs in manufacture. Thus, even when the upturn in output came, youths were no longer recruited in large numbers into apprenticeships.

In the female labour market the impact of the various processes of change was very different. Like the males, young females were increasingly excluded from the expanding occupations in the higher segments of the labour market. They were also adversely affected by the industry shifts, as many of the jobs as operatives in the labour-intensive industries were lost for good. In addition they also lost many middle-level clerical jobs. Yet, unlike the males, the growth of the service sector more than compensated for the loss of jobs in manufacturing. But not all female service sector jobs were open to young females. In the middle and higher segments they were being displaced by adults. As a result of this they were increasingly concentrated in the low-level, unskilled and semi-skilled jobs in areas such as Selling and Catering. These are the new deskilled service sector jobs which are one of the main areas of job growth. Yet even here, the success of young females in securing access to these jobs has been aided by massive Government intervention in the form of the Youth Training Scheme. This has helped counteract one of the major forces of change acting on the female youth labour market, namely the competition from married women.

Once we treat the male and female labour markets separately, it is also clear that within each of them the long-term structural trends we have identified are having a differential impact. In the male labour market, the decline of manufacturing industry has meant that industry shifts have been the major source of change. In the female labour market the major source of change has been the growth of Commerce, Retail, Hotels and Tourism. But unlike young males, young females face intense competition from older (married) females who often only want part-time work.

While we have identified a number of such processes of change which are affecting the manufacturing and service sectors, it is clear that they are not all moving at the same speed. The long-term decline of employment in manufacturing was accelerated during the recession. This was because the existence of mass unemployment and the Government's efforts to weaken organised labour facilitated employers' attempts to rationalise labour and introduce new technology. Such changes are unlikely to continue at the same pace in the future. In the service sector however, for reasons we shall discuss later, the rationalisation of labour is likely to continue well into the future. In addition, the recession has induced political change in the form of government schemes, which has made youth labour available on new terms. This is likely to remain a permanent feature of the labour market for the foreseeable future and has helped make youth labour particularly attractive to some service sector employers. However, while these processes of change may not all continue at the same pace in the future, their combined effect has been to introduce major changes into the structure of the (youth) labour market.

The implication of all this for our understanding of the youth labour market is that as we have emerged from the depths of the recession, the structure of opportunities facing 16-year-old school-leavers is very different from that which existed before. In general, it points to the prospect of fewer opportunities in a narrower range of unskilled and semi-skilled jobs. In the next four chapters we move on to a more detailed examination of some of the processes responsible for this change.

ANNEX

The Adjustment of the LFS Data

The classification of Government schemes in the LFS causes problems for comparability over time. In the LFSs of 1979 and 1981, those on Government schemes were considered to be economically inactive, and are therefore not included in the earlier tables. In 1983 they were considered to be inactive if they specifically stated that they were on Government schemes. Otherwise they were classified as being in employment. In 1984, all those on schemes were considered to be in employment.

In order to compare the LFS data for different years, it would therefore be necessary to either add those who were on Government schemes on to the 1979 and 1981 LFS figures or subtract those on Government schemes from the 1984 figures. Whichever path was chosen would still leave an element of confusion over 1983 figures. For our purposes the adjustment of the 1984 figures was considered to be the more satisfactory option, although it is conceded that there is some imprecision. The vast majority of young people on Government schemes in 1984 were on YTS, and so in estimating the figure to be subtracted, it was assumed that they were all on YTS. Estimations were made of the numbers to be subtracted from the LFS totals for each age group, by gender, on the basis of the knowledge that of those entering YTS in 1984/5, 56 per cent were males and 44 per cent were females, 91.7 per cent were 16-year-old school-leavers, 8 per cent were 17-year-olds and 0.32 per cent were 18–21-year-olds. For the industrial distribution, for which no accurate gender breakdown is given, the figures for the male and female combined sex structure have been imposed on the separate male and female components. Also, in the absence of data on the occupational distribution of YTS work placements, only the industrial distribution is used to calculate the effects of YTS.

Having made these assumptions and adjustments, the analysis is restricted to the figures for the 16–19-year-old group.

NOTES

1. We use the term recession to refer to the short-term downturns in the business cycle. In this instance we refer to the dramatic drop in business

activity which took place in the period 1980–81. We acknowledge that although business activity increased after that period, indicators such as the output of manufacturing industry failed to reach the pre-recession levels until 1988. Nevertheless, we refer to the period following 1981 as the recovery in that the level of business activity had started to rise from the previous low. In later chapters we refer to some of the reasons why manufacturing output and unemployment failed to reach their pre-recession levels in this period.

2. Unless stated otherwise, the figures in this section are derived from various issues of the Employment Gazette.
3. These figures are from the Institute for Employment Research, Warwick, quoted in the *Labour Market Quarterly*, November 1987.
4. Our findings with regard to the thesis of de-grading are partly at variance with those of Goldthorpe and Payne (1986). They confirm the tendency for the unskilled jobs in manufacturing to decline. However, the growth of 'less skill intensive' (Rajan and Pearson, 1986) jobs in the service sector points to the operation of a process of de-grading in that part of the economy. This appears to be a process which has been overlooked by Goldthorpe and Payne because of their concentration on male occupations. The growth of professional, managerial and technical workers supports the up-grading thesis, but is not solely due to the growth of the service sector as Goldthorpe and Payne argue in recent years. It is also a product of the more direct effect of technological change and the re-structuring of jobs which this has stimulated.
5. The OECD (1985) analysis of women's employment using different measures of occupational segregation reveals relatively little change in the degree of segregation over time although there are differences between societies.
6. The major problem we faced was that the 1979 LFS is coded in the 1968 Standard Industrial Classification (SIC) while the 1981, 1983 and 1984 LFSs are coded in the revised 1980 SIC. To facilitate comparison over the whole period a conversion was made for the 1979 data into the 1980 SIC. Details of this are available on application to the Labour Market Studies Group, University of Leicester.

   There were some problems involved in the conversion of the 1979 data. Firstly, there are the normal rounding errors. This results in the total, that is, overall employment, not quite equalling the sum of the individual parts, namely, industrial sector employment. To ease the analysis the overall total has therefore been reduced to equal the sum of its parts. This means that the totals for 1979 are not always exactly the same, but the difference is very minor (less than a quarter of one per cent). Further problems are that the conversion is based on an all-age distribution. For example, the industrial distribution of school-leavers is notoriously skewed towards a few industrial sectors. This conversion will result in it resembling the all-age industrial distribution more than would normally be the case. Despite these problems the conversion is invaluable for providing information on industrial trends from 1979 onwards which would otherwise be unavailable for different age groups. Caution should be exercised, however, when 1979 is used for differing age groups.

7. The formula for calculating the RCR is:

$$RCR = \frac{Nij/Nj}{Ni/N}$$

where N = level of employment
i = a demographic group
j = an industrial sector or occupational order.

8. The use of the RCR in this context can cause some confusion. Because the total RCR must equal unity it appears that some individual RCRs must increase and others decrease, thus making the test invalid. However, at the sector level, where this analysis is focussed, the average of the individual sector RCRs does not necessarily equal one, so maintaining the validity of the test.
9. During the recession output and employment fell substantially and it appears that YOP encouraged the recruitment of youths as cheap labour during the period 1979–82 while their proportions fell after 1983 with the introduction of YTS.

3 Determinants of the General Demand for Labour at the Level of the Firm

Having identified how, at the macro level, cyclical and structural changes combine to affect the overall demand for labour, we now move down to the level of the firm. At this level we are concerned to identify the factors which are perceived by managers of employing organisations to affect their demand for labour. Interviews were carried out with senior managers. Within a capitalist economy it is a precondition for the long-term viability of a firm and the employment it sustains that it remains profitable. Against this background the results of the interviews pointed to a number of inter-related factors, which can help determine the numbers employed. The major factors which will be discussed in this chapter are: (i) the product market; (ii) the actions of the state; (iii) the employment-output relationship; (iv) wage levels; and (v) ownership. At the outset it is important to stress the complexity of the relationship between these factors. For example, their relative weight can vary from firm to firm, even within the same industry. Also, as employers are operating in conditions of uncertainty then the relationship between the factors tends to change over time. Our attempt to point to what we believe to be the main factors impinging on different types of employers inevitably leads to an oversimplification of the complexity of the situation. Nevertheless, it provides an appropriate framework within which to address the central issues.

PRODUCT MARKET

A firm's position in its product market, and the state of that product market, was regarded by our respondents as the single most important factor in determining the level of labour demand.[1]

Manufacturing Sector

In the manufacturing sector, many of the firms we visited had been forced to reduce the size of their labour force, as a result of the impact of the recession. As the level of output was directly related to the level of demand for the firm's products, then any reduction in market size, or loss of market share led to workers being made redundant. This had been the case in all but one of the firms visited. However, to present this merely as firms responding to a fall in aggregate demand by reducing their labour force is a gross oversimplification of the reality, for it is possible to distinguish at least four different sets of conditions which caused a reduction in demand for individual companies' products.

Firstly, some companies were manufacturing products for which there was a substantial fall in demand due to the reduction in aggregate demand associated with the recession. This was the case in the chemical and vehicle manufacture industries, where the general fall in demand also affected component suppliers, and in the printing industry. As demand for advertising fell, so too did the demand for printed material through which the adverts were carried. These conditions approximate most closely to the idea of cyclical changes in demand discussed in the earlier chapters.

Of course, some companies operate in markets which have been in decline for a number of years. A good example of this is the tobacco industry, where, because of a concerted anti-smoking campaign, the British market for cigarettes has been declining for over ten years as consumption has fallen. This is an industry in structural decline.

A third set of conditions concerns the failure of companies to maintain their share of existing markets. In our research, this was often due to foreign competition. We visited companies involved in the manufacture of metal products, glass products, machine tools, footwear and textiles, which had been affected in this way. There were a number of underlying causes for the loss of market share. For a firm in the textile industry it was due to changes in fashion. The company had invested heavily in the production of nylon in the 1970s. This process has a long lead time before the investment pays off. A change in fashion to rayon left them with a greatly diminished product market. In other instances companies had failed to innovate and had been overtaken in the markets by superior products. However, one of the major causes was the relatively high cost of labour in advanced industrial societies making the product uncompetitive in terms of price. This was particularly noticeable in footwear and textiles, where the capital involved was being located in low-labour-cost countries. Although the overall size of the product market may continue to grow, the higher labour costs of firms based in the advanced industrial societies makes it increasingly difficult for them to compete. This situation is not dissimilar to that confronting those firms in the second category.

These categories are not mutually exclusive, for it was often the case that firms producing for a market which had been affected by the general fall in demand characteristic of a recession were also facing intensified competition from foreign companies with a superior product. This indicates the complexity of the relationship involved. It is interesting, in this respect, that we found it easier using statistical techniques to estimate the overall impact of cyclical and structural factors on the national labour markets than at the level of the individual firm.

Because of our concern to examine the effect of recession on the demand for labour we have focused primarily on factors leading to a decline in demand for products. Of course, even during the recession some companies continued to expand. In the manufacturing sector this may have been through diversification, product innovation, the company obtaining a larger share of existing markets or a combination of these. While individual employers pointed to the significance of the market for their product or service, the type of product market, whether it was domestic or international, was also important in determining the possibility of expanding the market and hence employment.

The numbers employed in a firm operating in a predominantly national market, such as that for confectionery or house construction, is influenced by the general level of demand and the ability of the firm to maintain its market share. The general level of demand in the domestic economy, subject to import penetration, will in theory set limits to the total employment levels in the industry. This is not the case in those firms operating in international markets. There, it is the level of world demand that is important, while the employment levels in Britain will be determined by the proportion of the total output which is manufactured in Britain. Firms operating in international markets thus have a greater potential for increasing employment, or conversely for losing it.

Service Sector

In the service sector there is not the same degree of international competition as in the manufacturing sector. Moreover, in the early 1980s only 18 per cent of world trade was in services, while the proportion of that trade held by the UK has been declining from 18 per cent in 1968 to 7 per cent in 1983.[2] Only in financial services and tourism do British companies compete in global markets to any significant degree. It follows from this that any expansion of employment in this sector is reliant upon an increase in domestic demand. This has been the case in retailing where the demand for goods has grown with the increase in the purchasing power of those in employment. Similarly, as the demand for leisure provision has grown so this has provided new markets in leisure services and fast food. Many of the companies operating in these product markets experienced a fall of demand at the height of the recession but this did not pose such a threat to their existence as it did in the manufacturing sector.

In this sector managers were also conscious of the relationship between the level of employment and the demand for the firm's output. This was particularly evident in those companies which had lost a substantial share of the market and been forced to make redundancies, as in the case of one distribution company which had seen its labour force halved over the period of the recession. However, a general increase in demand or an increase in their market share would not necessarily be capable of creating more jobs. Different factors associated with the structure of the product market in specific industries could explain this.

In the financial services sector there was the increased competition which occurred as a result of the deregulation of that industry. As the banks and building societies competed for the same customers the pressure was put on both to reduce costs in the fight to retain and attract customers. This created an additional stimulus to adopt labour-saving technology. The result was an attempt to sustain growth with a minimal addition of staff.

Changes also occurred in the market for retail goods and the hotel, catering and leisure industries. Here the changes were largely attributable to the emergence of large corporations which, in part, created a national market for their own products as in the retail trade and the leisure industry. Companies were successful in capturing a larger share of a growing market and putting smaller independent companies out of business or absorbing them through acquisition. This process will be discussed in detail in Chapter 4. Here it is sufficient to note that from the point of view of the managers of such companies, growth in profits and turnover was not necessarily associated with increases in employment. Indeed, in the leisure industry, companies taking over traditional family owned firms to increase their share of the market, tended to instigate quickly a process of rationalisation which reduced the number of employees required to provide an equivalent or even better service. Even where there may appear to be an increase in output accompanied by an increase in employment, close inspection can reveal a more complex situation. For example, a major brewery company, whose number of employees had increased in recent years, had effectively shifted its direction into new markets. Thus, although there had been reductions in the numbers engaged in the production of beer, this had been more than offset by the substantial increase in the workers employed in hotels and fast food outlets, which were becoming more significant areas of the business.

In view of these changes in the structure of product markets, it is not surprising that few of the large companies anticipated major growth in their labour force size. It may well be that the increase in numbers employed in this sector is stemming from the growth of smaller companies (Rajan and Pearson, 1986).

THE ACTIONS OF THE STATE

A firm's market share may also be susceptible to the effects of the actions of the state. In the same way that the state plays a role in regulating the conditions under which labour is bought and sold, so it plays a crucial role in regulating product markets. In the domestic market the state determines the conditions under which companies compete. An outstanding recent example of this in Britain was what is sometimes referred to as the deregulation of the financial markets, whereby the banks and building societies were permitted to compete across a range of financial services.

The state may also influence the operation of global markets, through its ability to determine the access of foreign companies to domestic markets. An obvious example is the power of the state to regulate air routes. This can also be achieved by the imposition of tariffs or, more indirectly, in the manner of the Japanese, by introducing regulations which make it difficult for foreign companies to get their products into the domestic market. Thus, special taxes may be imposed on foreign goods, such as Scotch whisky, or regulations introduced with which it is almost impossible for foreign manufacturers to comply. Japanese stipulations about the exhaust systems required on imported cars is a good example.

The Government's policy on exchange rates can directly affect a firm's market share, as can the provision of hidden subsidies to manufacturers. For example, cheap fuel may be provided to organisations requiring large inputs of energy to their manufacturing process. In a number of our case studies the companies claimed that the failure of the British Government to subsidise the cost of energy was putting some of their plants at risk. Companies in the cement and glass industries, both of which are large consumers of energy, argued that the provision of cheap energy to their foreign competitors by their governments was threatening the ability of the British plants to maintain competitiveness. In another case the imposition by the European Economic Community of restrictions on the processing of cane for sugar in order to protect European beet production was putting at risk a plant which was designed to process cane sugar. Some industries are regulated at the international level to prevent a free-for-all between competing nations; for example, the Multi-Fibre Agreement regulates the world's trade in cloth. It is clear from interviews that such political factors, far from being external constraints which may occasionally intrude upon the market for a product, are often important in defining the structure of the markets and hence the viability of continuing production.

Public Sector Employers

In the public sector the level of demand for a service is also seen as an element in determining employment levels, although its importance is partly dependent upon the outcome of political decisions. Decisions about the level of state expenditure are of crucial importance in determining the level of employment in this sector. However, at the local level the influence of central government is mediated by the political composition of the local authority. In recent years Labour-controlled authorities have tended to safeguard the level of employment within the limits of their powers, while Conservative and Alliance-controlled authorities have imposed greater restrictions on spending and so on the level of employment. Once again, other factors intrude to prevent the formulation of any neat deterministic models. For example, the reduction in the numbers of teachers employed by local education authorities could be said to be partly in response to falling rolls in schools. Opponents of this strategy may argue that maintaining the level of employment would reduce the teacher/pupil ratio, and thereby, hopefully, improve the quality of education. As another example, Social Services departments have been under considerable pressure to expand their staff numbers to cope with increased demand created by an aging population and political decisions to encourage greater community care as an alternative to hospitalising patients. A personnel manager interviewed in one authority explained how a series of Acts of Parliament had placed extra demands on the local authority which required additional staff if these demands were to be met. For example, the Mental Health Act had increased the involvement of social workers in the field of mental health, requiring the recruitment of extra social workers. The Education Act required that the authority publish information on schools' performance which again required extra staff. However, given the effect of cuts in the rate support grant, changes in the formula through which it was calculated, and rate capping, the authority was not in a position to recruit staff either to meet the perceived demand for social services or to fulfil its legal obligations. A similar situation can be found in the National Health Service, where the level of demand for a particular service is not always taken as the major determinant of the level of provision.

The influence of political pressures in determining employment levels can also be felt in public services such as the utilities. As a response to such pressures the relevant authorities have been attempting to cut costs and consequently restrict recruitment. As was the case with the local authorities, the water authorities have been encouraged to sub-contract much of their work, stop recruitment of staff and cut down on their capital investment. Here again, there is still a demand, in the form of the need to renew sewers and water-mains, but the decision about how much to invest in this area is influenced by political considerations.

THE EMPLOYMENT-OUTPUT RELATIONSHIP

Types of Employment-Output Relationship

After the product market, the employment-output relationship was the factor most frequently mentioned by managers as influencing

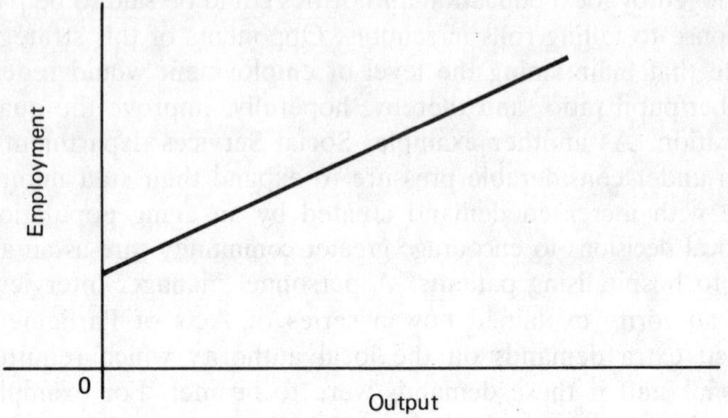

FIGURE 3.1 *The basic employment – output curve*

their employment levels. In fact, the capacity for changes in demand at the macro level to alter the demand for labour at the establishment level is largely dependent on the character of the employment-output relationship. There are an infinite number of employment-output relationships which we depict as existing between two extreme types. In one, capital is infinitely divisible, while in the other it is offered in 'chunks'. Figure 3.1 shows the first of these as a smooth employment-output curve. To produce more output, further labour is required. This is most closely approximated in traditional labour-intensive industries such as clothing, footwear and furniture and in the service sector in retail, and in hotel and catering. For example, in clothing manufacture, assuming that the firm is working to capacity, any increase in the output of, say, dresses requires the purchase of additional sewing machines and the recruitment of machinists to work them. In these industries a change in the demand for the product is immediately reflected in a change in the demand for labour. As output increases labour is taken on, while as it falls labour is laid off. The previous chapter showed how this is reflected in the recruitment practices of employers in these industries.

In the second type of employment-output relationship, capital, rather than being infinitely divisible, is available only in large units, so that any increase in capital (such as new plant) requires an initial disproportionate increase in employment. Employment then remains relatively stable irrespective of any increase in the level of output.

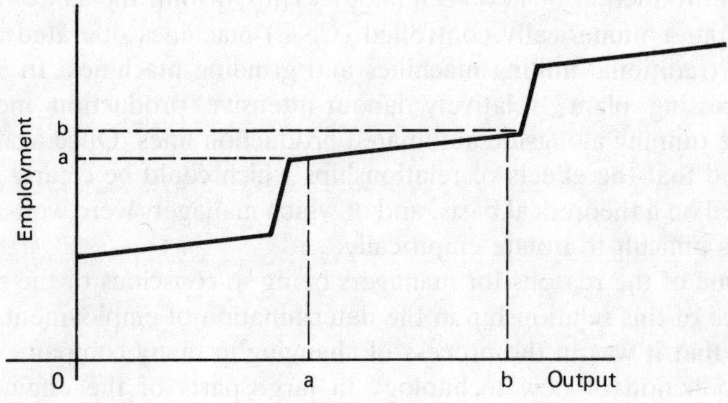

FIGURE 3.2 *The 'stepped' employment – output curve*

This is referred to as a step change in the relationship and is represented diagrammatically in Figure 3.2. This type is typically found in the process industries, such as in the manufacture of chemicals and man-made fibres. There, if a company is running its plant at full capacity and wishes to increase its output, it has to set up a new plant. This represents a major investment. Once that investment has been made then, irrespective of whether the plant is running at full capacity, the same number of operatives will be required. Thus, one of the companies we visited was operating its plant at 60 per cent capacity and could increase its output to 90 per cent without taking on any additional labour. This means that output can be varied without requiring a dramatic rise in employment. For example, in Figure 3.2 output may range from Oa to Ob with the requirement of labour only varying from La to Lb. When output required is Oa the firm can produce that amount, but it is producing under the firm's capacity. If output required rises then the amount of capacity used rises without any significant increase in employment. It is only when output moves beyond these limits that major changes in employment levels are necessary. In these circumstances employment levels will not vary directly with changes in output.

Within any one firm it was often difficult to establish with any precision which of the two types of relationship between output and employment predominated. In some instances this was because the relationship between employment and output was being changed by the introduction of new technology. Thus, within the same factory computer numerically controlled (CNC) machines operated alongside traditional milling machines and grinding machines. In a food processing plant, relatively labour-intensive production methods were running alongside automated production lines. Once again, we found that the effects of relationships which could be clearly established on a theoretical basis, and of which managers were well aware, were difficult to isolate empirically.

One of the reasons for managers being so conscious of the significance of this relationship in the determination of employment levels was that it was in the process of changing in many companies. The introduction of new technology in large parts of the engineering industry was creating rapid change while in the financial sector, the utilisation of information technology was having the same effect.

Management Strategies

One way of changing the employment-output relationship is by reducing the input of labour. All managers displayed a concern with minimising labour costs, but it was evident that many companies had used the opportunities provided by the recession deliberately to reduce the size of the labour force. Thus, a company in the petrochemical industry was able to achieve a reduction of 33 per cent in manning levels at one of its establishments without any effect on output. Even in the Financial Services sector increased competition was placing pressure on managements to do the same thing. In the retail and hotel and catering industries, management strategies *vis-à-vis* the use of labour, were one of the reasons for the competitive advantage of larger organisations over smaller independent operations. As already stated, in the public sector staffing levels are susceptible to the influence of political decisions. Among local authorities, Conservative-controlled authorities have tended to establish a policy of 'good housekeeping', ensuring that the staffing levels are 'finance-led,' whereas Labour-controlled authorities have a policy of minimising redundancies and staffing levels are more 'need-led'.

In concluding this section we would stress that across all industries employers had a range of discretion available to them in determining the precise level of staffing. The type of employment-output relationship which predominated in the firm was important but so too were a number of other factors. These included the degree of competition in the product market, the strength of unions and the political influences to which they were subject. However, within these constraints, management retained a degree of autonomy in determining which strategy it adopted in relation to its workforce.

OWNERSHIP

With the increasing penetration of British markets by transnational companies, ownership has become an important factor in determining a firm's investment and employment strategy. The investment policies of transnational companies, when seen from a British or European perspective, are more volatile than their national counterparts. Transnational companies owe no allegiance to any one nation state and investment decisions about where to locate manufacturing capacity are taken with reference to conditions in the global market. We found this to be the case in a number of such companies. For example, one company manufacturing pharmaceutical products could shift production and research and development from one country to another in order to maximise their competitive advantage in the global market.

In contrast, a British-owned family-controlled company had an explicit policy to locate manufacturing capacity in Britain wherever possible, even though they were competing in a global product market. As transnational companies increasingly dominate manufacturing industry such national loyalties will cease to operate. At a national level decisions concerning the domestic level of employment are increasingly being taken outside the confines of the national economy and being made by transnational companies (the implications of this are discussed in Chapter 6). This does not, as yet, apply extensively in the service sector, which is not so closely involved in global product markets.

THE EFFECTS OF WAGES ON EMPLOYMENT LEVELS

Given the prominence which economic theorists attach to the level of wages concerning the determination of employment levels, it is surprising that relatively few of the managers we interviewed mentioned it as a major influence on labour demand at the level of the firm. Labour costs were seen as important components of total costs and as such there was pressure on managers to minimise them.

However, wage levels were rarely mentioned. If a firm had to reduce labour costs this was done by reducing staffing levels or switching between types of labour, for example, by replacing full-time workers with part-timers. Only in companies operating in the low-paid areas of the service sector, such as hotels, catering, and fast food, did wage levels figure prominently in what they perceived as the major determinants of the level of employment.

The demand for labour is derived from the overall demand for the goods or services produced. At the level of the firm, however, the demand curve for labour is the marginal revenue productivity curve. It is the intersection of this curve and the supply curve which determines the equilibrium wage and employment levels. Each firm is assumed to maximise profits and to do so they are assumed to produce output at a minimum cost, which is referred to as the least cost combination. Other things being equal, if wage rates rise, the employment level in the firm will fall as firms switch from using labour to new, relatively less expensive capital. Hence, it is usually held that the wage level is an important determinant of the employment level. For many firms this may not be true. They may not be profit maximisers, seeking instead to maximise some other objective such as growth, sales revenue or some managerial utility function. There is a considerable literature on these alternative motivating factors which need not be repeated here. However, any theory other than profit maximisation, gives the firm leeway to be other than a seeker of least-cost combinations, and the wage may not be as important as first suggested. An example of such an alternative is output. Firms tend to concentrate on a given required level of output and will try to employ whatever amount of labour is required to produce that output. Within this they will still attempt to reduce costs as far as possible, but will do so subject to other pressures such as the smooth running of the factory, the necessity to meet demand on time, and so on.

Technology is always used as a substitute for labour, but it is open to question how much wage levels affect this investment decision. Given the pace of technological change many employers have to update their production methods or go out of business. If the wage were reduced by a high percentage it is doubtful whether it would be sufficient to counter the increase in production (and quality) which could be effected by the new technology. Indeed, the managing director of one of the largest employers in the textile industry argued precisely this case. He justified his decision to invest in expensive new machinery which required fewer workers, rather than to employ more workers on existing machinery, by claiming that the old production methods were slow and produced goods of inferior quality. The continuation of lengthy delivery dates and a poor-quality output would lead to the company losing its markets. Given the speed with which textile markets now change, the adoption of the latest technology is a prerequisite for being in a position to compete.

Thus, while accepting that in some sectors of the labour market there is an inverse relationship between the level of wages and employment, we do not believe that this relationship holds throughout the labour market. The employers in our sample did not necessarily regard the level of wages as a key factor in employment. Managements were more concerned with levels of output. Of far greater significance in determining the level of output were factors such as the state of the product market, the pattern of ownership, foreign exchange rates, the type of technology used and the Government regulation of product markets. Indeed, if, as our results suggest, the labour market is not a homogeneous whole, but is segmented along several dimensions, then economic and social forces which operate on wages and employment in one segment or part of the labour market may not operate on them in another segment. Chapter 2 presented evidence which suggested that changes taking place during the recession were having just such a differential impact. Chapters 4 and 5 will examine in greater detail their impact on the various segments of the labour market.

CONCLUSION

At the beginning of this chapter we stressed the ways in which, at the level of the individual firm, many of the factors we have identified were inter-related. Having dealt with them in isolation for analytic purposes we return to the question of their inter-relationship. Perhaps the best way of demonstrating this is through one of our case studies. This was a company manufacturing machine tools, of which a substantial proportion were exported. With the rise in the value of the pound in the early 1980s the company was faced with an effective increase in its prices of export goods of one third. At the same time, it found itself facing intense competition in its traditional markets from European and Japanese manufacturers, which were producing innovative CNC machines. Moreover, as machine tools are a capital investment, the effects of the recession were reducing demand. The company responded by changing its business strategy, reducing the number of models it made, and redesigning those it intended to continue to produce. This involved substantial job losses which stemmed from a number of the features we have identified; Government exchange rate policy, the fall in the general demand associated with the recession, and a change in the structure of competition in its product markets. In addition, the company introduced CNC machine tools into their own manufacturing process so that, following the depths of the recession, it was able to increase output without taking on the level of additional labour it would have required in the past. In this company, as in others, it was virtually impossible to quantify the contribution that each of the variable factors made to the change in the demand for labour that took place.

In our endeavours to simplify this complex inter-relationship we have identified how some of the factors which were found to affect the demand for labour at the national or macro level operate at the level of the firm. We have shown how cyclical changes in the pattern of demand interact with structural changes to reduce, or in some instances, increase the size of the workforce. However, the use of open-ended interviews has done more than just 'flesh out' the explanation produced by the quantitative analysis of labour force data, for it has revealed a number of factors that are important in structuring the demand for labour, but which are not evident from a quantitative approach. Among these are the actions of the state, changes in the structure of product markets, ownership and managements' labour market strategies. When seen from the perspective of individual companies, the actions of the state appear somewhat arbitrary, as, for example, in the decision not to intervene when the value of the pound sterling rose, and the decision not to subsidise energy costs. However, as with companies, so governments have a business strategy, which in Britain in the 1980s is to leave the economy to the operation of market forces. By contrast the Japanese and to a lesser extent the French, German and Swedish approaches are to use the powers of the state in conjunction with those of industry to encourage industrial growth in areas where it is felt the country has a competitive advantage. At a macro level such differences may prove to be a powerful factor affecting the general level of demand in the economy. Similarly, ownership proved to be an important factor in influencing investment decisions. In later chapters we shall continue this theme and show how ownership and changes in the structure of product markets are also important in influencing management's labour force strategy, and, through that, the type of jobs created. All of these have important implications for the demand for youth labour.

NOTES

1. The only qualification we would add here is that we focused primarily on the factors which managers perceived to be important as affecting their decisions. There are, of course, a number of factors which may affect their decisions without them being aware of it. Such factors are part of their 'taken for granted world'. For example, Blackburn (1987), has shown how companies do not meet the full costs of unemployment when declaring redundancies. The direct costs to the firm are small, being carried by other firms through taxes which are used to meet the costs of maintaining those made unemployed by specific employers. The analysis of managers' 'taken for granted worlds' is discussed in more detail in Chapter 6.
2. This issue is discussed in the Bank of England *Quarterly Bulletin*, September 1985.

4 Structuring the Supply of Workers

In Chapter 3 we identified a number of pressures which operated on employers to determine the number of workers employed. We now turn to a consideration of the factors which influence the supply of labour. In view of our concern with understanding the operation of the youth labour market the emphasis is on the supply of new entrants, especially school-leavers. We argue that the institutional structures which regulate the supply of workers, notably the educational and training arrangements, provide external constraints which influence employers' recruitment practices and the type of labour recruited for diferent types of jobs.

However, employers are not passive agents. Their interpretation of worker characteristics and especially the position of the person in the family are also important forces which serve to differentiate labour. The interplay of these two sources of differentiation leads to the segmentation of the youth and adult labour markets.

INSTITUTIONAL STRUCTURES

Education

In recruiting young workers, employers face a complex set of institutional arrangements through which young people are prepared for work. It is not widely appreciated how these arrangements structure the choices that are available to employers when making decisions about the groups at which their recruitment is targeted. The educational institutions are the most powerful in that they both prepare young people for work and, through a variety of mechanisms, regulate their aspirations and behaviour in accordance with the structure of opportunities available in the local labour market. It is useful here to make an intitial distinction between the institutions of higher education, which prepare young people for employment in the higher occupational segments, such as management and the professions, in what is essentially a national market, and the schools and further education colleges, which prepare youths for jobs at lower occupational levels in the local labour market. As we saw in Chapter 2, the number of jobs in the higher segments has expanded considerably throughout the recession. For those entering the middle and lower segments, the comprehensive schools, like the grammar and secondary modern schools which preceded them, give very clear signals to pupils about the segment of the labour market they could 'realistically' expect to enter (Ashton and Field, 1976). Those 16-year-olds from the middle streams of the comprehensives tend to enter the skilled manual and clerical segments while those from the lower streams enter the lower segments.

These features of the organisation of education which have functioned to structure the aspirations of pupils, have been reinforced by the academic curriculum. In higher education, the curriculum, which is controlled by the universities, has been closely linked to the requirements of the professions and the upper echelons of the Civil Service. In the grammar schools and upper streams of the comprehensive schools, which were seen as preparation for higher education, this curriculum also appeared well suited. For those in the middle streams destined for skilled manual and clerical work, it was largely irrelevant. The curriculum was negotiated by pupils in an instrumental manner, exchanging a minimal commitment and compliance to the school in exchange for the credentials that would ensure access to such jobs (Brown, 1987). Those in the lower streams, who were destined for semi-skilled and unskilled jobs, regarded this type of curriculum, even in a watered-down form, as irrelevant and often offered resistance, either individually through truancy or collectively through a counter-culture.[1]

These relationships between education and the labour market were almost ruptured by the severity of the recession and the mass youth unemployment which accompanied it (Wallace, 1987 and 1987a). The result was a series of major interventions by the state, culminating in the two-year YTS programme. This has effectively extended the period of transition for many youths (i.e., approximately half the 16-year-old leavers) and created a new pre-entry period as they wait to obtain access to permanent full-time paid employment. From the youths' perspective, they have had to develop new strategies. Increasing proportions have chosen to stay on at school. Others have sought to use the 'better' YTS schemes, which offer the promise of eventual entry to a skilled or clerical job, as a means of realising ambitions they were unable to achieve on first leaving school. Others who failed to enter the 'better' schemes have either made do with whatever scheme was available or rejected them altogether and tried their luck in the labour market (Furlong, 1987).[2]

Yet throughout this period of radical change, some features of the relationship between education and the labour market have remained constant. Youths in Britain still leave school earlier than those in other advanced industrial societies. The Technical and Vocational Education Initiative (TVEI) has succeeded in introducing a more relevant and interesting curriculum for some but, given the instrumental orientation of the pupils, this has had little impact on decisions to leave at 16.[3] At the same time the relationship between the organisation of education and the labour market segments into which the different types of education feed remains the same. Indeed, proposed reforms of the educational system are likely to make the links even more apparent through the introduction of selective schools feeding into the middle segments. In this sense all that YTS has done is to extend the period of transition from a matter of months to one of years, thereby slowing down the absorption of youths into the labour market. Other institutionalised forms of training which function to prepare youths for the labour market also remain intact. The most important of these has been the apprenticeship system operating in such industries as Engineering, Construction and Hairdressing. Although the numbers of apprentices in Engineering fell dramatically over the period 1978/9 to 1983/4 from 24 500 to 9800, the institutional arrangements which govern apprenticeship training were effectively reinforced by the introduction of YTS.

The introduction of YTS, through employers rather than through the education system, meant that employers received a subsidy to take on and train young people. The provision of the subsidy was not contingent upon plans to change their existing recruitment and training systems. Consequently, most employers incorporated the young people who entered the scheme into their existing practices. Thus, in Engineering and Construction, YTS was incorporated into the first year of the apprenticeship, thereby reinforcing the practice of recruiting young people at 16.

Training

The British system of training has traditionally been centred around the apprenticeship. Organised by employers and unions, apprenticeships have historically represented the peak of attainment for most of working-class youth. The transferable skills offered provided the route to relatively high and secure earnings and status. This, together with age restrictions on entry, encouraged youths to seek the minimal qualifications necessary for entry (which was often no more than a satisfactory school performance) and enter a trade before they were 17 or 18 years of age.[4] The apprenticeship has served the interests of workers by regulating the flow of labour into the occupation while providing employers with a predictable supply of skilled labour. More recently, age restrictions have been lifted and a modular system of training has replaced the time-served basis. In practice, however, 16 is still the age at which recruitment takes place. Any employer who wishes to secure the services of the more able school-leaver as a trainee has to recruit at 16, as that is when other employers are competing for the 'best' labour. Once established, the system develops its own dynamics and puts pressure on other employers to conform. Often, this competition for the 'best' school-leaver recruits results in the main employers in a locality bringing forward their recruitment campaigns in order to ensure that they have the pick of potential candidates. Offers of jobs may be made in the first term of an applicant's last year at school.

Although the apprenticeship system remains central to the British system of training, political and economic changes have led to modifications. Occupations which have developed in the twentieth century, notably secretarial and clerical work and service industry occupations (such as chefs and receptionists), had no such institutional mechanisms to provide training. In response to demands from the market, private courses and courses in Colleges of Further Education were established to provide secretarial training. The large employers in the financial sector provided their own training, and recruited those with some academic achievement directly from school. In parts of the Retail, Hotel and Catering sector, which was traditionally characterised by small firms, the training for chefs, receptionists and, more recently, managers, was left to local colleges. Recently, the advent of mass unemployment has encouraged the state to provide training for early school-leavers through YOP and YTS. YTS has incorporated some aspects of traditional forms of work preparation, such as the apprenticeship. However, the degree to which YTS has replaced traditional routes into work, sometimes with a considerably enlarged training component, is variable (Turbin, 1987). Some employers still recruit youths without recourse to the scheme, especially in economically buoyant areas, where competition for labour is intense.

Thus, when recruiting young people, employers may be faced with widely differing institutional constraints, depending on their industrial sector, the occupation for which they are recruiting, and the geographical location of the plant. Besides influencing employers' recruitment practices, these institutional arrangements also play an important part in structuring the firm's internal labour market.

Occupational Labour Markets and Firm Internal Labour Markets

In industries such as Engineering, Construction and Printing, the employers' recruitment and training policies are shaped by well-established institutional arrangements, which underpin occupational labour markets. The Engineering industry has the tripartite arrangement between the employer, unions and the Engineering Industry Training Board (EITB), which provides the framework within which the recruitment and training of skilled manual and technician workers takes place. As mentioned in Chapter 2, this performs important functions not only in spreading the costs of training across the industry, but also in constraining the options available to employers in their choice of labour and in the composition of their internal labour markets. Employers' recruitment policies are affected by important aspects of the provision of training being 'external' to the firm. This is especially so where there are strong union agreements which specify the appropriate apprenticeship qualification necessary for anyone wishing to work in a given occupational specialism. In these circumstances a company wishing to train skilled manual and technician labour is obliged to restrict recruitment to 16- and 17-year-olds. The establishment of such a separate channel of recruitment into skilled manual occupations prohibits these skilled jobs from being part of an internal career ladder. The internal labour market is characterised by rigid horizontal barriers which separate the skilled workers from other manual workers. In this way the training institutions influence the internal structure of the organisation. However, not all companies adhere to such practices and so will promote experienced workers into skilled jobs, creating an informal internal labour market. It is unclear just how widespread this practice is, but for a minority of young adults it does provide an alternative route to skilled status that is discussed in Chapter 7.

Other manufacturing industries have fewer external constraints on recruitment and training activities, especially since the disbanding of many of the Industrial Training Boards. For example, the Textile, Footwear and Food Processing industries are characterised by firm internal labour markets, and relatively weak trade unions, in terms of bargaining power. This allows the employer greater control over the provision and organisation of training, and the function it performs in the internal labour market. Consequently, recruitment will be targeted at those whose level of training and previous experience is appropriate for the degree of post-entry training provided.

In the service sector, employers in Retail, Hotels, Catering and Leisure have been able to rely on the state to fund a minimal level of training. However, the recent emergence within those industries of large national corporations has meant that employers are now in a position to use their internal labour markets and exert far greater control over the structure of training for the industry as a whole. In the past, apart from training offered in Colleges of Further Education, recruits in this industry picked up their knowledge through on-the-job experience. As we show in Chapter 6, because these large corporations now control a significant proportion of the labour force they are able to systematise training. Instead of individuals moving from one small employer to another for better pay or more interesting work, the large corporations can offer internal promotion. Thus, YTS has been incorporated as the main port of entry into an internal labour market which can offer progression up the career ladder within the firm. Similarly, at management level, the professionalisation of the occupation is being encouraged in order to raise standards of performance in Catering. Employers in Banking and Finance have always maintained control over the training of their personnel and integrated it into their internal labour markets. This is also true of the police force.

The labour market for typists and secretaries transcends industrial boundaries, but, unlike in most male-dominated occupations, there are no unions or professional organisations which control training. In Marsden's (1986) terms this is an 'unregulated occupational labour market.' The result is that employees are recruited into specific posts, which represent enclaves within the internal labour market, often with little or no prospect of internal promotion.

All the training arrangements we have discussed so far, have been influential in determining the pattern of entry to the middle and lower segments of the labour market. With the exception of the Engineering, Construction and Printing industries, trades unions have only played a minor role. In the higher segments, the professional bodies have been much more influential in determining the pattern of recruitment and the provision of training. The medical and legal professions are the most obvious examples of this. In medicine the profession has been able to dictate the structure of training and thereby define the internal labour markets of the health organisations. The professional bodies in engineering have been less influential in controlling entry, although they have played an important part in determining the content of training. The power of such professional bodies in creating horizontal divisions within organisations has already been illustrated. In this respect the internal labour markets of the various local authorities and health services may be appropriately conceptualised as local parts of one national labour market jointly controlled by employers and professional bodies.

The strength of the constraints imposed on management's behaviour by institutional arrangements for training are clearly variable both between occupations and industries. If employers wish to train their own typists and secretaries they can do so with relative ease. In the higher segments it is far more difficult, if not impossible, to ignore the constraints imposed by some of the stronger professional associations on the form and content of training and indirectly on recruitment and the structure of the internal labour market.

WORKER CHARACTERISTICS

When deciding from which groups to recruit, employers' assessments will often be influenced by their perceptions of worker characteristics. Age, gender and expertise are of major importance. Through their control over the recruitment process, they are able to impose their own, sometimes idiosyncratic, definitions, which effectively determine the access of different groups to jobs. It is the ability of employers to enforce their definitions of worker characteristics that provides one of the most important mechanisms linking the position a person occupies in the family to their position in the labour market.

Gender

Employers' perceptions of the characteristics of males and females as potential recruits, are related to traditional values about domestic circumstances, notably about the domestic division of labour. Males who have family responsibilities in the form of mortgage repayments and children to maintain, are regarded as the most desirable recruits for routine operative jobs, as it is felt that their domestic commitments will ensure that they work regularly and in a disciplined manner. A standard response to requests to define the 'ideal' manual worker is: 'A male aged between 25 and 35, married with two kids, a mortgage and repayments on a car.' By contrast females are seen as more committed to their domestic role. In the event of a clash of loyalties, such as when a child is ill, the domestic role is expected to have first claim on the person's loyalties. For this reason employers perceive females as being less committed and hence less stable employees than males. Consequently, an employer recruiting labour for a capital intensive plant which requires a series of cohesive work groups, which have to work shifts to ensure continuity of production, will deem the extra cost of the labour of prime age males worth while. On the other hand, in industries such as Hosiery and Footwear, where the work is individual machine based, and where high rates of labour turnover can allow adjustments to be made to the size of the workforce to match seasonal fluctuations in demand, the perceived personal characteristics of females, in addition to their lower wages, can be seen as advantageous.

High labour turnover is not necessarily regarded as a problem in very routine jobs with low skill content. Recruitment will often be targeted at females working part-time. A minimum of commitment is expected from the employee, while the flexibility of working hours, possibly between 10.00 a.m. and 3.00 p.m., while the children are at school, or an evening 'twilight' shift, after the husband has returned home from work, means that the intrusion which work makes on the married woman's domestic responsibilities is minimised. However, this does not apply to young females whose suitability is questioned, because it is believed that 'they want full-time jobs' and will therefore be likely to leave should full-time work become available, especially in areas of full employment. This is not necessarily the case in areas of long-standing high unemployment, where the scarcity of full-time jobs has led employers to re-assess their ideas concerning the personal characteristics of youths, and to accept them as suitable candidates for part-time jobs. Another factor which works to the detriment of young people, however, is that a larger increase in jobs in recent years has been among clerical workers employed part-time in parts of the service sector, such as banks and building societies. More often than not, older women returning to the labour market are preferred to young people, as they have previous experience and are perceived to be better at customer relations, especially when this involves handling cash transactions.[5]

For higher status professional, administrative and management jobs, adult males have traditionally been stereotyped as being more committed to a career in the organisation than are females. In the eyes of employers the possibility of females interrupting their career to have children renders them potentially less likely to repay fully any investment made in their training, especially if they decide to return to work only on a part-time basis.

Thus for many years banks and other financial institutions used to make a distinction between males as career employees and females as non-career employees. For this reason males were recruited into career grades as future managers and technical experts, while females predominantly entered non-career grade jobs as cashiers and clerks. In recent years, the combined influence of equal opportunities legislation and a fear of future labour shortages at the career level, has led to the diminution in importance of this division. Increasingly females are being accepted into career positions. This change coincides with a trend amongst female workers to spend less time out of the labour force for the purpose of childbirth and child-rearing (Martin and Roberts, 1984; Dex, 1987). We are not in a position to determine whether the stereotypes reported here accord with 'objective' observable differences or whether they are a result of personal or structural characteristics. There is evidence which suggests that many married women do give their domestic responsibilities highest priority when choosing work, but whether this affects their behaviour once at work is an open question (Chaney, 1981). Similarly, there is evidence that some males place their commitment to their career higher than that to their domestic responsibilities (Pahl and Pahl, 1971), but so too do some women. The point of reporting these sex stereotypes is to demonstrate their significance in reproducing the subordination of females in the labour market. However, employers are not the only agents responsible for the reproduction of gender inequalities. The recent work of Griffin (1985) and Cockburn (1987) among others, has begun to unravel the complexities of the issues, which involve fundamental questions of patriarchy and identity.

Their conclusions are supported by the results of our interviews. Respondents in two large companies in the textile and footwear industries claimed to have attempted to introduce males into what were seen as traditional female jobs. In both instances a small number of males had been recruited as machinists, but pressure from the female work group led the males to leave. At one plant the influx into the area of a new ethnic group with different cultural traditions had provided management with the opportunity of breaking down gender role stereotypes. Asian males were recruited as machinists, albeit in the more highly skilled jobs, but, after a period of harassment by the female workforce, the males left and were not replaced. In this instance racial prejudice may also have been a factor.

At the local level, the traditions of what are appropriate male and female jobs are usually so strong that they rarely need to be enforced through such collective worker behaviour. Once established, they acquire a degree of autonomy and are transmitted via family socialisation from one generation to the next. Young females acquire from their mothers appropriate aspirations which will either reinforce, or at least not damage, their gender identity (Griffin, 1985). Young males on the other hand, acquire their occupational aspirations from their fathers (Furlong, 1987a). For both sexes, the school tends to reinforce their gender identities with the result that on entering the labour market, young males apply for one type of job and young females for another. Most employers accept the traditions and work within them, by expecting these differentials in applications.

From a sociological perspective these stereotypes are important in that they form one of the mechanisms through which differences in the social location of males and females, particularly in relation to the domestic division of labour, are transformed into differential opportunities in the labour market. In so doing they also point to some of the reasons why the substitution of male for female labour, and vice versa, is so difficult.

Any attempt to challenge the powerful forces which maintain the existing level of sex segregation in the labour market means acting on several separate fronts. Firstly, the maintenance of these sex stereotypes ensures that women are concentrated in relatively powerless positions in the labour market, providing employers with a large pool of relatively cheap labour. Secondly, the present distribution of sex inequalities in jobs provides support for the gender identity of both sexes so that changes are likely to be resisted. For men, doing 'women's' work would expose them to jibes from their male friends and so create a threat to their masculinity, while for young women in particular, gaining access to a traditionally male occupation may threaten their identity and possibly damage their chances in the marriage market. Thirdly, the introduction of women may pose a threat to the males' monopoly of the higher-paid jobs. Finally, the current organisation of the division of labour within the family creates different pressures on both sexes, forcing many females to accept the more marginal occupations, on returning to the labour market.

Age

Stereotyping plays an equally important role in differentiating youth jobs from adult jobs. Once again we are reporting managers' opinions or perceptions of young adults. These are important because they form the basis of decisions which lead to young adults being excluded from some jobs while being preferred for others. Unqualified male youths are often seen by managers as irresponsible, lacking in commitment to the organisation, unreliable and likely to be a disruptive influence in the work group. This was especially the case among managers recruiting for jobs in high-technology firms, where young males were seen as totally unsuitable labour when compared with prime age adult males. Such a stereotype emphasises certain aspects of the social location of youths, notably their transitory status between their family of origin and their family of destination, when they have few responsibilities and when their courting and leisure activities may take priority over their obligations to their employer.

When recruiting young people for skilled manual and clerical work different criteria are utilised. The potential recruit is regarded differently, being someone who has achieved something at school, demonstrated a capacity for hard work and shown that he or she has the ability and aptitude to learn. It is for this reason that employers use educational qualifications to discriminate between applicants. Although the particular academic subjects in which the certificates are obtained may well be irrelevant for the performance of the work tasks, educational certification does signify a general level of ability and a willingness to learn which, in the absence of previous work experience, are important signals to the employers.[6] Moreover, after being appointed, the job provides considerable rewards for completing the training and so encourages stability.

One advantage which youth labour is seen to have over that of adults is that youths are easier to train, as they do not have to 'unlearn' previous work habits and attitudes. In today's parlance they are 'flexible' and can be easily adapted to the requirements of the organisation. This is regarded as a particularly advantageous characteristic when recruiting for jobs which require familiarity with word processors and computers. Youths also often have the added advantage of familiarity with such technology. This concern among employers in Britain with the adaptability and trainability of young people when recruiting for skilled manual and clerical jobs, is not found in all societies. For example, Canadian employers do not recruit for such jobs until applicants have first demonstrated their abilities on the job. After being recruited at 18-plus, young adults spend a probationary period in less skilled work before receiving training as a skilled worker. This suggests that the stereotype may be a product of the institutional regulation of the labour market in Great Britain, in which management and union agreements and training arrangements place the emphasis on recruitment to jobs entailing lengthy training periods at 16 or 17.

It is clear from these findings that statements from employers about the characteristics of young workers need to be placed in the context of the labour market segment within which the employers are recruiting if they are to help us understand the operation of the labour market. In the absence of such knowledge general questions asked in surveys about the qualities employers seek in the labour they recruit are almost meaningless and may even be misleading. The characteristics which different groups of workers are perceived to possess in common, only become important in relation to the demands of the occupation in the particular segment for which recruitment is taking place.

CONCLUSION

In Chapter 3 we explored the factors which influence the amount of labour recruited by firms. In this chapter we have attempted to identify some of the factors which differentiate the supply of labour and so influence the type of labour recruited. The importance of this for our understanding of the structure of the labour market is twofold. Firstly, it shows some of the mechanisms which serve to differentiate and segment the labour force. As we saw in Chapter 1, in spite of initial attempts to distinguish non-competing groups in the labour market, neo-classical economists and some sociologists still tend to treat labour as a relatively undifferentiated and easily substitutable commodity. In view of this we have identified some of the main sources of sex and age discrimination. One of the most important of these is the employers' definitions of worker characteristics in terms of the position the person occupies in the domestic division of labour and life cycle. The existence of these discriminatory mechanisms explain the difficulties which employers face in trying to substitute different types of labour and which reformers face in their attempts to secure greater equality of access to jobs. Secondly, in differentiating the supply of labour, schools and training institutions impose conditions on employers which affect their behaviour. Thus, in Britain the training system subjects employers to pressures which leads them to recruit 16- and 17-year-olds as apprentices and trainees and excludes adults from such positions. These arrangements lead employers to compete for the labour of the 'best' 16-year-olds as trainees. However, for the more prestigious jobs in the professions, technology and administration, the training arrangements lead to the exclusion of all school-leavers. From this it follows that, overall, the institutional arrangements for the provision of education and training play just as crucial a role in determining the opportunities available for school-leavers as do the pressures which operate on employers from the demand side.

These findings suggest that if we are to understand the impact of the institutional arrangements for training on educational provision, and on the structure of opportunities available to youths, it is important to conceptualise them as a system of relations. This means abandoning attempts to treat education and training as separate, autonomous activities and focus instead on the relationship between the two. Thus, we cannot explain the desire among youths to leave school at 16 and enter the labour maket, even when few jobs are available, without reference to the organisation of training and the competition this generates among employers to secure the best recruits. The policy implications of this are discussed in Chapter 9. Here the main objective has been to establish the importance of both the educational and training systems and employers' definitions of worker characteristics in segmenting the labour market.

NOTES

1. There is considerable debate about whether the origins of this resistance lay in the organisation of school or in the social class culture of the pupils. See P. Brown, 1987.
2. Similar strategies have been adopted by German youth as they have come to terms with the declining demand for youth labour and the introduction of new Government schemes. See W.L. Heinz, 1987.
3. The introduction of the Technical and Vocational Education Initiative has

changed the curriculum of those predominantly working-class pupils who enter the lower segments. Those destined for further and higher education still tend to opt for the more academic curriculum. The facility for schools to opt out of the local authority and the introduction of city colleges are both likely to strengthen the links between the leavers from such schools and entry to the middle and higher segments.

4. We refer here to the majority of those entering apprenticeships; in some trades, such as knitting mechanics, entry cannot take place until aged 18.
5. Here we are referring to part-time jobs. When recruiting for full-time jobs as secretaries and receptionists, employers may prefer younger women.
6. For a more extensive discussion of these issues see Ashton and Maguire (1980) and Maguire and Ashton (1981).

5 Determinants of the Type of Labour Employed at the Level of the Firm

INTRODUCTION

Having examined the factors which determined the general demand for labour and explored some of the mechanisms which functioned to differentiate those people seeking jobs, our primary concern in this chapter is to explain the position of youths in the labour market. Given the sex segregation of the labour market we will also attempt to account for the concentration of young males and females in different parts of the youth labour market.

While it is commonplace to make a theoretical distinction between factors which determine the general level of demand and those which determine the type of labour employed, on an empirical level this distinction cannot always be sustained. The reason for this is that the factors which create a demand for one type of labour rather than another are mediated by a whole set of institutional and political factors, both within and outside the organisation, as well as by the struggle between capital and labour. For example, new technology has enabled banks and building societies to reduce the labour input required to process files, and has enabled engineering companies to reduce the labour required to machine parts. However, the degree to which this results in the deskilling of the operations and the possibility of substituting, say, unskilled females for more highly skilled males, or vice versa, depends on a whole number of other factors, such as the type of technology introduced, the availability of different types of labour, the willingness and ability of labour to resist such changes and the outcome of political struggles within the organisation. In view of this, it is perhaps surprising that, over time, a number of factors do appear to create pressures for the recruitment of one type of labour.

THE STATE

Any attempt to explain why employers use one type of labour rather than another in Western societies assumes that the state is committed to fostering the conditions of a market economy, with property rights being defined, maintained and defended. Without always being conscious of the fact, individual actors, such as employers and employees, take these structural conditions for granted. The role of the state is also crucial in maintaining the conditions of the labour contract, which ensures the subordination of labour to capital. This is regarded by employers as a facet of the 'natural order' of things. Employers are more aware of state intervention in determining the type of labour which can be recruited, or in specifying the conditions under which labour can be employed. For example, legislation restricts the ability of young people to work certain shifts or to serve alcohol, thereby creating barriers to their employment in parts of the labour market. Minimum wage legislation, operated through Wages Councils, may also determine the conditions under which youths can be hired.

EMPLOYERS OPERATING IN COMPETITIVE PRODUCT MARKETS

While these conditions operate throughout the market, some employers are more conscious of pressures on labour costs than others. Amongst the respondents in our sample, those whose firms were operating in a highly competitive product market were likely to regard cost as a significant determinant of the type of labour to be recruited, while those from firms in oligopolistic markets viewed other factors as being more important.

In highly competitive product markets, the pressure on labour costs is considerable, because the costs of entering the market, in terms of capital equipment, are often relatively low. Such a situation could be said to closely approximate that of perfect competition, and can be found in some of the traditional manufacturing industries such as Textiles, Footwear and Clothing and parts of the Plastics, Construction, Retail, Catering and Leisure industries. Wages form a large proportion of the total costs of production and firms of all sizes tend to be very conscious of their significance in determining the viability of the company or organisation.[1] Any major increase in the cost of labour which was not also incurred by their competitors could threaten the profitability of the firm. Similarly, any innovation which could reduce labour costs would provide a significant competitive advantage. Inevitably, this creates pressure on the employers to hire the cheapest type of labour available and generates a strong downward pressure on wages.

Previous governments, through the action of Wages Councils in these industries, have sought to provide a baseline below which wages should not fall, in order to counter this downward pressure. Indeed, some respondents from the larger organisations in these industries expressed a desire to have the wages of young workers excluded from such regulation in order that a lower starting wage could be introduced. Yet even were that to happen they did not anticipate recruiting more youths. Rather they hoped to contain existing labour costs. Reducing the starting rate would make it easier for them to introduce an internal market or career ladder which would enhance the commitment of their staff, and through that, provide a better quality of customer service than their competitors.

The Attraction of Youth Labour

In a highly segmented labour market the low wages paid to unqualified youths, relative to those paid to adults, make young people attractive to employers operating in competitive product markets.[2] Indeed, young people who are in employment are concentrated in the industrial orders of Other Manufacturing, Distribution, Hotels and Other Services, which are the sectors where pressure on wage costs is greatest, especially in smaller firms.

Although the relatively low wage costs of youths explain why they are attractive to employers, it does not follow that increasing the youth/adult wage differentials will thereby generate a significant increase in the number of jobs available to youths. In firms operating in domestic product markets a fall in the cost of youth labour, either forcing down wages or through the use of subsidies, will not necessarily increase the total demand for labour. As we saw in Chapter 3, that is determined by the overall level of demand in the domestic economy. A lowering of the relative cost of youth labour may encourage some substitution of adults by youths but not an overall increase in the numbers employed. A reduction in the cost of youth or adult labour will only lead to an increase in the number of jobs available in labour intensive firms operating in international product markets. In these product markets a national subsidy or direct reduction in wage costs in British firms will lower the cost of production in comparison to that of foreign competitors and so provide British firms with a competitive advantage. This will enable them to increase their share of the product market and hence the number of employees.

However, this strategy runs the danger of forcing down the level of wages in industries such as Textiles and Footwear to those prevalent in the low labour cost countries of the Far East. Thus, given the segmented character of both product and labour markets, attempts to reduce labour costs through state subsidies are unlikely to generate significant increases in the overall level of employment throughout the labour market. Only in those industries operating in international product markets can overall job gains be expected. Elsewhere, any gains in the number of youth jobs created by the lowering of youth wages will be at the expense of jobs for adults.

The search for cheap labour is not the only factor which leads to the recruitment of young workers, as there are a number of other considerations which influence employers. Some forms of payment structure do not provide youths with any cost advantage over adults. When employers are paying on a piece-work basis, as is often the case in Footwear, Hosiery, Food Manufacture and Other Manufacturing, the age of the person doing the work is virtually irrelevant, as the level of income received is dependent on 'the price of the job' and the operative's speed.

If the work involves a period of training before the person can be made fully productive, employers in small firms often refuse to recruit youths, no matter how cheap their labour. For these firms the cost of disruption to production incurred in supervising the 'trainee' is such that it outweighs any advantage to be derived from employing them. Even if the training should only consist of 'sitting next to Nellie', it means distracting other operatives and reducing their output. In addition, there are the costs of wasted materials and the wages of the trainee while he or she learns the trade. These employers are likely to recruit only experienced labour.

If it is not always attributable to a cost advantage, then how do we explain the presence of a large proportion of youths in the labour forces of firms in these manufacturing industries? A young person's perceived ability to learn quickly allied to a willingness to accept a low wage during the period of training may provide a further explanation. But this would only be for those firms which are prepared to undertake training. As we have seen, small firms will often refuse to train. However, this strategy is only possible if there is a ready supply of trained labour already available, as in local labour markets where particular industries are concentrated. For example, in the Hosiery and Knitwear industry in Leicester, the larger firms recruit youths for training, thereby providing a pool of skilled labour, from which the smaller firms recruit. Firms operating in local labour markets where there is no such pool of skilled labour are obliged to do their own training.

Employers may prefer young workers because of their flexibility. It is widely believed that where the tasks require manual dexterity, young workers can pick up the relevant skills much faster than older workers. Whether there is any scientific basis for such a belief, is beyond the scope of this enquiry but certainly many employers claimed that their experience had shown this to be true.

The Exclusion of Youth Labour

There are other pressures on employers which can lead them to exclude youths from unskilled and semi-skilled jobs even though the labour of youths would be cheap. If the work involved is heavy and the pay is subject to union regulation, which raises it above that of the average unskilled worker, then employers may limit their recruitment to adult males, as is the case in some of the Utilities. Similarly in the manufacturing sector, companies operating shifts, will usually exclude young people from consideration, and direct recruitment at prime age males with family responsibilities. The high cost of insurance may prevent young people gaining access to driving jobs or to those involving responsibility for handling money, while trade union bans on the employer participating in the Youth Training Scheme may also close jobs to youths.

The other major area from which both adult males and youths are largely excluded is that of part-time work. There, the labour of married females, besides providing a major cost advantage in that it is cheaper than employing full-time workers, has the added advantage of allowing greater flexibility. Employers, especially in the Retail and Hotel and Catering trades, can at short notice, adjust the hours of work required in order to meet fluctuations in the demand for the service on offer. In addition, young people are seen as being less reliable than females returning to the labour force on a part-time basis.

Other Sources of Labour Market Segmentation

Where pressures from a competitive product market combine with the need for a relatively skilled labour force, employers often seek to employ females, largely because of the substantially lower costs involved. However, the prevalence of equal opportunity legislation can prevent them from stating this to be the reason. Some jobs are classified as being naturally women's work, due to factors such as the requirement for 'nimble fingers' or certain keyboard skills. Two major employers in the Footwear and Knitwear industries went so far as to say that the availability of female labour was an important consideration when determining the location of their plants. Young females are regarded as suitable to be recruited as trainees in such industries for the reasons already mentioned, namely that the low initial wage does not act as a deterrent and also because they are seen as being easier to train. Moreover, once they are trained it may be from five to ten years before they leave for child-rearing. It may also be that Textile and Footwear are industries where employers have succeeded in defining certain jobs as semi-skilled, when, were they to be undertaken by males, they would be classified as skilled (Westwood, 1984). Young males are not usually considered for such jobs, and few apply. They do enter these industries but in different, more highly paid, 'skilled' occupations.

Prime age males with family responsibilities are also excluded from part-time jobs and the low-paid jobs found in the Catering, Hotel and Leisure industry, by virtue of the low level of wages paid. Adult males do not usually apply as the pay is frequently below that recognised by the state as necessary to maintain a family at the basic level of subsistence.

These then are some of the pressures which further segment the labour market when employers are recruiting semi-skilled and unskilled labour. The result is that even in the lowest segment of the labour market different types of labour are not always interchangeable. In fact the points of entry to the labour market where there is open competition between groups such as youths/adults, males/females or full-timers/part-timers, are limited. Employers usually direct their recruitment at specific groups or types of labour.

EMPLOYERS OPERATING UNDER CONDITIONS OF OLIGOPOLY

Firms operating in conditions which approximate those of oligopoly or monopoly do not experience the same pressure to recruit the cheapest labour. The fact that they operate within a capitalist economy ensures that the profit constraint operates, but the extent to which it dominates other objectives is unclear. It may be, as Scott (1979) suggests, that such firms are long-term profit seekers rather than short-term profit maximisers. The evidence from empirical studies of the motivations of employing organisations is inconclusive. Managers do not necessarily rank maximisation of profits as the major target, and will often deny that adequate information is available to make the appropriate marginal decisions. Much depends not just on the behaviour of the individual firm, but on that of its competitors. Managers are likely to be constrained not by a profit maximisation requirement, but by a minimum profit constraint. This is a minimum level of profit required to prevent shareholders from either directly replacing management or selling their shares due to dissatisfaction with returns. This latter could lead to a fall in the price of shares, and possibly the threat of a takeover. Our findings suggest that the extent to which the profit constraints affects managers' behaviour is variable. In times of recession or when the collapse of a domestic monopoly results in the integration of the domestic market into an international market, then the profit constraint is dominant. In periods of economic boom or under monopoly conditions, other objectives, such as sales revenue maximisation, or growth, may be the dominant goal.

The Exclusion of Youth Labour

When discussing the type of labour recruited, oligopolistic organisations show little concern with minimising labour costs by switching from one type of labour to another. The firms we visited were concerned with containing labour costs, but this was achieved by reducing staffing levels, improving productivity or delegating financial responsibility to the companies' operating units thereby creating individual cost centres and enhancing awareness of the importance of minimising costs. There was no suggestion of substituting young workers for prime age males. Some firms had introduced casual and temporary contracts as a way to cut labour costs, but these were usually for jobs which previously had been filled by females working full-time. Very rarely did these large manufacturing companies consider switching the type of labour used. Their main concern was to ensure that they recruited the right type of labour. In the case of many manufacturing companies this was a question of recruiting professionally or technically qualified adults, for as was shown in Chapter 2, these were the jobs which continued to expand throughout the recession. Young people were effectively excluded, due to the length of training required to obtain the appropriate certification.

Young people under 18 years are also usually excluded from capital-intensive manufacturing plants, which require round-the-clock operation. Here it is a case of recruiting mature, prime age males with domestic responsibilities, who can be relied upon to work conscientiously and accept the discipline of the workplace. Youths are not recruited, because of legal restrictions on their employment or because they are perceived as unreliable by the employers. None of the capital-intensive manufacturing plants that we visited employed 16-year-old school-leavers in routine operative jobs. One firm rejected them because they paid relatively high wages for the locality and managers saw it as improper to hire single youths when prime age males with domestic commitments were out of work. In addition, youths were seen as irresponsible and a possible source of disruption to the smooth running of the production process. So powerful were the barriers which created the segmentation of labour that even if the labour of youths was free, as it was on a number of Government schemes, employers would still not recruit 16–18-year-olds. They might, out of a sense of social responsibility, run a YTS scheme, but the placements were often in clerical work or outside the firm; the trainees were never used in the production process.

Another area where 16- and 17-year-old school-leavers are increasingly excluded is in recruitment to training for professional, managerial and technical jobs. Here the pressures for exclusion stem largely from the professional associations involved. As more occupations become all-graduate, this increases the competitive pressure on the remaining other occupations to do likewise, if they are to maintain their status and financial rewards. In some instances, as among the large employers in Hotel and Catering and Finance, this process is encouraged but in many areas of manufacturing, the employers tend to be dragged along more reluctantly by the professional bodies. The result is the fairly rapid closure of many opportunities, such as trainee accountant, that were once available to the qualified school-leaver.

The Attraction of Youth Labour

Large firms usually only consider recruiting young people for skilled manual and clerical jobs, for which substantial training is provided. The attraction of youths in this instance is that their labour is relatively cheap and they can be more easily trained in the ways of the firm, especially when the job involves the use of new technology. As the training is fairly extensive the firm incurs certain costs although these may now be offset by the subsidies offered through the Youth Training Scheme. Some employers choose to avoid these training costs and attract trained labour through offering higher wage rates. Those who undertake training do so in order to ensure a constant supply of skilled labour.

The fact that the training involved carries substantial costs to the firm and that many of the skills imparted are transferable, provides the rationale for the continuing existence of the remaining training boards. In Engineering and Construction, which account for a major proportion of the training provided for 16-year-old male school-leavers, the Training Boards play an important role in maintaining the long-standing pattern of entry into the middle segments of the occupational hierarchy. Indeed, we argue later that it is the existence of these institutional arrangements which helps to explain why employers in Britain persist in recruiting 16-year-olds into these occupational areas.

Having decided to train new recruits rather than 'buy in' trained adult labour, a firm will attempt to match the amount and content of that training to the requirement of maintaining a stock of skilled workers. During the recession many firms were unable to do this, as the uncertainty in product markets threatened their very existence. Fears about the financial viability of the organisation often resulted in cut-backs in training provision. If the profit constraint was dominant, then reducing labour costs was seen as a potential area of saving, and training was regarded as a luxury. For example, amongst the firms we visited, a medium-sized engineering company, which relied heavily on its skilled workforce for the manufacture of machine tools, was faced with the collapse of its product market. Management's response was to reduce the size of the workforce, halt the intake of trainees, and do away with the training department altogether, in an attempt to minimise costs. While economic theory may predict that the rational long-term response in a recession is to undertake more training, because of lower opportunity costs (for example, idle equipment which can be utilised), in fact the dynamics of market competition, and in particular, the vulnerability of British firms to changes in foreign exchange rates and product markets, created a crisis mentality in which the firm cut all costs in an effort to ensure its continued existence. Only when the order book looked healthier did the firm start to train again. Our results suggest that this was not an untypical reaction of British employers to changes in the product market. In companies which were not so adversely affected by the recession, the tendency was to place a freeze on the recruitment of apprentices and to redirect training efforts towards the retraining of the existing labour force. This strategy was also adopted partly in response to the changes that were taking place with the introduction of new technology. In addition, during a recession there is usually a pool of skilled labour to be found among the unemployed and so firms can afford to stop training labour. Only in those companies in which continuous training was regarded as an integral part of the everyday functioning of the firm was training unaffected by the impact of the recession.

In periods of growth and stability apprenticeship costs represent such a small proportion of total wage costs, and an even smaller proportion of total costs as to be almost insignificant when viewed in the light of the firm's requirements for skilled labour. Those employers which are particularly concerned about the cost of training young people are the smaller firms, operating in more competitive markets. For example, in the construction industry, the marginal cost of employing additional labour is much higher.

When discussing the question of training, British employers are almost invariably referring to the cost of training males. This is because they make a significant contribution to the costs of training males while that for females is primarily borne by the state. In the case of training for secretarial work and business skills, the state covers the cost through the Colleges of Further Education (FE) system, while the family is expected to subsidise the young person while they are in the educational system. Thus, employers are able to recruit females as relatively cheap labour for secretarial and administrative work, without directly contributing to the costs of training.

While many large firms operating in what we refer to here as oligopolistic markets attach little significance to the relative costs of youth labour or to the possibility of substituting it for that of adults, recent changes in their product markets have made them more conscious of the need to contain and reduce labour costs. The growing internationalisation of product markets in manufactured products is forcing them to reduce costs, while political changes have made it easier for them to do so. For the reasons spelt out above, they cannot do this by substituting different types of labour and so their response has been to restructure the use of the different types of labour. This process of change is discussed in detail in the following chapter.

EMPLOYERS IN THE NON-MARKET SECTOR

The significance of the non-market sector in segmenting the labour market is an issue that is rarely addressed in the literature. Many of the services administered through the local authorities, such as housing, the fire service, and education, are regulated through legislation rather than pressures stemming from competition in the market for such services. Politically, these have been removed from the market in the same way as much of the health service provision, although the degree of state as opposed to market regulation is a matter of some dispute between the political parties. This serves to underline the fact that the actions of central government significantly constrain the strategy these authorities adopt in relation to labour. During the period of our research the relationship between central and local government was dominated by the attempts of the Government to control and reduce the spending of local authorities, especially those controlled by the Labour Party. The effect of Government cuts was to create a downward pressure on both wages and the numbers employed.

What is also interesting about local authorities as employers is that their actions can be strongly influenced by local politics. Because of this they provide ideal opportunities to observe the effects of different political decisions on the same set of administrative functions. Our sample included one authority that was Conservative-controlled and one that was Labour-controlled.

The organisation of functions such as education, social services, police, transport, planning and finance were almost identical in the two authorities. Each of the services or functions had considerable autonomy and in neither of the authorities was there anything approaching a central manpower and training policy. To implement such a policy would require the agreement of all the main political parties, should there be a shift in the balance of political power, and this was difficult to obtain. The two authorities faced similar problems of falling rolls in education, and an aging population increasing the demands on the social services. However, the organisation of labour in each of the main service functions, such as education and social services, was greatly influenced by the respective professional bodies and the traditions they had established. The different grades of staff, with the exception of senior management, were fully unionised, thereby requiring the central personnel departments to deal with a large number of different worker organisations.

The result of these pressures in both authorities was a highly segmented labour force with stronger vertical and horizontal divisions than were typically found in most other employing organisations. Given the length of training and specialist expertise required for most professional posts, there was little or no horizontal movement between the police, education and social services. This helps to explain why local authorities are such loosely integrated structures. The strength of professional organisations in regulating access to these occupations also meant that for those without professional training, promotion chances were very limited.

These trends had resulted in the situation where even though the authorities in our sample each employed in excess of 30 000 people, there was little demand for school-leavers. As entry to higher level jobs was regulated by the professions, young people could only obtain access to a limited range of opportunities. For example, young people could compete for jobs as swimming pool instructors/attendants in leisure centres, gardeners in parks departments, and apprentices in engineering departments, and most significantly for lower-grade clerical jobs. Yet even for some of these jobs the departments concerned had a tradition of hiring mature females. We estimated on the basis of one authority's figures that even if all clerical jobs were included, only 15 per cent of full-time jobs were open to school-leavers.

TECHNOLOGY

Here we define technology as the means used to enable people to produce goods and services. In some instances the term refers to specific machines or tools, while in others it refers primarily to intellectual skills such as those of the craftsman or doctor. When defined in this manner, it is possible to model technologies in terms of a continuum, with those industries whose technologies are labour-intensive (e.g., medicine, handicrafts, teaching, hosiery, footwear), at one end, and those whose are capital-intensive (for example, cement, chemicals) at the other. Traditionally, medicine, teaching and the handicrafts have been labour-intensive in that they are concerned with applying a given body of knowledge to a specific problem. The vast majority of practitioners did not require capital-intensive tools to perform their tasks. This has changed over time, so that parts of modern medicine, such as surgery, require expensive capital equipment, while general practice does not. Similarly in teaching, the transmission of knowledge and skills in modern physics and engineering often requires expensive capital equipment, whereas the teaching of English relies much more heavily on books. Even some parts of modern manufacturing industry remain labour-intensive. For example, it is still possible to set up as a manufacturer of clothes or shoes with relatively little capital equipment. At the other extreme it requires tremendous capital resources to extract or refine oil, or produce chemicals. Unfortunately a great deal of our thinking about these issues tends to be formed on the basis of fixed notions of particular industries being high-technology or low-technology industries when, in fact, firms and industries are constantly moving along a continuum. Indeed, our research findings indicate that many establishments have shifted significantly in the last five years, largely through the introduction of new technology. Defined in this way technology covers the traditional mechanically based manufacturing processes and the 'new' information technology used in administration and parts of the service sector (Gill, 1985).

Technology is, of course, neutral in its effects on the type of labour employed. There is no inherent reason why males should not operate sewing machines, females lay bricks, young people serve alcohol, or older people serve hamburgers. The fact that certain techniques of production are associated with the labour of either males or females, or youths or adults, is entirely a social construction. However, there is a definite relationship between the techniques of production utilised by different companies and the type of labour they recruit. In general, there is an inverse relationship between capital intensity and the employment of youths. That is, the more capital-intensive the process of production the less likely it is that youths will be employed. There are two main reasons for this. The first is that firms operating expensive, automated plant and machinery need to be productive round the clock, working a 24-hour day, in order to recoup the capital costs involved. The shift patterns that the introduction of new capital-intensive equipment necessitates in industries such as Chemicals, Glass and Cement, and, increasingly, Engineering, lead to the exclusion of young people for the reasons cited earlier. In addition, because this machinery produces with such speed, any disruption to the production process, either because workers fail to turn up at work, or because technical faults are not rectified immediately, is very expensive. Idle machinery is expensive in terms of lost production, and a failure to rectify faults results in the production of very expensive scrap. Either way, 'reliability' and 'responsibility' are the prime characteristics required from employees and, for reasons discussed above, youths are not seen to possess these.

Young people may be favoured for jobs which demand a familiarity with aspects of new information technology, such as word processors, visual display units and computers. Many employers regard their prior acquaintance with this technology as giving young people an advantage over older workers who may be apprehensive about their ability to cope with new developments or are considered to be difficult to retrain. Also employers' often see older workers as having less potential in terms of possible years of service, for recouping their investment in training. However, this advantage may prove to be short-lived as familiarity with information technology becomes widespread in the same way that literacy did at the beginning of the twentieth century.

While there are good reasons for more capital-intensive operations not employing many 16- to 18-year-olds, it does not follow that all labour-intensive industries employ large numbers of such young people. Indeed, some of the most labour-intensive areas of work, such as Medicine, Teaching and Professional Services, employ very few, the obvious reason being that the operation of the tasks requires the application of a complex body of knowledge, for which a long period of training is seen as necessary.

INTRA-FIRMS DEMAND FOR DIFFERENT TYPES OF LABOUR

Although at the level of the firm, wages may not be a major determinant of the number of workers employed they may actually influence the type of labour recruited within the firm. That is, if there are discrete groups of potential employees which can easily be substituted for each other, then relative rates of pay may influence the level of employment for each group. This was the theme of work by Wells (1983, p. 48), who suggested that there was a significant relationship between the wages of 16–18-year-old males relative to those of adults, and rising youth unemployment. However, further work by Junankar and Neale (1987) cast doubt on the robustness of these findings.

In reviewing these studies Raffe (1987) argues that both the quality and quantity of available data are inadequate to sustain the interpretations placed on disequilibrium analysis, where conclusions are in any case highly sensitive to model specification. More generally, they are historically specific, being based on data from the 1970s or earlier and cannot take account of the influence of special measures on the youth labour market after 1978. 'The main conclusion of the time-series studies is that declining aggregate demand is a significant cause of rising youth unemployment: on all other factors, including the relative pay explanation, the evidence is equivocal' (Raffe, 1987, p. 237). This interpretation has recently received additional support from the work of Roberts, Dench and Richardson (1986, 1987). When they asked a sample of employers in three urban areas whether a drop in youth rates of pay would encourage them to recruit more young people, only 11 per cent would 'definitely' or even 'possibly' do so (1987). Further supportive evidence can be found in the work of Stern and Turbin (1986) who reported that only 12.5 per cent of employers in rural areas claimed that youth wages were too high.

Our own evidence pointed to the fact that most employers were operating under constraints which prevented them from changing the wage rates of youths in response to fluctuations in either labour supply or government policy. In the majority of companies only a very small proportion of the workforce is comprised of young people at any one point in time and so any savings to be made by lowering their wage levels would be marginal. As most large companies set rates through national collective bargaining procedures or nationally imposed company pay policies, then attempts to introduce changes either nationally or in selective localites in order to drive down youth rates would be counter-productive in terms of the industrial relations costs. In addition, many companies kept their rates relatively high in order to attract the right type of youth; their concern with the quality of the labour recruited overrode that of cost. The only persistent complaint from employers about youth wage rates concerns the age at which young people on training programmes move on to the adult rate. With the raising of the school leaving age and especially with the lowering of the age of majority, youths often move on to adult rates at the age of 18, before they have finished their training and become proficient workers. The only area where the pay of youths relative to that of adults was significant in encouraging substitution within firms was in Retail, Hotel and Catering establishments. This will be discussed in Chapter 6.

Does this mean that the level of youth wages is irrelevant to an understanding of their position within the labour market? In answering this question we have to take care in specifying just what it is that the relative level of youth pay is being used to explain. If it is the general demand for youth labour, then the weight of the evidence is clear; the relative pay of youths has not been a major factor in determining the general level of youth employment. There can be little doubt that the Conservative Government has succeeded in lowering the general level of youth wages, but this has not been translated into a surge of new jobs for youths throughout the labour market. As we saw in Chapter 2 the introduction of YTS merely accelerated existing trends. The subsidies it provides have slowed down the rate at which youths were being substituted by adult females. Yet, even with the availability of free youth labour, young people remain excluded from large parts of the labour market. This finding provides a measure of the strength of the barriers which segment the labour market.

CONCLUSION

Our concern throughout this chapter has been to explore the factors which determine the type of labour employers recruit, in order to explain why employment opportunities for 16-year-olds are so highly concentrated in a small part of the labour market. As segmentation theory would predict, factors such as the type of product market, the labour intensity of the production process, technology and the organisation of the labour process, were all found to be important in leading employers to prefer one type of labour rather than another.

Pressures which lead to the exclusion of youths are greatest in firms operating in conditions of oligopoly with capital-intensive technologies. Few, if any, of these employers would consider recruiting youths for semi-skilled and unskilled jobs. The only opportunities for young people in such firms were in occupations in the middle and higher segments where training was required. In their decisions to exclude youths from some jobs, wage costs played a negligible role.

The pressures which led to the decision to focus recruitment on 16-year-old school-leavers were greatest in those firms operating in competitive product markets, where labour costs were a significant part of total costs and where the production process was deskilled. In these circumstances the cost of youth labour relative to that of adult labour made youths an attractive source of labour to employers, especially if these costs could be reduced further by state subsidies. These pressures provide an explanation for the concentration of youths in such a limited number of occupations and industries.

The other major finding which emerges from this exploration of employers' demand for different types of labour, is that it is a mistake to look upon employers as operating with a single set of criteria in the recruitment process. What this means is that we must move beyond conceptualising their recruitment decisions as operating in the context of a single job queue. At the moment competition between youths and adults is typically viewed in terms of a single job queue (Raffe, 1987), with young people occupying a position at the rear of the queue by virtue of their lack of experience and personal characteristics. What we have identified above is a whole series of job queues. As we indicated in Chapter 2, in recruiting for each of the segments employers utilise different criteria. In the middle segments they are looking for evidence of specific skills or, where young people are concerned, the ability to acquire them. In the lower segments they are more concerned that the recruits have the appropriate industrial discipline and attitude to work. This means that the same person can be ranked differently depending on the segment to which they are seeking entry. For example, a bright young person with a good record of educational achievement, will be ranked highly by an employer recruiting technician apprentices. The same person will be ranked lowly by an employer recruiting a labourer or semi-skilled machinist as he or she will be seen as being overqualified and unlikely to settle in the job.

It is not just between segments that the queues differ. Even within segments there are different job queues, with applicants being judged in accordance with different criteria. Thus, in the lower segments where jobs have been deskilled, all that is required is a very basic education and the acceptance of industrial discipline. Employers put youths at the head of the job queue because their labour is the cheapest, especially if it is also subsidised. This may mean excluding adults altogether. For other jobs in the lower segments, youths are excluded, as the requirements of the production process demand a level of concentration and commitment which youths are seen to lack. They are therefore placed outside the job queue. In the middle segments, youths may be placed at the top of the job queue, in part because they are seen as being easily trainable but also because the institutional arrangements for training such as age restrictions on recruitment to apprenticeships, shelter youths from competition by excluding adults. The idea of a single queue is misleading as is the idea that employers have a uniform set of criteria against which prospective recruits are evaluated.

NOTES

1. The information on smaller employers is derived from our earlier study of 360 employing establishments of varying sizes across a wide range of industries (see Ashton, Maguire and Garland, 1982).
2. We have avoided the use of the term 'secondary' market to refer to this situation for a number of reasons. One is that it is sometimes used to imply that workers are in this market because of their personal characteristics. We would not want to endorse this position. A further reason is that earlier research (Ashton and Maguire, 1984) suggested that the idea of a simple dichotomy between primary and secondary labour markets was a crude oversimplification.

6 Changes in Labour Demand during the Recession

In this chapter the aim is to distinguish short-term pressures such as seasonal fluctuations in the demand for products, from more fundamental structural changes which will continue to develop beyond the limited period of a business cycle. Our results suggest that four major structural changes are currently affecting employers. Each of these is dealt with separately in this chapter, where it is argued that knowledge of this process of change is essential for an understanding of the contemporary transformation of the labour market.

Firstly, the widespread development of global markets is changing the terms of competition in many product markets and is having a profound impact on the larger corporations. It is transforming multinational companies which have a strong national base from which they export to other national product markets, into transnational companies, which have largely uprooted themselves from their national base and regard the world as their market. Production is organised across national boundaries. As a result, some leading large firms have abandoned labour-intensive production in Britain, while others have established specialised market niches for their products. These decisions have important implications both for the demand for labour and for the organisation of the labour force.

Secondly, parts of the service sector, notably Distribution, and Hotel and Catering, are experiencing a process of increasing industrial concentration. This process has its origins in changes in domestic product markets, where a shift towards larger units of production has established oligopolies. As the companies concerned have developed very different systems of labour management and utilisation to those which characterised the family firms they displaced, the result has been a rapid transformation of labour demand.

Thirdly, there has been the diffusion of new technology. The introduction of information technology is having a major impact on the pattern of labour demand in commerce, while in the manufacturing sector the combination of information technology and advances in machine design to produce CNC machines, robots and flexible manufacturing systems is having an equally profound effect on the demand for labour.

At the level of the firm there can be great difficulty in disentangling the effects of these factors. Changes in the organisation of product markets and in the industrial structure interact with the effects of new technology. However, the impact of global product markets has been primarily confined to manufacturing, whereas changes in the industrial structure are largely found in parts of the service sector. It has, therefore, proved possible to isolate these two factors. Then, within each sector we have been able to examine the interaction of the relevant factors with the impact of new technology on the demand for labour.[1]

Fourthly, there have been the outcomes of the political process. Although not usually examined in detail in analyses of labour markets, their effects are of importance in a number of ways. Government legislation and pressures on public sector employers have had a significant impact on both the general level of demand for labour and on the type of labour recruited. In addition, political changes in the institutional structures of the labour market, notably in the provision of work placements and training, have been of particular relevance for the youth labour market, affecting, as we have already seen, the type of labour some employers use. The labour market has also been susceptible to the consequences of developments in the industrial relations framework, wherein the balance of power between management and labour has shifted, as a result of political decisions during the 1980s. The industrial relations issue is not explicitly addressed in this chapter, although its importance is recognised. We have attempted to incorporate it into our analysis, wherever the ensuing weakness of labour has enlarged management's scope for action in determining the type of labour employed.

Of course, these are not the only changes which are affecting the demand for different types of labour. This chapter merely seeks to identify the major sources of structural change in the labour market. Even within a particular sector or industry, firms may respond to these changes in different ways, especially when it comes to adapting their labour force management strategies. Here we hope to achieve a better understanding of the underlying direction of change in the composition of the labour force which results from these processes. The chapter concludes with a discussion of the implications of these long-term structural changes on the demand for youth labour.

THE INCORPORATION OF NATIONAL MARKETS INTO INTERNATIONAL MARKETS

The effect of the world recession and the Government's exchange rate policy on the competitiveness of British industry and on employment levels in manufacturing firms has already been noted. Yet our findings indicated that the effects of the recession were masking other fundamental changes taking place in the structure of product markets, namely the gradual incorporation of what had hitherto been predominantly British markets into global markets, such as that for automobiles.[2]

The reasons for the emergence of global markets are connected with accelerated technological diffusion, the integration of capital markets, reduced information and transportation costs, the liberalisation of trade barriers and the growth of the multinational corporation as the dominant form of economic organisation (Ballance and Sinclair, 1983).[3] The impact of these processes on British manufacturers was accelerated by the onset of the recession. Although global restructuring had been taking place in many industries over the previous two decades, it took the events of the early 1980s, and the demise of large numbers of manufacturing firms, to bring home to many companies the changed circumstances in which they were now operating.

The process involved is similar to that which occurred in the nineteenth century when craft production, organised by family businesses serving local markets, was replaced by mass production in large corporations serving national markets. What we are witnessing now is the displacement of these national corporations by transnational corporations which organise production, distribution and sales for a global market. At each stage in this process the level of integration of economic activities, the division of labour and the bonds of interdependence change. As the bonds of interdependence now extend across national boundaries, this has produced a higher level of integration, which is that of the global market. The transnational companies which operate in these markets no longer organise production within the confines of a single nation's boundaries. They design for a worldwide market, organise production in different countries and market on a world scale. In doing this, they also play an important role in integrating national markets into global markets.

This is not a uniform process in all industries. The electronics and car industries have already achieved a high degree of global integration in both production and distribution. Other industries, such as metal manufacture, machine tools and food processing, are still in the early stages of moving from production organised for national markets to production organised for global markets. It should also be restated here that our investigations were restricted to large firms. While the effects of these profound changes in product markets may ultimately impinge on the operations of small and medium-sized firms, it is fair to say that many smaller companies effectively still regard themselves as being involved in a national market. Larger firms, however, account for a high proportion of national output and employment.

In this section we first examine the implications of global markets for the organisation of production and the level of demand in the national economy. This is followed by an examination of the response of firms which have been adjusting to the incorporation of national into international or global markets.

THE IMPLICATION OF GLOBAL MARKETS FOR THE ORGANISATION OF PRODUCTION AND THE DEMAND FOR LABOUR

The significance of global markets for our understanding of national labour markets is that they weaken the link between the level of product demand in the national economy and the level of demand for labour. As the focus of a firm's business strategy shifts from that of a single national market, from which it may export, to that of a global market, fundamental changes take place in investment and marketing strategies. Decisions made by Japanese and American companies about whether to invest in Britain are made not with reference to the UK market but with reference to the European and world markets. Nissan, a Japanese multinational company, invested in Britain out of political necessity, in that it had to locate manufacturing capacity in Europe or face the possibility of losing its European market. This is symptomatic of the fact that in these global markets political factors, such as tariff barriers and industrial subsidies, come to play a more important role in determining investment strategies. Similarly, a factor such as the quality of the labour force, in terms of level of education, which was a constant for firms operating within a national economy, now becomes a variable factor, which has to be taken into account by multinationals when deciding on where to locate their plant (Reich, 1983). A growing awareness of the need to establish manufacturing bases in more than one country was leading a number of the British companies we visited to locate plants overseas. The majority of those companies we visited which were operating in well-integrated global or European markets, were foreign-owned, with overall decisions on strategy being taken at the Head Office based outside Britain.

Managers in individual establishments of these transnational companies were not responding solely to the pressures of market forces, or Adam Smith's 'Invisible Hand', but rather to what in a slightly different context Chandler (1977) called the visible hand of the corporation. The difference, in this context, is that the visible hand of management co-ordinates production, distribution and markets across, as well as within, national boundaries. Production is organised in accordance with the rules and procedures laid down by Headquarters, where corporate strategy is determined. Thus, the target level of output and the amount and type of labour needed to meet that requirement are determined by the administrative system operated by Head Office. When questioned about their product market and its influence on their employment and manpower policies, responses focused not on the organisation of a product market, but the internal administrative arrangements of a multinational company. Within these companies individual plants frequently compete against each other for allocation of the right to be responsible for the manufacture of particular products in the company's whole product range. If successful, they then produce units for a world market. We found examples of this in firms producing pharmaceuticals, computers and tyres.

This system of organising production has very important implications for our understanding of the relationship between the level of demand in the national economy and the level of employment. It means that output and employment levels can no longer be determined to a large extent by fluctuations in the level of demand for goods and services within the national economy. A manufacturing company in our sample found that, although demand in Britain fell during the recession, output and employment levels were increased due to the system through which the parent company allocated production. The British plant we visited had succeeded in obtaining the order to produce a new generation of machines for the European market.

The converse is also possible. For example, a British plant of a transnational company producing for the European vehicle components industry lost a substantial proportion of its labour force due to a decision by Head Office to transfer production to other plants in Europe. The job losses incurred were far in excess of those to be expected on the basis of the fall in demand for the product. In terms of the earlier discussion of the output-employment curve this represented a decision by the firm to move down a step. If each of the horizontal lines between the steps is assumed to represent a single plant, then when demand falls the company descends a 'step' and closes down a particular plant. In this case it was the British plant. The choice of which plant to close may also be affected by factors other than the overall level of demand, such as levels of productivity, industrial relations and transportation costs. A further consequence of this ability of international capital to move production from one country to another is that it introduces into jobs at managerial level a degree of uncertainty which was formally more characteristic of manual occupations.

The Role of the State

When production was predominantly organised on a national basis, the state, by affecting the level of domestic demand, could exert a strong influence on the aggregate level of employment. Now, as decisions about investment are increasingly made on the basis of the interests of multinational companies in the context of international markets, the influence which the state can exercise through its fiscal policy on the general level of employment is diminishing. Major decisions about employment are now taken outside the jurisdiction or the influence of the state. Yet, as we saw in the previous chapter, the actions of the state, through its political decisions, are still of importance in influencing both the product market and the ability of individual establishments to compete. Thus, the sphere of effective state action is changing. Although it is less able to use fiscal policy to affect the general level of employment, it can still exert some influence by supporting the development of firms which have the possibility of playing a significant part in world markets. The success of many Japanese companies has been aided by the willingness of the state to use its powers to encourage and support the development of those industries whose firms are deemed capable of competing in international markets. The domestic economy has been used as the basis for their growth into multinational companies. In the new circumstances of international markets the position of the state changes in relation to both the economy and the wider division of labour, of which the national economy is a part. If the political elite who control the machinery of state choose to rely solely on fiscal measures to regulate a national economy which has relatively few companies playing a significant role in international markets, this affects the types of jobs that are generated.

The Process of Incorporation

While some global markets, such as those for electronics and vehicles, are highly integrated, others, such as those for machine tools and metal goods, are in the early stages of the process of incorporating national markets. A number of companies in our sample were involved in this process. This entailed much more than merely reorientating the design of their products to meet the needs of larger markets. They were moving from a domestic market in which production and distribution were relatively highly organised within national boundaries by a small number of companies, to an international market in which production and distribution were only loosely organised, with no company or group of companies able to dominate.

An example from our sample of a firm which found itself caught up in this process was a large capital-intensive manufacturing organisation which had enjoyed a dominant position in the British container goods market, but now faced increasing competition from an American company which had established manufacturing plants in Britain. This competition led to a decline in its share of the market, which, together with the introduction of more modern capital-intensive equipment, brought about a massive reduction in the size of its labour force, from 40 000 in 1976 to 21 000 in 1985. The company was transformed from being primarily geared towards supplying a stable national product market in which it was dominant, to a situation where great emphasis was placed on more technologically advanced products for an international market. Internally, this necessitated the establishment of greater flexibility and decentralisation in the organisation in order to respond effectively to a more competitive and dynamic international market over which it had far less control. Similarly, a company in the machine tool industry found its market share in both home and export markets increasingly threatened by European and Japanese manufacturers. The response was to undertake a radical restructuring of both its product mix and internal organisation in order to survive. It subsequently merged with a competitor in order to provide a larger base from which to compete in the new international market.

The incorporation into global markets has resulted in some companies being bought up by foreign or British firms and reorganised as a unit within a multinational organisation. In some cases the object of the acquisition has been to gain access to the firm's markets, so that the manufacturing process has been dispensed with, and production switched to another of the company's plants.

Labour-Intensive Industries

As was suggested in Chapter 3, firms operating in product markets characterised by manufacturers with labour-intensive modes of production were confronted with a different situation. Many British manufacturers foresaw themselves being unable to compete with producers based in developing societies where labour costs were so much lower than in the UK. A common response was to withdraw from such markets and develop new product market strategies.

One strategy was to establish a niche in the market where the company felt it had a competitive advantage. As an example, a major British footwear manufacturer had lost some of its market to foreign manufacturers during the 1970s. Its initial response was to create a distinctive segment in the British market. This was done by investing heavily in research and development, and moving up-market with a distinctive product. From this base it is now starting to expand into the European market. This process was accompanied by significant job losses as production capacity was cut back, and the introduction of major changes in organisational design. The company's strategy had been successful and at the time of the interview it was starting to take on additional production staff.

An alternative strategy, developed by a textile company facing similar problems, as imports from low labour cost countries ate into its markets, was to cut back on its 'making up' operations which had traditionally been its 'bread and butter', and to diversify into completely new product markets in medical supplies and electronics. As with the footwear company's strategy, this involved investment in research and development and exploiting technological advantages.

We stress the complex nature of the changes taking place in the product market because although many of them are linked to the transformation of what were relatively closed British markets into global markets, they are also inextricably linked to other changes in product markets. Some of these, such as fashion changes in footwear, are specific to one product market. In other instances companies can operate in a variety of product markets. For example, the container manufacturer cited above was operating in a global market against giant American corporations with one of its products, and against small, locally-based plastic extrusion companies with another product. In emphasising the growth of international markets we are merely highlighting what we perceive to be the dominant factor affecting employment.

IMPLICATIONS FOR THE ORGANISATION OF THE FIRM AND MANAGEMENT STRATEGIES

Changes in product markets have implications for at least two aspects of a firm's organisational structure. These are its organisational design, in terms of whether this is functional, divisional or matrix, and its labour force strategies. In our sample, those firms already operating in global markets which were making changes, were modifying their labour force strategies. Firms in the process of being incorporated into global markets were more likely to be changing their organisational design as well as their labour force strategies.

The greater uncertainty in these product markets was forcing some firms to abandon functional and centralised divisional forms of organisation in an attempt to obtain a more effective response to the demands of the market. For example, one large manufacturing company had a centralised divisional structure based on its manufacturing processes, which it had found effective in producing for the British market where it had a dominant position. As this became integrated into an international market, it adapted by changing the basis of its divisions from process-based to market-based divisions in order that the individual manufacturing plants could respond more rapidly to changes in specific markets. In addition, it decentralised the decision-making process, shifting responsibility for collective bargaining and profitability from head office to divisional heads. Similar changes were taking place in other companies where the emphasis was on increasing the flexibility of the organisational structure to meet the demands of what was seen as a much more competitive and hence uncertain product market. In the case of the footwear company this flexibility was achieved by integrating the manufacturing and retail functions in order that it could respond more rapidly to changes in fashion. This was part of a broader response to changes in the product market, for whereas 20 years ago 8 per cent of their lines were changed each year, this had progressed to 25 per cent each year.

Those companies we visited which were operating in global markets were becoming increasingly conscious of the high productivity levels achieved by their competitors, particularly those from the Far East. This often acted as the trigger for a reassessment of their strategies towards the management of labour. To succeed in world markets against companies from Japan, West Germany, Taiwan and elsewhere, it was seen as essential to obtain both a higher level of commitment from their existing labour force and greater flexibility in the deployment of labour. To this end, one transnational company was attempting to break down the social division between manual workers and staff in an attempt to secure greater loyalty and commitment from all employees. In addition, they were attempting to reduce lines of demarcation and introduce forms of continuous training to improve the overall skill level of their labour force.

Such an exercise is expensive and in a competitive situation, where pressure is on labour costs, a number of companies were attempting to achieve this greater commitment and flexibility from their labour forces while simultaneously cutting labour costs. The solution which a number of companies sought was to reduce the number of permanent employees. However, in order to enhance the commitment of those who remained, the companies offered assurances of long-term employment provided that the workers adopted more flexible working practices. These, it was claimed, would enhance the long-term viability of the company and secure the remaining jobs. Wherever possible, additional labour costs were minimised either by contracting out functions or using short-term contracts or temporary workers. Thus, most firms were contracting out functions such as catering, cleaning, and in some cases maintenance, which had previously been performed by permanent employees.

INDUSTRIAL CONCENTRATION IN THE SERVICE SECTOR

The discussion has so far concentrated on firms in manufacturing. The markets for distribution, construction, leisure and catering are still largely met by the production of services organised on a national basis. However, these domestic product markets are being affected by an increasing level of industrial concentration, rather than from the extension of global markets.[4] As these are essentially domestic markets, in which the production of the services remains relatively labour-intensive, levels of employment respond more directly to changes in the overall level of demand in the domestic economy. The growth in the standard of living of those in employment has generated a continuing increase in the demand for consumer goods, while the increasing proportion of income spent on leisure and prepared food has created new markets for those industries. The result has been the growth in employment in this part of the service sector which was outlined in Chapter 2. At the same time the increasing industrial concentration has led to changes in the typical organisational structure of firms in these industries and in the type of labour required.

Traditionally, the market for services in the Hotel, Catering, Leisure and Retail distribution industries has been served by relatively small to medium-sized family firms. Over the last two decades this has started to change, with the emergence of nationally based organisations with a greatly enhanced capital base.

In Retailing, the national chain and department stores have incorporated and displaced the small family firm. What were previously highly competitive local retail markets have been transformed into national markets dominated by relatively few organisations. The most obvious example of this is in food retailing where the retailing giants, such as Sainsbury and Tesco, now dominate the market. This has involved an increasing degree of control by the firm over their suppliers and the production process. In some parts of the industry, such as fast food outlets, this has been associated with the extension of a form of sub-contracting, namely franchising, but the general tendency in retail distribution and hotels and catering has been for the larger units of production to expand at the expense of the smaller ones. For example, the growth of the national food retailers has virtually eradicated the independent grocer. The distribution of food is now administered centrally by these companies rather than through wholesalers, transport companies and retailers.

The process which is taking place in the service sector is similar to what Chandler (1977) highlighted in the manufacturing sector during the early decades of this century; what was previously organised through a whole series of markets is now administered more efficiently through a central bureaucracy. This process is not the only reason for the success of these companies. Their size and capital resources create a purchasing power which often makes the manufacturers dependent upon them, and enables them to undercut family stores. From the point of view of their impact on the labour market, their ability to rationalise the use of labour, besides enabling them to reduce labour costs, has also been the cause of the restructuring of the labour market.

In the Hotel and Catering trade this transformation of the industrial structure has been a more recent phenomenon, although the pattern of change has been similar. The small family-owned hotels, pubs, and other catering and fast food establishments have been incorporated or displaced by national companies which are able to provide higher and more uniform standards of provision and service. In the leisure industry the growth of more capital-intensive holiday and leisure centres of various types has been pioneered by the larger organisations such as Ladbrokes and the Rank Organisation.

The impact of these changes on the organisation of the labour force has stemmed less from the adoption of new labour management strategies by existing companies than from the displacement of traditional forms of family management by the new corporations. Control of the traditional family firm was vested in family members, with a functional form of organisation being adopted and full-time staff employed. Typically, recruitment was targeted at school-leavers, some of whom (usually the males) were promoted into managerial positions after several years of service. Such firms were usually depicted as having a pyramidal structure as in Figure 6.1.

Some of the main differences between this traditional structure and that of the large corporation which is replacing it, are illustrated by Figure 6.1 B. Although this does not illustrate that the corporations usually have a strong divisional structure, it does show how the internal labour market has changed. The corporations have identified the precise peaks and troughs in the daily, weekly or seasonal demand for services and replaced the full-time workers with part-time or temporary workers. In the retail trade this often took the form of replacing many full-time sales staff with part-timers, who were often married women returning to the labour market after childrearing, and who would cover the peak period of demand during weekdays, of between 11:00 a.m. and 3:00 p.m. These were then supported by a small core of more highly trained managers and

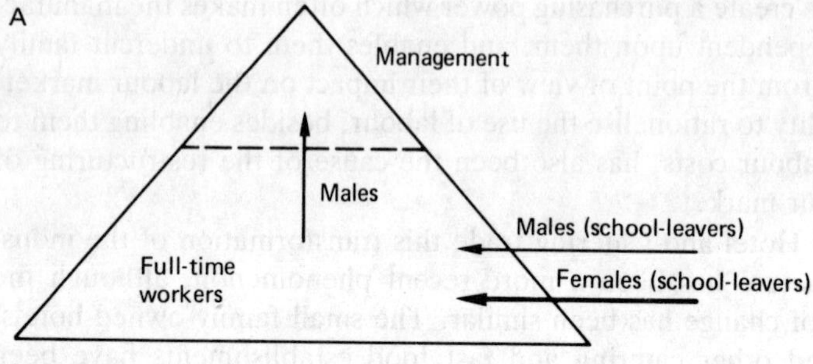

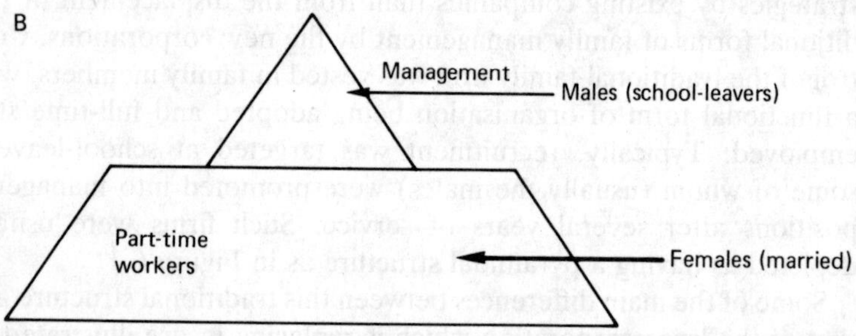

FIGURE 6.1 *The impact of labour rationalisation strategies on the internal labour markets of retail stores*

supervisors. The result was a more professional managerial staff and a more intensive use of labour, thereby cutting the operating costs.

As new outlets were established, firms adopted this form of labour strategy from the outset. This led to the rapid growth of female jobs which was identified in Chapter 2, and the enhanced competition between single and married women for these jobs.

TECHNOLOGY AND THE EMPLOYMENT-OUTPUT RELATIONSHIP

It was evident from our interviews that the heightened competition taking place within product markets was accelerating changes that were already under way in the relationship between output and levels of employment in large parts of British industry. These changes could be attributed to either investment in new technology or to a process of intensification, whereby the productivity of individual workers was increased without the introduction of new technology (Massey and Meegan, 1982). In labour-intensive manufacturing industries, the amount of labour required for a given output was largely unaffected by technological change. For example, in the footwear industry, although micro-electronic technology was being used to automate the design and cutting processes, it had, as yet, had little impact on the relationship between employment and output.

The situation in the engineering industry was very different, for, in addition to the changes being brought about by office automation and computer-aided design and computer-aided manufacturing (CAD/CAM) systems, the introduction of micro-electronic technology into the manufacturing process, in the form of Computer Numerically Controlled machines, Flexible Machining Systems and robotics, was dramatically reducing the amount of labour required. The old milling and grinding machines were being replaced by units which operated at speeds in excess of those attainable previously, and to standards of quality which were higher than those achieved by traditional craft methods. Each unit, operated by one worker, effectively displaced five or six craftsmen. The result was a quantum leap in the relationship between labour and output. Moreover, the new technology involved a substantial capital investment which often necessitated the machinery to be run continuously for 24 hours a day in order to be cost-effective. Also, as the setting-up process was automated, the amount of 'down time' previously associated with batch runs, when switching from one batch to another, was drastically reduced. Thus, batch production started to take on the characteristics of process production.

Not all sectors of the engineering industry were being affected in the same way by these changes. In mechanical engineering, the result was a continuous reduction in the labour input required so that no additional recruitment took place even when output was being increased. Other sectors, such as electrical instruments, continued to recruit additional labour in order to increase the output of control systems.

The introduction of new information technology was having a significant impact on the relationship between employment and output in the Financial Services sector. Whereas during the greater part of the 1970s rising staffing levels had accompanied increases in the volume of business, from the early 1980s new computing systems and widespread use of word processors had enabled the main banks, building societies and insurance companies to expand their output without a proportionate increase in staff. They foresaw this trend continuing in the future (Rajan, 1984).

As far as the retailing and hotel and catering industries were concerned, new information technology had made some impact, although it had less potential for reducing the labour input than did the process of rationalisation resulting from the industrial restructuring which was referred to earlier. The incorporation of family firms into the bureaucratic national organisations in Hotel, Catering and Leisure involved the eradication of whole levels of management and the rationalisation of labour. In some cases this radically reduced the amount of labour involved in producing a given service. For example, when a large hotel chain took over smaller family businesses a typical policy was to reduce the number of layers of management, cut back on the use of full-time labour and hire part-timers to meet fluctuations in demand for services.

EXPLAINING CHANGES IN EMPLOYERS' USE OF LABOUR

The Flexible Firm

In the contemporary literature the effect of changes in employment strategies is often referred to in terms of the introduction of core and periphery forms of organisation or as a model of the 'flexible firm' (NEDO, 1986, p. 3). Atkinson (1984), of the Institute of Manpower Studies, has argued that we are witnessing the emergence of a dichotomy between core and periphery workers within employing organisations. Core workers are normally full-time employees who are offered security of employment. In return they agree to provide functional flexibility, by undertaking whatever work is required by the company. This may entail performing tasks which would at one time have been outside their job description, or previously jealously guarded demarcation lines. This core workforce is then supplemented by recruiting peripheral workers, who provide numerical flexibility, in that their numbers can be adjusted to accommodate fluctuations in product demand and, therefore, output. They have no long-term security of employment, and may be on temporary or fixed-term contracts, or work on a part-time, casual or sub-contract basis. The NEDO report emphasises that 'the flexible firm is an analytical construct, which brings together into a common framework the changes which are occurring (often on a fragmented basis) and reveals their commonalities and the relations between them. It is presented neither as an example of a type of organisation which already exists nor as an ideal for organisations to aim at. A key question for this research is to ask how far such changes are actually taking place and how far they represent a conscious strategy to restructure the workforce into core and periphery' (NEDO, 1986, p. 5). The authors see three main sources of change pushing in the direction of core and periphery organisation: (a) the consolidation of productivity gains; (b) market volatility and uncertainty; (c) technological change. Our main reservation about embracing wholeheartedly this 'analytical construct' is that it seems to assume that all companies are adopting a similar form of organisation.

We would certainly accept that the trends highlighted by the core/periphery model are very important in understanding the restructuring of the labour market. Indeed, during our interviewing in employing organisations, we found many examples of practices, often of recent origin, which were akin to those discussed by Atkinson. For example, one firm in the retail trade, when faced with a loss of sales and the threat of closure, had responded by getting rid of all of its full-time employees, with the exception of management. In their place they had recruited part-time and casual, female workers. A list of available workers, who could be called in for a given number of hours' work at short notice was retained. This enabled the company to match precisely the number of hours worked with variations in their demand for labour.

There are limitations, however, in conceptualising the consequences of change in a single model. By omitting to analyse fully the reasons for the introduction of these employment strategies, one could assume that the forces which have generated these changes are common to all industries and firms. We have shown that the sources of change, and their implications for labour management strategies, vary between industrial sectors and between individual firms. The pressures for flexibility in manufacturing and financial services companies stem from the incorporation of domestic into international markets, although the responses of individual firms may be very different. The increasing propensity to recruit part-time and casual labour in Retailing, Hotel and Catering, and Leisure Services stems, not from 'external' market pressures, but from changes in the pattern of ownership, with large corporations becoming ever more dominant over smaller family firms, and their type of internal organisation becoming standard. Thus, part-time and casual working have been imposed on an ever greater proportion of the workforce because they have already proved successful in reducing labour costs. In contrast, the growth of 'peripheral' workforces in manufacturing firms is partly attributable to the greater degree of unpredictability they have experienced, as relatively small units in a global market. This uncertainty in predicting future manpower requirements has been exacerbated, in some cases, by the need to make redundancies during the recession of the early 1980s, and by the pace of technological change. A common response to this uncertainty has been to introduce temporary or fixed-term contracts for any additional labour recruited.

The model of the 'flexible firm' based on the idea of core and periphery employees has already been subjected to a detailed critique which echoes some of these other points (Pollert, 1987). While concurring with the call to abandon the model as representing a uniform response on the part of management, we believe that it does represent a valuable initial attempt to conceptualise the impact of significant structural changes on management's behaviour. In the polemics of academic debate there is often a tendency to disregard the significance of change because of the inadequacy of the initial conceptualisation. This can foster a temptation to 'throw out the baby with the bathwater'. Here, we argue that the structural changes we have identified are leading to alterations in managements' labour strategies. However, these changes differ across industries and sectors and the initial attempt to bring together their consequences in terms of a single model has greatly oversimplified the processes involved. In what follows we attempt to 'unpack' the ideas and trace the impact of the various structural changes on employers' use of labour. We distinguish four major developments in the management of labour which our interviews identified.

These are (i) the use of sub-contracting, which involved a change in the employer's control of the production process; (ii) the shift away from the use of full-time permanent employees; (iii) attempts to introduce multi-skilling into the existing labour force; and (iv) changes in the culture of the company. Each of these is linked to the various structural changes that were producing them. For this reason the changes in manufacturing and commerce which stem from the growth of global markets are discussed separately from those in Distribution and Hotel and Catering, which stem from industrial concentration.

MANUFACTURING AND COMMERCE

Sub-contracting

The pressure from the internationalisation of markets and the resultant intensified competition in the manufacturing sector has caused many firms to rethink their labour management strategies and introduce sub-contracting as a means of slimming down. In itself this is not a new strategy. There is a long history of employers in competitive product markets using sub-contracting as a means of dealing with uncertainties and fluctuations in the product market. For example, a major footwear manufacturer formerly had a policy of sub-contracting the initial runs of new product lines as a means of testing the market. Only when the line had been proved a success in the market would its own productive capacity be committed. Firms in the textile, hosiery and knitwear industries would contact their local competitors, or reroute orders through the manufacturers' federation, when seasonal fluctuations in demand exceeded their manufacturing capacity. We found some evidence of similar sub-contracting among engineering firms shortly before the onset of the recession, although by the mid-1980s this technique was being used more extensively throughout parts of the engineering industry.

The need to cut labour costs, in the face of enhanced competition and an adverse exchange rate, has led many companies to off-load as many aspects of the production process as possible to agencies, the self-employed and sub-contractors. Car manufacturers have been sub-contracting many of the component parts, leaving themselves to concentrate on assembling the finished product. In other areas of engineering, companies have increasingly sub-contracted service work, such as maintenance, canteen provision and training, as well as specialist work, such as tool-making.

Sub-contracting is not necessarily an option which is open to all manufacturing companies. Where the establishment is involved in process production such as in the manufacture of rubber or pharmaceuticals, the technological requirements prohibit the production process from being sub-divided in this way. The capital equipment required for production is too expensive to be left idle for any length of time. Seasonal fluctuations in demand have to be met either by storing the finished product or reducing the flow of materials through the plant. Thus, sub-contracting is only one possible response to the problems of intensified international competition, and requires specific conditions under which to operate.

The sub-contracting of services is a more widespread phenomenon, involving firms throughout the manufacturing sector, and is more likely to be a response to the integration of the domestic market into the international market. The proliferation of this phenomenon partly explains the growth of service sector employment highlighted in Chapter 2.

In the Financial Services sector, the deregulation of product markets and intensification of competition have not led to an extension of sub-contracting, although banks and building societies have expanded their services into new areas, such as that which was previously the province of estate agents.

The Use of Part-time, Casual and Temporary Labour

The move away from using full-time permanent employees to hiring workers on part-time and temporary or fixed-term contracts is a means by which employers are able to minimise their commitments to the labour force and reduce the costs of adjusting the size of that labour force to suit fluctuations in the demand for the product or service. The introduction of part-time work has been most extensive in those industries which employ a large female labour force, notably in the service sector. Part-time working is less widely used in the manufacturing sector, although one employer in the food industry in our sample had, in one plant, switched almost completely to the use of part-time labour in the production process. Engineering firms often reported that they preferred to recruit part-timers wherever possible. This was usually with regard to female employees, although one Personnel Officer remarked, 'We take on part-time workers wherever possible because they are cheaper and there is a possibility of getting a grant for job-sharing. This policy has been introduced because "people will take any job now"'. However, there were counter-trends, as illustrated by one large organisation operating a process production plant which had recently got rid of its female part-time employees. The firm was looking for a greater commitment among its labour force in order to improve its performance, and felt that it was more likely to secure this from a full-time male labour force.

Fixed-term contracts have been introduced for a number of reasons. They may provide a means of screening recruits before offering a permanent contract, while in other instances they are used to meet seasonal or periodic increases in demand. In some industries union pressure has been effective in restricting the use of fixed-term contracts, but in general the most important factor restricting the spread of this type of contract is the complexity of the production process. Temporary workers are not usually considered suitable for some jobs in manufacturing, which demand a high level of skill or commitment. In these circumstances firms maintain flexibility in their use of labour through shift working and overtime. Temporary workers are sometimes used in areas of skill shortages, such as computing. The difficulties experienced by firms in recruiting highly skilled employees on a permanent basis allows these sought-after workers to exploit a situation of excess demand to their advantage.

In Financial Services, as part of the transformation of the employment-output relationship, firms have phased out large numbers of full-time routine clerical jobs. Many of the jobs which replaced them have been part-time, enabling firms to adjust their labour forces more precisely to fluctuations in demand and thereby lower labour costs. At the upper occupational levels, the increased demand for professional services has led to a growth in the requirement for highly trained personnel. However, even here, some of the higher level entry jobs for graduates in, for example, finance, are now available only on a short-term contract basis. The use of fixed-term contracts provides the firm with the chance to assess new entrants before offering them a permanent job in much the same way that YTS is often used in the lower level jobs.

Multi-skilling

The introduction of multi-skilling has usually reflected an attempt by management to respond to pressures on the firm to enhance labour productivity and/or to increase the flexibility of its workers. Manufacturers of textiles and footwear in our sample had experimented with multi-skilling among semi-skilled operatives, with the objective of enhancing the flexibility of the labour force by enabling management to switch labour between different types of operation. Although there was no opposition from unions, there was a history of resistance from operatives. As the jobs were paid on a piece-rate basis, operatives required continuous practice at one operation to keep up their speed and hence their income. The introduction of multi-skilling required them to switch to new operations and it took time before they could work up the speed necessary to achieve a comparable income. Resistance by workers to the introduction of multi-skilling was, therefore, to be expected. One textile company had gained agreement for its introduction from a group of workers, but was unable to persuade newcomers to the shop to adopt it. While the introduction of multi-skilling achieved flexibility in the use of personnel in the companies cited here, it did not necessarily lead to higher levels of productivity. Also, firms in these industries could rely on the high turnover of female personnel as an alternative method of adjusting the size of the labour force to changes in labour demand.

Productivity gains which could be derived from multi-skilling agreements were most apparent in engineering and the more capital-intensive industries. In these industries the introduction of new technology required workers to be conversant with a number of different skills for the sophisticated and expensive machinery to be efficiently utilised from management's point of view (Cross, 1985). This inevitably led to multi-skilling involving the dismantling or eradication of traditional lines of demarcation. The pressure to introduce multi-skilling appears to be greatest in the transnational companies competing largely against Japanese companies whose levels of productivity are so much higher. However, its introduction is more problematic, and worker resistance stronger, where traditional craftworkers are involved in servicing the technology, as in vehicle manufacture. Here, trade unions have offered resistance to what they perceive to be a threat to the status of their members, who stand to lose control over their work tasks. This has not, however, prevented the emergence of a new type of craftworker in mass production industries. In contrast, craftworkers in small batch and continuous process production industries are more directly involved in the process of production.

In firms operating batch production the processes of technological change associated with the introduction of CNC type machines have created a new type of craftworker, who needs to be conversant with both mechanical and electronic skills. The new technology has required the worker to acquire additional skills. Some trade unions have sought to resist this trend, while others, such as the EEPTU, have been more encouraging. Thus, where the technology directly involves the craftworker in the process of production, new technology does not constitute such a threat to established lines of demarcation as it does in those industries where craftworkers merely provide a maintenance function.

A move towards multi-skilling has also been evident in banks and building societies, and our findings support those of Rajan (1984). The introduction of information technology has facilitated a reorganisation of work tasks, so that one person is no longer responsible for single specific tasks, such as handling cash or filing. For example, the new technology now allows the person at the counter to follow through the various stages of a transaction.

The Culture of the Firm

Fear of the advantages which competitors had achieved by virtue of their higher levels of productivity has caused some firms to attempt to introduce changes in the culture of the firm. Greater commitment to the organisation, on the part of the worker, is seen as essential in order to improve productivity and enhance the flexibility of the organisation. However, the strategies adopted by the firms in our sample to achieve greater commitment varied. In some cases more participative forms of management, which placed greater emphasis on teamwork and a willingness to question and accept criticism from others had been introduced. Another strategy was to pay more attention to the selection of recruits and offer security of employment to the employees in return for greater flexibility and a willingness to retrain. The companies involved were using leading US and Japanese firms as their models and attempting to adopt aspects of their management techniques. Such changes affect the type of labour recruited by transforming the values attached to worker characteristics. Whereas employers would once have required recruits to possess specific skills, they were now looking for a stronger identification with the company and a willingness to accept change, as well as evidence of the intellectual skills which would enable the recruit to accommodate continuing redefinition of work tasks. Often this translated itself into a desire for a higher level of general education among recruits.

CONSTRUCTION, DISTRIBUTION, HOTELS AND CATERING

Sub-contracting

Sub-contracting has long been established in the construction industry, whereas in Hotel and Catering developments have been more recent and by no means uniform. Some companies are growing rapidly on the basis of sub-contracting or franchise agreements, notably in the fast-food industry. Yet at the same time, in the public houses and catering outlets, there is a tendency for the independent landlords who bought their way into a tied house, to be replaced by managers who are more dependent on the company and subject to greater central control. This latter group is also being encouraged to become more professional by the companies involved.

The Use of Part-time, Casual and Temporary Labour

The main change taking place in the Hotel, Catering, Leisure and Retail industries has been the rationalisation of the use of labour, often involving the employment of fewer full-time workers and more part-time workers. A similar process to that which, as we have indicated, is taking place in retailing, has also been occurring in other parts of the service sector. The capital-intensive companies which have become increasingly dominant have been able to establish more precisely when peaks in demand occur and deploy the labour force accordingly. This may involve dispensing with, or reducing the hours of, full-time staff, or, more frequently, introducing only part-time staff when a new investment is made. In general, this process has been most prevalent among the less skilled sales and catering staff in the hotel and catering industry. Unlike the traditional use of seasonal labour where the period of employment could amount to several months, this new form can involve employment for a matter of only hours or days at a time.

While the labour management techniques of the large corporations is undoubtedly one of the main factors responsible for the growth of part-time working, it does not follow that all part-time workers are regarded as peripheral to the organisation. The need for the larger retail stores and catering companies, with their chains of branded-name restaurants and pubs, to move up-market in relation to their competitors, has meant that they have to improve their standard of service. This is difficult to achieve while jobs as cashiers, waiters, waitresses and cooks are regarded as casual jobs with a high level of turnover. To obtain a greater commitment from their staff, and hence a greater degree of control over the behaviour of the people involved, the companies have started to invest in more training, and to devise ways of reducing turnover by retaining workers in the organisation. Part-time staff have been given the same terms and conditions as the full-time staff and the chance of promotion. The result has been the introduction of career ladders into these jobs in order to provide the employee with an incentive to stay in the job and comply with the requirements of the company. Thus, bureaucratic career ladders offering promotion within one organisation, are starting to replace the casual movement of staff from one relatively small employer to another which previously characterised the industry. Again, it is a similar process to that which occurred in the manufacturing sector as large corporations started to dominate the industries and sought to introduce a greater degree of control over the labour force (Gordon, Edwards and Reich, 1982).

In pursuing these strategies companies have encountered little worker opposition, as neither unions nor professional bodies have established a significant presence in these industries. Rather than having to accommodate strong professional organisations, as in health administration, the problem for firms has been to professionalise management. Having invested considerable capital in creating a brand name, the companies want to ensure that the customer is not 'put off' from purchasing because of a poor standard of service or management in the particular establishment they visit. To achieve this objective in all their establishments they need to ensure that all their managers have achieved minimal standards of competence and that all staff 'know how to behave in relation to customers'. This requires establishing minimum standards of performance and systems of training. Only in a limited number of areas, such as the training of chefs and receptionists, has the state or any external agency had control over the definition of the skills involved. It may well be that the introduction of career ladders into what had previously been casual jobs, will create the conditions for more effective unionisation of those employees than has hitherto been the case. For as companies start to impose standard conditions of pay and service among employees, improvements in the individual's pay and conditions are going to be less dependent on their ability to move between employers, which are fewer in number. Instead they will be contingent on the workers' ability to improve collectively their conditions with their current employers. Also, from the unions' point of view, the increasing concentration of workers in large units facilitates the process of organisation.

Multi-skilling and the Culture of the Firm

Multi-skilling is not a significant issue within the service sector, primarily because workers' organisations, with the exception of the professions, have never been successful in establishing control over occupational tasks. This has provided management with considerable discretion over the ways in which they can combine tasks and organise the labour force. Similarly, the question of changing the culture of the company to enhance worker commitment and productivity has only been of importance when a large corporation has absorbed smaller units, as has occurred in Hotel and Catering and Leisure. Management has then attempted to incorporate the key workers from the new units into the organisation by stressing the importance of establishing a common company identity and culture. This has essentially been an issue concerned with company growth, and is very different to those problems facing established manufacturing companies which have been under threat from foreign competitors.

POLITICAL CHANGES

The Public Sector

The most significant change in the public sector in the 1980s has been the continuous pressure from central government to reduce expenditure, and to privatise services wherever possible. The public utilities, which were subjected to stringent constraints, attempted to reduce labour costs. In the face of strong union opposition to compulsory redundancies, virtual bans on recruitment were introduced in order to reduce employment levels through natural wastage. This policy continued over the period 1979–84.

We have already seen how local councils can mediate the impact of central government policy at the local level. In the Labour-controlled council we studied the politicians had attempted to avoid privatising services by entering into a productivity deal with the unions and by seeking to reduce labour costs while minimising the number of compulsory redundancies. For example, the school meals service was reorganised, with many full-time jobs being converted into part-time jobs and some staff being made redundant. The direct labour departments, such as Highways and Transport, had to take a cut in staff and compete with outside organisations for contracts from the authority. The authority instituted a freeze on recruitment, and encouraged early retirements and voluntary redundancies. Whenever jobs became vacant they were carefully assessed, and, wherever possible, the hours of work reduced. The result was a reduction in the size of the labour force over the period 1979–84 from 45 000 to 37 000 and a large increase in the proportion of part-time workers.

The local youth labour market was badly affected by the introduction of a block on new recruitment. In addition, the main white-collar union in the authority was opposed to YTS. Therefore, to counter the detrimental effects on the employment prospects for youths, the personnel department of the local authority introduced a scheme whereby school-leavers could be recruited on a part-time basis for a limited number of posts of fixed duration. Once in these jobs young people were entitled to apply for other posts within the authority and so the scheme provided young people with a new point of access to the internal labour market for youths. However, the numbers recruited in this way remained relatively small.

The other local authority, which had traditionally been governed by the Conservative Party, had pursued a different policy. Subcontracting of services had always been attempted, wherever possible, so that central government policy in this respect had little impact. In response to calls for financial cuts the authority instituted a policy of compulsory and voluntary redundancies. Staff at all levels were either sacked or encouraged to leave. The unions opposed the scheme but were unable to prevent its implementation. The result was the rapid loss of jobs and, as in the other authority, the conversion of many full-time jobs into part-time jobs. As far as young people's job opportunities were concerned, the loss was not as great as in the Labour authority, because recruitment soon recommenced into the remaining jobs to combat the effects of natural wastage. YTS was absent, not because of union opposition, but because of the administrative costs which would have been incurred by the authority. With the absence of a powerful, centralised personnel department, there was no internal pressure to develop a YTS scheme. Each of the Council's divisions had its own budget and no one wanted the additional responsibility and work involved in administering a YTS scheme.

CHANGES IN THE INSTITUTIONAL STRUCTURE OF THE YOUTH LABOUR MARKET

The first part of this chapter has provided a discussion of the pressures on employers to change the organisation of labour and the type of labour employed. However, these changes were, in many respects, facilitated by events which were taking place in the broader labour market. First and foremost of these was the massive growth in unemployment which took place during this period (Raffe, 1987). As unemployment soared above the three million mark, youths were finding it more and more difficult to secure entry to their first jobs, and encountering more intense competition from adults in those areas of the labour market where both groups competed for jobs (Roberts *et al.*, 1987). These conditions provided employers with a much greater degree of choice when recruiting labour than they had had previously and this enabled them, in certain circumstances, to switch more easily from one type of labour to another. In addition, while unions were reeling from the impact of job losses in manufacturing on their membership numbers, they were further weakened by legislative changes which restricted their powers to constrain or influence managerial prerogative. Other legal restrictions on managerial control over the hiring and firing of labour were also removed or modified through Government legislation on employment protection. The result was a substantial shift in the balance of power towards management in what was already an asymmetrical relationship. It was in this context that the Government also sought to modify the operation of the labour market by introducing various schemes for youths, culminating in the two-year YTS. Such schemes were intended, either directly, as in the Young Worker Scheme, or indirectly, as in YTS, to lower youth wages.

YTS, and the schemes which preceded it, have affected the labour market in a number of different ways. Our evidence suggests that they have reinforced and extended the segmentation of the youth labour market. Lee *et al*. (1987) have gone so far as to refer to YTS as constituting a 'surrogate labour market', which is itself highly stratified. Thus, in the middle level occupational segments the first two years of many apprenticeships are now undertaken on YTS, leaving employers free, in some cases, to determine which of the recruits should be offered a full apprenticeship. In other instances, where employers recruit YTS trainees directly into an apprenticeship and make up the wages to the same level as that of conventional apprentices, the young person may be unaware that they are on YTS. It must also be remembered that in areas of high unemployment, YTS has become virtually the only route into jobs in the lower segments for youths. Even where this is the case, however, schemes are further differentiated in the eyes of young people into those which offer a good prospect of leading to a 'real' job at the end and those which may have few, if any jobs, to offer (Roberts *et al*., 1986). Clearly, in terms of both training given and the prospects of jobs, there are good schemes and bad schemes. Much depends on the local labour market.

Another effect of YTS has been to reinforce the age segmentation which was already a distinctive feature of the British youth labour market. By adopting an employer-led response the scheme has reinforced the tendency of British employers to recruit youths at an early age. In contrast to North American practice, where recruitment to apprenticeships and good-quality white-collar jobs takes place between the ages of 18 and the mid-20s, YTS encourages British employers to continue recruiting 16-year-olds (Ashton, 1988). Access to these jobs is very difficult after the age of 16, which is when the bulk of recruitment for YTS takes place.

Employers also use YTS in very different ways. As already indicated, for some it provides a useful screening device as they are able to take on youths for two years, or a part thereof, during which time they can assess the trainee's suitability for employment, without any obligation to offer a permanent job. For those who do not normally recruit youths, participation in the schemes may be out of a sense of moral responsibility. It must also be admitted that in some instances, especially among smaller firms, YTS provides, through the managing agents, very cheap labour, towards which the employer has few, if any, obligations. This labour can be used for a time and dispensed with in the knowledge that there will be replacements available next year. Roberts *et al*. (1986) have referred to these as 'new juvenile jobs'.

Although YTS has had a profound impact on the youth labour market it still falls short of providing a bridge to work for all 16-year-olds. Three years after the introduction of YTS almost a half of all school-leavers did not undertake schemes and a significant proportion still went directly into employment. The greater economic buoyancy experienced in 1987 and 1988, particularly in the South East of England, coupled with the declining numbers of 16-year-olds in the population, has led to greater competition for 16-year-olds from employers, YTS managing agents, school sixth forms, and Further and Higher Education. Where demand for labour is high, many employers have by-passed YTS and tempted school-leavers to go directly into employment, often with little or no training content, by offering high wages. As a result, recruitment into YTS in London and the South East has been reduced. This contrasts with increases in recruitment in Scotland, the North, the North West, Yorkshire and Humberside, and Wales (*Financial Times*, 20 January 1989, p. 9). Thus the impact varies in relation to the general level of employment in the local labour market. Although fewer young people enter YTS in the more prosperous areas, those who do stand a good chance of securing employment at the end. In areas of high unemployment the greater numbers who enter have less chance of securing a job at the end. The scheme continues to evolve, and as a training measure it has certainly improved the training of those who enter jobs in the lower segment. However, as a solution to the unemployment problem the scheme merely delays the onset of unemployment for youths in the deprived areas. These issues are addressed in more detail in Chapter 9.

CONCLUSIONS – THE IMPLICATIONS FOR YOUTH

The Demand for Youth Labour in Manufacturing and Commerce

The continuation of the trends identified in this chapter will reduce further the demand for the labour of less qualified 16-year-old leavers which was highlighted in Chapter 2. This is due to the relocation of labour-intensive industries, and the effects of technological change in certain manufacturing industries. These losses will be partly offset by the growth of jobs in the service sector, although the extent to which youths rather than adult females will benefit from these changes will depend in part on the ability of YTS to counter the trend towards the use of part-time labour. Yet while the market for unqualified young people is declining, due to long-term labour market trends, the same social and economic forces are increasing the demand for more highly qualified labour.

One of the major areas where further job losses can be expected is in the labour-intensive manufacturing industries which have traditionally employed a high proportion of school-leavers. The relocation of capital to low labour cost countries is likely to sustain the reduction in the demand for young people as unskilled and semi-skilled manual workers. A residual demand for unqualified youth labour will remain as some of the smaller companies replicate the working conditions of their competitors abroad or find their own market niches. However, as the source of this change is structural in character, being a product of changes in the international division of labour, it can be expected to continue into the foreseeable future.

There is a similar trend within the rest of manufacturing industry, albeit for different reasons. The introduction of new technology is causing substantial job losses. For example, tasks on production lines in the car industry which were previously carried out by operatives, have been taken over by robots, while CNC machines enhance the productivity of craftworkers at the skilled level and information technology in the office is eradicating clerical jobs. However, the impact on employers' demand for youths is mediated by other factors. Thus, one of the reasons for employers being obliged to adopt new technology has been the expansion of global markets and the intensified competition associated with it. Yet this pressure is not always sufficient to explain its introduction. Often both the type of technological innovation and the speed with which it is introduced have to be negotiated with unions. In these circumstances the existence of widespread unemployment has weakened union resistence to change. Another factor is the struggle for power within the firm. Thus, in one of our case studies, even after the introduction of new machinery, the decision to use highly skilled rather than semi-skilled labour to run it was a result of a struggle between the line manager who wished to continue using apprentice-trained labour and the training manager who wanted to use semi-skilled labour. However, there was agreement on the fact that, because of the higher levels of productivity of the new machines, fewer workers would be required for a given level of output. The result was a substantial and permanent fall in the level of demand for apprentices.

At the operative level, male youths were traditionally excluded from most of the jobs in the mass production industries that have now been lost. By contrast the automation of packing and other routine manual operations in the food processing and printing industries has eliminated jobs previously done by unqualified female school-leavers. This goes a long way towards explaining the gender differences in recruitment noted in Chapter 2 and the decline of unskilled jobs in manufacturing industry.

The introduction of word processors and computer systems to office work is reducing the demand for female clerical workers as typists or filing clerks. As noted in Chapter 2, this is creating a major change in the opportunities available to females in the middle segments of the occupational hierarchy. For example, at one extreme a large manufacturing plant had a workforce of 3000, of which 2500 were indirect labour, with clerical support provided by six females operating word processors. Other firms have achieved a similar effect by introducing networked systems of micros. For the more sophisticated forms of operation, involving the control and application of computers, young males have usually been recruited. The general implication of the introduction of new technology in the office, besides the loss of female jobs, has been the transformation of the skills required for the remaining female jobs and the creation of new male jobs.

Overall, the impact of new technology on manufacturing has been to eradicate jobs and to enhance the productivity of the existing labour force. This change has affected the youth labour market in different ways depending, in part, on the sexual division of work. The impact on job content has been to maintain the relevance of some skills, such as knowledge of the mechanical process by which articles are produced in engineering and of keyboard skills in clerical work, while also introducing new skills, such as the ability to manipulate and control computer systems and programmes. Whether these new skills are more complex is open to question. What is clear is that the relatively unskilled machine-minding jobs in the manufacturing sector, which formerly provided a means of access to employment for unqualified youths, are disappearing.

Many of the jobs which remain in manufacturing have been susceptible to the effects of technological change, so that the skills required to operate and control the machinery have had to be upgraded. For example, breweries, which used to recruit apprentices in substantial numbers, now require graduates to oversee the ever more sophisticated process of brewing. Traditional craft apprenticeships in engineering have given way to the need for workers possessing a combination of mechanical skills and knowledge of micro-electronic control systems. Due to the increasing cost and complexity of the machinery, the ability to identify and diagnose faults is of prime concern.

Other pressures, which stem from the spread of global markets, are working in the same direction. The more extensive use of subcontracting is encouraging the growth of self-employment, although in the case of skilled manual occupations this may lead to fewer training opportunities for young people, as the self-employed are less likely to take on apprentices. Where the work that is sub-contracted is less skilled, jobs which may in the past have been part of an internal market, to which youths may have had access, are now in areas of employment where youths find it difficult to obtain access. Self-employment and the establishment of businesses are usually undertaken by people with considerable work experience.

In the commercial sector, our results suggest that where the jobs involve responsibility, as for example cashiers in banks and building societies, adult females are displacing youths. The employers' concern about the need for responsibility among cashiers in their handling of large sums of money, and the need for the organisation to present an image of maturity in dealings with customers, have led employers to prefer married women as recruits. These are the jobs which are growing in numbers and this in itself represents a form of structural change.

Changes in the content of jobs are leading employers to reappraise the criteria used when recruiting into the various segments of the labour force. For those seeking entry to the middle and higher segments emphasis is placed on the development of abstract conceptual thinking and the associated diagnostic ability. Similarly, changes in organisational culture are resulting in recruits being required to demonstrate the ability to maintain flexibility in thinking, to relate tasks to the broader context within which they are located, and to place a higher value on collective, as opposed to individual, objectives. However, it must be emphasised that these are marginal changes within the overall structure of the manufacturing sector, and are only likely to affect those who succeed in entering permanent employment in the large companies.

The Demand for Youth Labour in Distribution, Hotel and Catering and other Service Industries

While the long-term contraction of the manufacturing sector has caused a substantial reduction in the demand for young males and, to a lesser extent, young females, the growth of parts of the service sector has provided a source of new jobs. As was shown in Chapter 2, this growth was sufficient to encourage employers to increase the proportions of youths recruited during the recession. None the less, one of the most significant trends in the demand for labour has been the growth of part-time jobs and, in some instances, the replacement of full-time jobs by part-time jobs, for which employers are often reluctant to recruit young school-leavers. This is having a profound effect on the youth labour market. This displacement of youths by older females accounts for most of the unemployment found among young females during the recession when the demand for female labour was increasing.

The competition between all-age females and youths is most acute in the case of unskilled and semi-skilled jobs in retail stores, hotels and catering. There the trend for full-time jobs to be replaced by part-time jobs, and for new job growth to be predominantly among part-timers, has not produced such a massive substitution of youths by older women. This is largely due to the impact of the Youth Training Scheme. These jobs are largely deskilled and labour may be regarded as interchangeable. The main reason for employers preferring married women for part-time jobs is their perceived greater stability (due in part to the restrictions imposed by their domestic commitments). Also, youths have been expected to look for full-time work. However, given the introduction of either free or heavily subsidised youth labour through YTS, employers are faced with a choice. The decision to take YTS trainees may be explicitly on the grounds that the labour of the trainee is subsidised and therefore cheap or because the company believes it has a moral duty to help provide jobs for youths; neither in fact excludes the other. Thus, one major retail organisation which we visited has issued a directive for individual stores to switch from recruiting married women to YTS trainees. Traditionally, married women had been preferred because of their perceived maturity, greater reliability and flexibility. Now the company wished to be seen to be contributing towards alleviating the youth unemployment problem and so, local labour market conditions permitting, the switch was made and married women were no longer to be considered. If this strategy had been adopted on a large scale by employers, it would explain the trends revealed by our analysis of the Labour Force Survey (Chapter 2) which showed married women being displaced by single women in the less skilled service sector jobs. Without trade union opposition and with a surplus of labour in the local labour market, such a switch can easily be implemented, without any formal announcement of a change in policy. Recruitment becomes channelled through YTS, rather than through local press advertising. Given a fairly high turnover among staff, the age composition of the labour force will soon change as youths are substituted for adults. This could, of course, easily be reversed if the subsidies for youth labour were withdrawn.

There is some evidence that employers may be changing their attitude towards the recruitment of youths and beginning to regard them as acceptable as part-time workers. This change in employers' beliefs is a consequence of the recession. As unemployment levels rose, youths found it increasingly difficult to get any job, so that a part-time job which paid more than Supplementary Benefit became more attractive. The absence of available alternatives has enhanced the stability of youths who enter part-time jobs. It is not that they do not want a full-time job, it is just that none are available. Employers' fears about the instability and unreliability of youths have receded, resulting in their increasing recruitment into part-time jobs.

While the rationalisation of the labour force in retailing and hotel and catering has created new low skilled jobs, a drive for greater professionalisation in the management of these enterprises is causing employers to increase the educational qualifications they demand as a condition of entry for the more prestigious jobs.

The Impact of YTS

It is against the background of these changes in the demand for youth labour which took place during the recession that we now assess the impact of the political attempt to increase the demand for youth labour through YTS. At the higher occupational levels, the availability of free youth labour has not been sufficient inducement to counter the trend towards increasing the educational requirements necessary for entry, thereby encouraging youths to stay on at school. The pressure of qualification inflation has proved stronger than the attraction of the schemes.

In the middle segments YTS has provided a subsidy for the recruitment of youths into apprenticeship and trainee positions. This led to an increase in the recruitment of 16-year-olds in the construction industry during the recession. However, YTS has been unable to halt the decline in the total number of apprenticeships, which reflects the radically reduced demand for skilled labour as industries have contracted. Moreover, the widespread adoption of new technology has created a counter-trend for an increase in the demand for technicians and technologists. These jobs usually require higher educational qualifications and therefore YTS has had only a limited impact in this area.

Overall, the scheme has not succeeded in opening a wide range of different types of job to youths. It has failed to arrest the underlying trend towards a greater concentration of entry points for school-leavers. Its main achievement as an agent of change has been to increase awareness of training and to keep the doors open to young females in the less skilled service sector occupations.

NOTES

1. The recent work of Rajan and Pearson (1986) and Rajan (1987) has also suggested that these factors have been an important source of change in occupational and employment trends. Their work was based on a survey of over 3000 companies and provides a more detailed account of the occupational changes discussed here. However, their primary concern was to identify occupational changes and so less consideration was given to an analysis of the underlying causes. Thus, in the engineering industry they identify lack of output growth due to international competition, changes in working methods, new technology and a reliance on sub-contracting as the four main causes. Our position differs from this, for we argue that the change in the structure of international competition is closely related to the other changes which are partly driven by it. Thus, new working practices, new technology and sub-contracting have been introduced in part as a response to changes in the structure of product markets.
2. On global or transnational, as opposed to multinational corporations, see Taylor and Thrift (1982). Lash and Urry (1987) also discuss this issue, but look at the problem of global markets from the perspective of national markets, and develop the idea of the deconcentration of capital and disorganised capital. This perspective means that they fail to appreciate the effects of the restructuring and reorganisation of capital which is taking place at the higher level, that of the international division of labour.
3. Following Ballance and Sinclair (1983) we do not argue that this process is complete. The emergence of global markets is a long-term process stretching back many years. While it has accelerated in recent years this acceleration is not uniform in all the constituent elements. Thus, the General Agreement on Tariffs and Trade (GATT) has removed some barriers but, as with all long-term processes of change, other counter-pressures exist. Examples of other forms of protectionism are the periodic devaluations which countries make to enhance their competitiveness. In the area of technological diffusion change is more rapid and uniform.

4. Rajan and Pearson (1986) and Rajan (1987) also point to industrial concentration as one of the causes of occupational change in the service sector, together with externalising or sub-contracting, organic business growth, new technologies and working methods and changing job status. Our results again suggest that these other factors are closely linked to, and partly driven by the increasing domination of the product market by the larger employers.

7 The Segmentation of the Youth Labour Market

In this chapter we move on from the analysis of broad structural changes to an examination of how they affect the work histories of young adults, that is, the movement of young people within the labour market and their experience of it. Throughout this aspect of our research the focus has been firmly on placing individuals within structured work histories rather than merely identifying them by occupation. As we have seen the pressures of labour market segmentation are currently creating major structural changes in the labour market. In order to establish their impact on the way in which young people experience employment we need to distinguish between changes which affect the relative size of the various segments and changes which affect the composition of the jobs which comprise the segments. With regard to the former, we have already seen how the proportion of apprenticeships available to males has shrunk and how the proportion of white-collar, especially professional, technical and administrative jobs, has increased. Similarly, for females we have noted how the proportion of clerical jobs has declined and the proportion of semi-skilled and unskilled service sector jobs has increased. Because of such changes, the overall configuration of the youth labour market is undergoing a major transformation.

With regard to the change in the composition of the jobs, we have noted a number of features. Many of the new male clerical jobs now involve the manipulation or control of computerised systems, apprenticeships now demand a greater knowledge of computers, and many of the remaining female clerical jobs require keyboard skills for working VDUs. In the service sector we have also noted how some jobs are becoming further deskilled with the introduction of fast-food outlets and EPOS systems.

It is important that we are aware of these changes in the configuration of the youth labour market because they form the context within which young people's labour market histories are shaped. Some will follow highly structured 'careers', while others will experience a series of unrelated, semi-skilled and unskilled jobs, interspersed with periods of unemployment or moves out of the labour market.[1] In what follows we focus on how the various labour market segments structure job movement, although it is important to remember, in the course of the analysis, that the very structures of the segments are changing.

THE CHARACTERISTICS OF LABOUR MARKET SEGMENTS

One consequence of the pressure of labour market segmentation is that once entered, labour market segments exert their own influence on the young person's subsequent experience of the labour market. Conceptually this means treating each particular segment as having its own characteristic features which are independent of those of the individuals who, at any one point in time, may pass through it. This is a familiar distinction in the literature (Stewart, Prandy and Blackburn, 1980), but one that is frequently lost sight of in empirical analysis (Borus, 1984). Our evidence leads us to suggest that each segment offers different career opportunities, chances of unemployment and distinctive pattern of inflow and outflow. In this way each segment constrains the life chances of the individuals who enter it almost independently of their personal characteristics. For example, the pattern of job movement of most teachers is explained by the structure of the teaching career ladder and the rules which determine movement up it. New members enter at the lowest level and movement up the hierarchy is determined by the application of certain criteria used in promotion and the availability of places. It is, of course, possible for people to enter teaching after several years in the labour market and leave for other jobs. However, the basic structure of the teacher's career could persist through time with a substantial inflow and outflow of personnel. The numbers moving through it may affect the rate of mobility within the profession, but will not affect the direction of movement, as this is determined by the hierarchical structure of the career.

On the other hand, the pattern of inflow and outflow will be strongly influenced by the relationship between segments. For example, once having trained as a teacher it is usually too late to subsequently retrain for an occupation requiring a substantial initial training period, such as for a skilled craft worker or a doctor. In what follows we identify the basic structure of movement within the segments and the life chances associated with them, and then move on to analyse how the relations between segments influence movement between them. The evidence on which the discussion is based is the data from the 'Young Adults in the Labour Market' study, which comprised interviews with 1786 18 to 24-year-olds.

Few of the respondents had had more than three jobs, so that tracing career paths was not difficult. This lack of job movement was partly due to the impact of the recession but also due to the fact that the respondents were still in their early years in the labour market. The data enabled us to follow through the movements of individuals at each stage of their career up to the time of interview, by coding every change of status in an individual's labour market experience as a different event. Thus, a person who left school, went to college, became unemployed, took an unskilled job and then moved to a clerical job would be coded as having four events. For each event, the position in relation to the labour market, such as the type of job done, attendance at an FE College, being unemployed, or being out of the labour market, is referred to as a status.

Our own and other research (Spilsbury, 1986; Blau and Duncan, 1967; and Breen, 1984) indicated that the occupational level of the first job a person entered had a significant influence on the direction of subsequent job movement. It was therefore decided to trace the career paths of those who started in each of our occupational categories. This technique has been advocated by Spilerman (1977).[2] The assumption was that the pattern of subsequent movement would be imposed by constraints in the labour market, which could encourage or prohibit movement in a given direction. If a large proportion who started from a given position had a similar pattern and sequence of events it would be realistic to assume that these were in response to labour market constraints.

This technique inevitably focuses attention on first jobs, and as such can provide only a partial understanding of subsequent job movement. It is adequate when the first job is part of a career ladder, as in the case of an apprentice who then becomes a skilled worker and perhaps a foreman. It is less effective in mapping the movement of those who may stay on in Further Education or take a job as an unskilled worker before entering a technician, professional or administrative job. These latter jobs provide a career, but cannot be entered on leaving school because of age restrictions. As a result, the early labour market experience of the young person will bear no relation to their subsequent career. In order to counter this and assess the impact of mobility on respondents' careers as they entered the adult labour market, the routes taken to achieve the career destinations at the time of interview were traced. This technique highlighted the various avenues of mobility into the higher status occupations. It also produced new insights into the dynamics of the youth labour market.

Our results suggest that each of the segments has characteristics which distinguish it from the others and which structure the labour market experience of those who enter. Here we focus only on five such characteristics, the level of job stability; career chances; unemployment chances; learning time; and the pattern of job movement within the segment. These we argue to be most appropriately conceptualised as a function of the position rather than of the incumbent.[3]

Job Stability, Promotion Chances and Unemployment Chances

If we look first at the influence of the various segments on the job stability of those who enter, significant differences are revealed. Not all 16-year-old school-leavers enter jobs on leaving school. Some continue within Further Education, others enter Government schemes, while some fail to find any employment. Moreover, once they enter the labour market the majority will either change jobs, become unemployed or leave the labour force before their mid-twenties. In fact only a small majority (57 per cent) of the 24-year-olds in the sample were still in employment at the time of interview. The other 43 per cent had either left the labour force or were unemployed. The picture, even during a recession, is one of considerable fluidity within the labour market. However, unlike the 1960s and 1970s when the movement was between jobs, in the early part of the 1980s there was less movement between jobs but more movement into and out of unemployment and Government schemes. Our data provided a series of snapshots of the flows of young people moving between these various statuses. Table 7.1 provides the results of two such snapshots illustrating the percentage of all those who entered each segment during their early years in the labour market and stayed in that position until the time of interview.

The first two columns show the percentage of males and females in the sample who entered each job category on first leaving school and remained in that job until the time of interview. The other columns show the proportions who entered each category as their second, third and fourth event or move in the labour market. These moves were primarily from Further Education, other jobs, unemployment or Government schemes.

TABLE 7.1: *Percentage who remained in their job or were unemployed at the time of interview*

Status Category	Stage in the young adults work history at which they entered their last status: 1st Event F	M	2nd Event F	M	3rd Event F	M	4th Event F	M
Prof, Man, Tech.	51	73	55	67	54	59	52	69
Clerical	33	61	33	56	43	40	41	67
Skilled	31	44	39	29	17	32	35	22
Semi-skilled	11	20	26	27	12	32	23	24
Unskilled	9	11	21	15	22	14	28	8
Sales	18	24	26	11	20	57	28	40
Unemployed	*	*	18	27	24	43	23	37
N =	128	204	157	167	113	122	83	90

* for an explanation of the absence of any young adults in this category see Footnote 2

The table shows a high level of stability in the higher segments, so that the majority of those who entered these jobs, whether as their first, second or third event, tended to stick in them. Females tended to move on more frequently than males, possibly because of the lower status of many of the professional and technical jobs entered by women. Entrants to the clerical segments exhibited a lower level of stability, albeit one that was much higher than that experienced by those who entered semi-skilled, unskilled and sales jobs in the lower segment. Again, females were less stable, possibly because of the male jobs being of higher status and being more likely to be a part of an internal labour market. Differences in the opportunities for promotion would seem to bear this out (Table 7.2). Overall, entrants to the skilled segments exhibited a slightly lower level of stability than did those in the clerical segments, and there was less difference between males and females. Other evidence from the research suggests that the lack of gender differential is a consequence of the recession which had a more dramatic effect on the male jobs, with many apprentices and skilled workers being made redundant as a result of the collapse of manufacturing industry in this period. There was a high level of instability in all jobs in the lower segments. With the exception of males who entered sales jobs, few respondents had remained in the first job they took in these segments. This suggests that no matter at which point in their labour market experience a

TABLE 7.2: *Are there any chances of promotion in your present job? (those in full-time jobs who replied 'yes')*

	Prof./Man. Tech.		Clerical		Sales		Skilled		Semi-skilled		Unskilled	
	%	No.	%	No.	%	No.	%	No.	%	No.	%	No.
Males	73	(153)	75	(68)	75	(16)	48	(121)	62	(93)	24	(21)
Females	69	(89)	63	(190)	41	(56)	33	(33)	24	(62)	23	(52)

person enters a particular segment, their chances of remaining within it are powerfully influenced by the characteristics of the jobs they take.

A similar pattern of results was obtained using other measures of job stability. The proportion of respondents who left a job within twelve months of starting it was lowest in the upper segments, at less than a third, compared to between half and three-quarters in the lower segments.

Part of the reason for these differences in the levels of job stability evident in the various segments, lay in the length of time taken to learn the appropriate skills. Becker and Carper (1956) have argued that, in the process of learning the more complex skills required for jobs in the higher segments, people learn to identify with the occupation and so become committed to it. In addition, such jobs provide greater rewards in the form of income and status. If we look at the first jobs entered by the respondents, almost 80 per cent of all unskilled jobs were learnt within a month of starting. Other jobs within the lower segment also had a short learning time, 60 per cent of those entering sales jobs learnt them within a month, as did 50 per cent of those entering semi-skilled work. By contrast, the vast majority entering jobs in the skilled and higher segments were either still learning their jobs at the time of interview, or had taken more than a year to learn them. Thus, in order to obtain the higher rewards and status that accrue to those in professional and technician jobs, young people had to invest a considerable period of time in training, thereby committing themselves to the job in order to realise that 'investment'. For those in the lower segments learning time was so short that these mechanisms could not come into play.

Another factor which influences job stability is the career chances attached to the position. Table 7.2 shows how these differed significantly between the various segments and in different categories within the segment. As expected, the higher and clerical segments

TABLE 7.3: *Percentage of those entering each job status who became unemployed immediately after leaving**

	Event 2		Event 3		Event 4		Event 5	
	F	M	F	M	F	M	F	M
Prof/Man/Admin & Tech.	9	15	6	10	9	10	19	23
Clerical	15	17	15	6	17	20	5	17
Skill	14	28	16	37	9	32	12	50
Semi. Sk.	25	37	22	25	36	25	27	42
Unsk.	30	33	29	38	35	58	36	64
Sales	16	26	19	37	15	14	24	40

* Excludes self-employed.

appear to offer good promotion prospects for both sexes. In the skilled segment, less than one half of respondents thought there were chances of promotion in their present job, with a noticeably lower proportion of females reporting this to be the case. Of those in semi-skilled work, a significantly higher proportion of males (62 per cent) than of females (24 per cent) claimed to have chances of promotion. This suggests that in sales and semi-skilled work the male jobs were more likely to be part of an internal labour market. This would also help to explain the greater stability of males in these jobs as they had greater future prospects. In unskilled jobs the chances of promotion for members of both sexes were very low. Overall, however, in most segments fewer females than males foresaw any career prospects.

Finally, from an examination of what happened to young adults when they left the job they entered as their first event on leaving school, it is clear that a much smaller proportion of those leaving the higher segments became unemployed when compared to those leaving the lower segments (Table 7.3). Moreover, these differences tended to persist with each successive inflow into the various segments, which again suggests that it is the characteristics of the jobs rather than the individuals who enter them which determines the young adults' chances of becoming unemployed. Those leaving the higher segments, which offer career prospects and training, are unlikely to leave their job until they have secured an alternative. In the lower segment the greater insecurity of the jobs is reflected in a higher proportion being forced to leave through redundancy and the termination of casual and short-term jobs and so being more exposed to unemployment. The relatively high proportion of male skilled workers who became unemployed was a result of redundancies associated with the decline of manufacturing during this period.

We are not arguing that individual characteristics, in the form of educational qualifications, ambition, attitude, and so on, are irrelevant to an explanation of these results. They clearly play a part in explaining why some people are more likely to experience spells of unemployment, but they only become meaningful in the context of the relationship with employers and the characteristics of the jobs they provide (Schervish, 1983). When selecting young people for entry to the various segments, employers tend to choose on the basis of these individual characteristics. Educational qualifications and ambition are virtually essential for entry to the higher segment, but once in that segment then other factors, such as the length of training offered by the job, and the availability of promotion opportunities, come into operation in determining the young adult's experience of the labour market. In the lower segment educational qualifications are irrelevant for entry to most jobs,[4] but the insecurity of many of these jobs renders young people who enter them more susceptible to unemployment, irrespective of their previous educational attainment.

The Pattern of Job Movement

The effect of the pressures of segmentation can be witnessed in the pattern of job movement. Tracing the movement between jobs of all those in our sample who started in a particular occupation, revealed that the single most frequent move was to another job in the same segment.

The distinctive patterns followed by those who entered each segment are illustrated in a series of diagrams, which trace the subsequent movement of entrants to each of the occupations which comprise the various segments as their first job (event) on leaving school. In order to simplify the presentation, and to illustrate the direction of the main flows, a number of conventions have been introduced. The main directions of movement have been indicated by lines. These have been drawn when the destination to which the line refers represents 5 per cent or more of the total outflow from a given category and accounts for more than three respondents. Different types of line have been used to represent different magnitudes of flow. In order to further simplify presentation and because their

FIGURE 7.1 *Patterns of job movement – males who entered jobs as technicians as their first event*

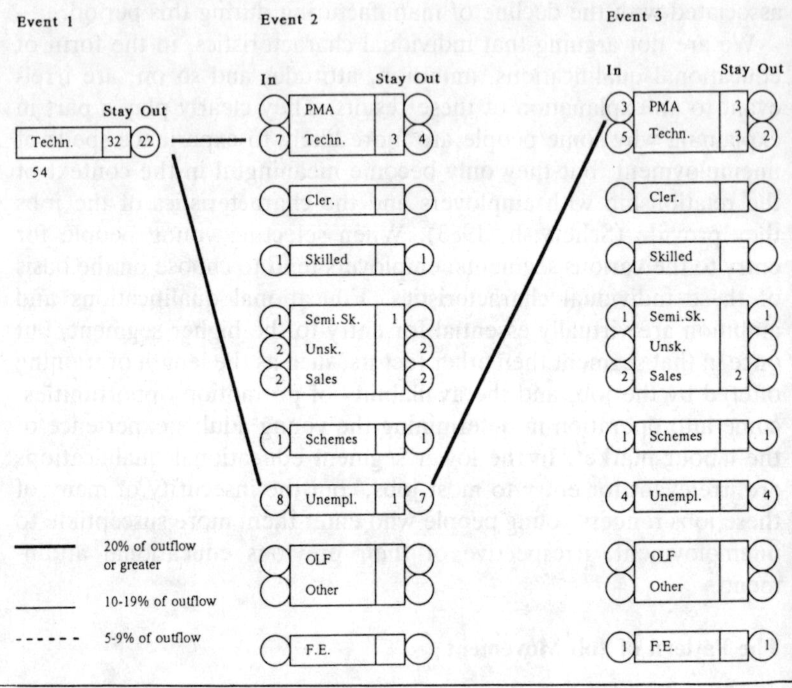

Note: This diagram only refers to the first three events (moves) as the numbers involved in the fourth were very small

numbers were very small, the self-employed have been excluded. Therefore, the total numbers entering each event may differ slightly from those leaving the previous event.

Figure 7.1 presents the results for males whose first job was in the technician category. This pattern was typical of all those of both sexes who entered the higher segment. In this, and the subsequent diagrams, the predominant direction of outflow is indicated by thick lines, and the secondary direction by a thin line. The numbers involved in either moves are indicated in the circles. Thus, in Figure 7.1, of the 54 males who entered technician posts as their first job, the majority remained in them.

But of those who did move into another job, the most frequent move was to another job in the same segment. The alternative was, of course, a move downward, either into a job in a lower segment, or into unemployment, but even these moves followed a distinctive pattern. For those who were downwardly mobile, certain occupations, such as skilled manual, were virtually closed, or were avoided, as in the case of unskilled work in the lower segment. For those who became unemployed a distinctive feature of their subsequent movement was that a high proportion succeeded in re-entering the higher segment by the time of the interview. Of course, the numbers involved are only small, but our confidence in these results is sustained by the fact that the pattern of movement of those who entered professional and managerial posts was almost identical.

The pattern of movement for those who entered the clerical segment was different. Figure 7.2 illustrates the pattern found among females entering clerical work. In comparison to the higher segment a greater proportion of both sexes moved jobs, but the most common destination was still to another job within the same segment. For females who became unemployed, the subsequent move was either back into clerical work or into a job in the lower segment. For males the movement out of unemployment was to either the higher or skilled segments rather than the lower segment. In the case of both sexes the movement was by no means random.

Figure 7.2 also illustrates a distinctive feature of the females' job histories, namely the high proportion moving out of the labour force. As the sample consisted of young adults, many of whom were in the early stages of the process of family formation, a significant number of females left the labour force for the purpose of childbirth. This was the case among females from all segments, although those who entered the lower segments tended to move out of the labour force earlier.

In the skilled segment, the experience of females was very different to that of males, and for this reason we present figures for both sexes. Of females who took their first job in this segment, 53 per cent had their work experience confined to it. Of those who subsequently moved, most went either into unemployment or out of the labour force. Those who entered another job tended to move either into the lower segment or another skilled job. For males a similar proportion remained in their first job, but thereafter the pattern of movement was more highly structured than in the case of females. The main direction was either to another skilled job or unemployment, reflecting the effects of the recession on manufacturing industry. The proportion who were successful in re-entering the skilled segment after becoming unemployed was smaller than was the case among those whose first job was in the higher segment (see Figure 7.1). The majority moved into jobs in the lower segment. This reflects the

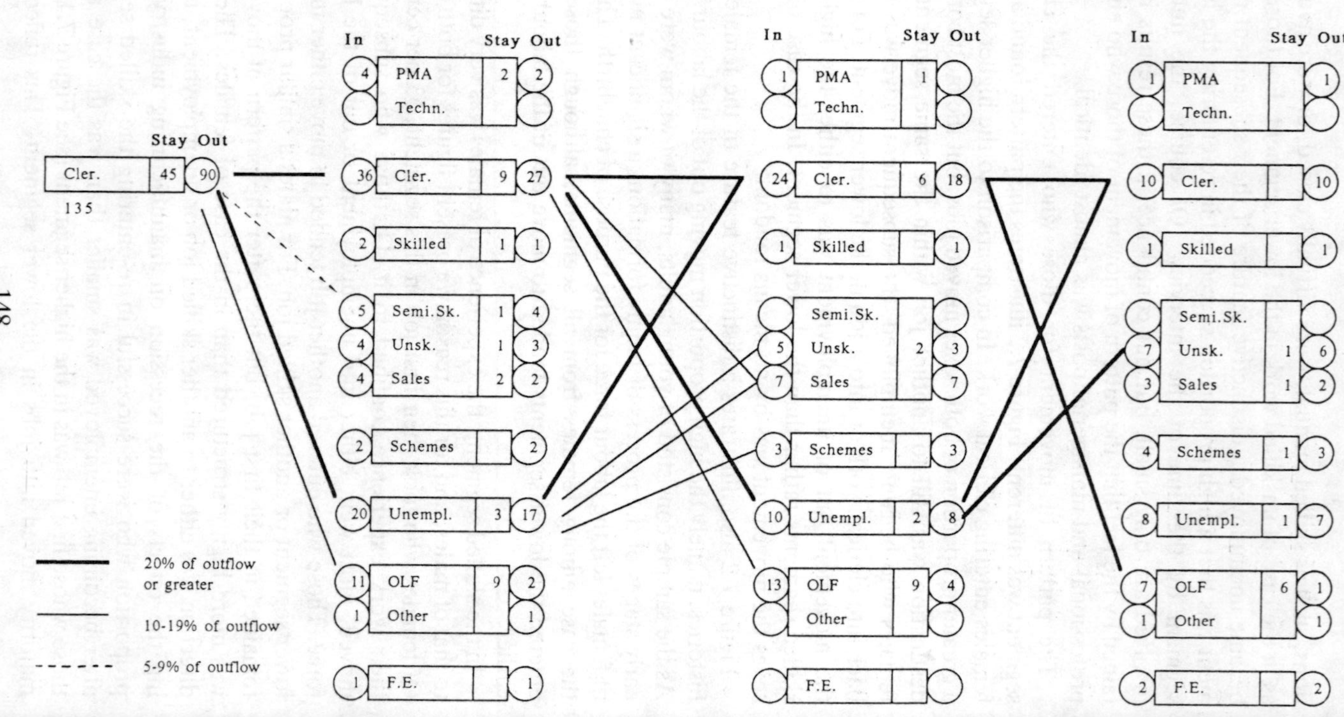

FIGURE 7.2 *Patterns of job movement – females who entered jobs as clerical workers as their first event*

FIGURE 7.3 *Patterns of job movement – females entering skilled manual work as their first event*

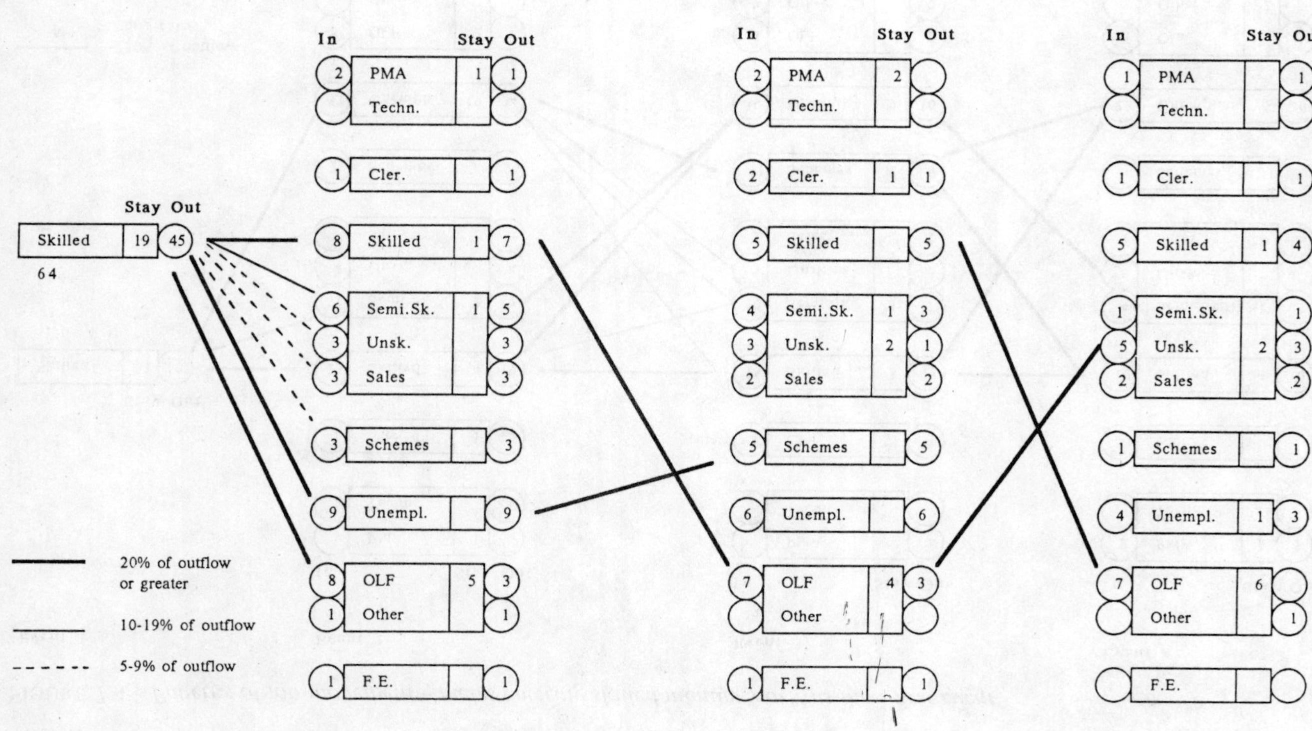

FIGURE 7.4 *Patterns of job movement – males entering skilled manual work as their first event*

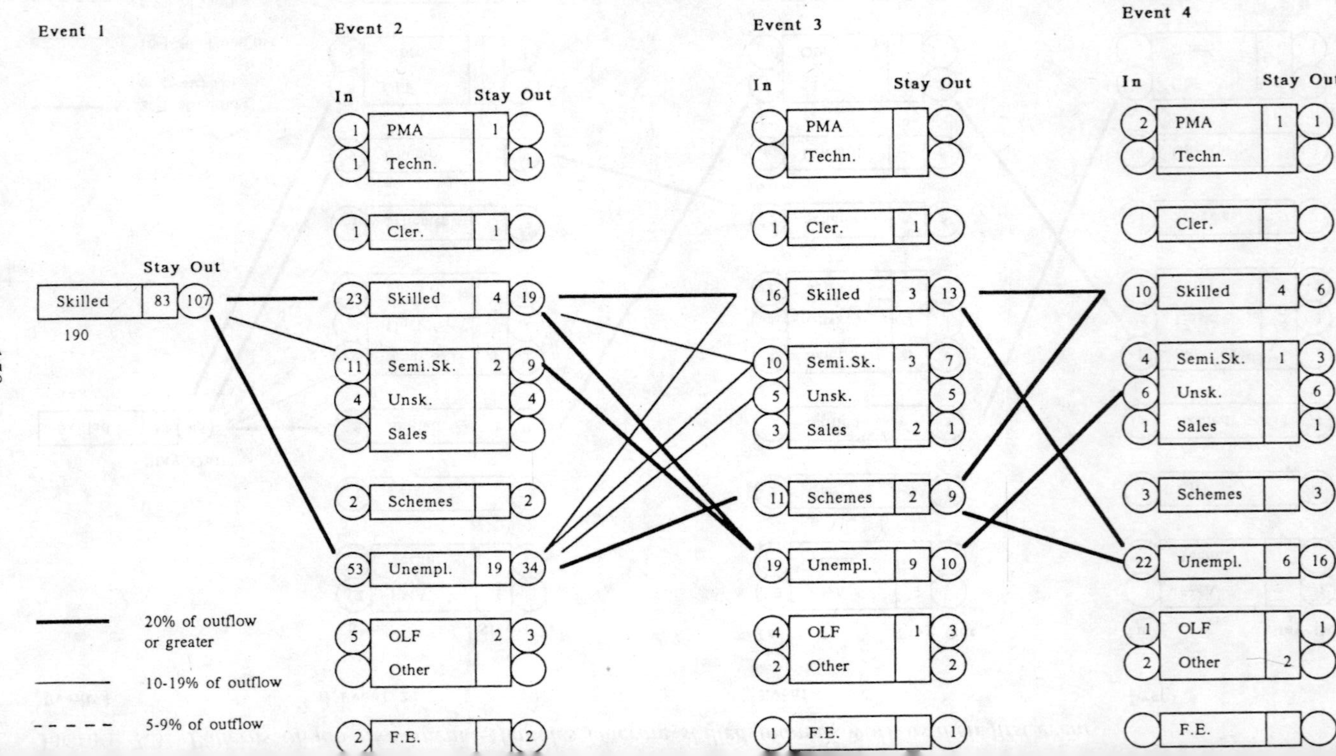

reduction in the size of this segment which took place during the recession.

Relatively few young people who took their first job in the lower segment (Figures 7.5–7.8), stayed in that job until the time of interview, although the labour market experience of the majority was confined to that segment. The general pattern of movement was highly structured, taking them from one semi-skilled, unskilled or sales job to another, interspersed by periods of unemployment or experience of Government schemes. Thus, while these job histories cannot be described as 'careers', in the conventional sense, the pattern of movement within the segment was similar. The point at which the person entered the segment did have some influence on the subsequent movement of the worker. Those entering semi-skilled work were more likely to return to that work following periods of unemployment. This may be a result of the fact that many women in semi-skilled jobs (Figure 7.5) had acquired a fairly extensive set of skills, for example, as machinists in textiles, and so strove to re-enter that type of work rather than take unskilled or sales jobs. Similarly, males (Figure 7.6) may have acquired tacit skills which provided a greater monetary value than that obtained from other jobs within the segment. In addition, a few males did succeed in moving up into skilled jobs, either directly, or after a spell of unemployment.

A small proportion of both sexes who took a first job in unskilled work used it as a fill-in job before moving into the higher segment. For the majority, however, the next move was to unemployment or a Government scheme, followed by another job in the lower segment (Figure 7.7). The only difference between the sexes was that for some males it was a prelude to movement into skilled work. Females who first entered sales jobs had noticeably less chance of becoming unemployed than those who entered unskilled and semi-skilled jobs. This was a consequence of the continued expansion of such jobs throughout the recession. Some young females entering sales work also used it as a prelude to securing work in the clerical segment (Figure 7.8). For males in sales work, the movement upwards was into skilled work. Of those whose first labour market experience was on a Government scheme, a few males later succeeded in entering skilled work, while a few females entered clerical work. Overwhelmingly, however, as Figure 7.9 illustrates, it was a matter of subsequent movement being between unskilled, semi-skilled and sales jobs interspersed with periods of unemployment for the majority; a situation more appropriately described as sub-employment (Norris, 1978).

FIGURE 7.5 *Patterns of job movement – females entering semi-skilled work as their first event*

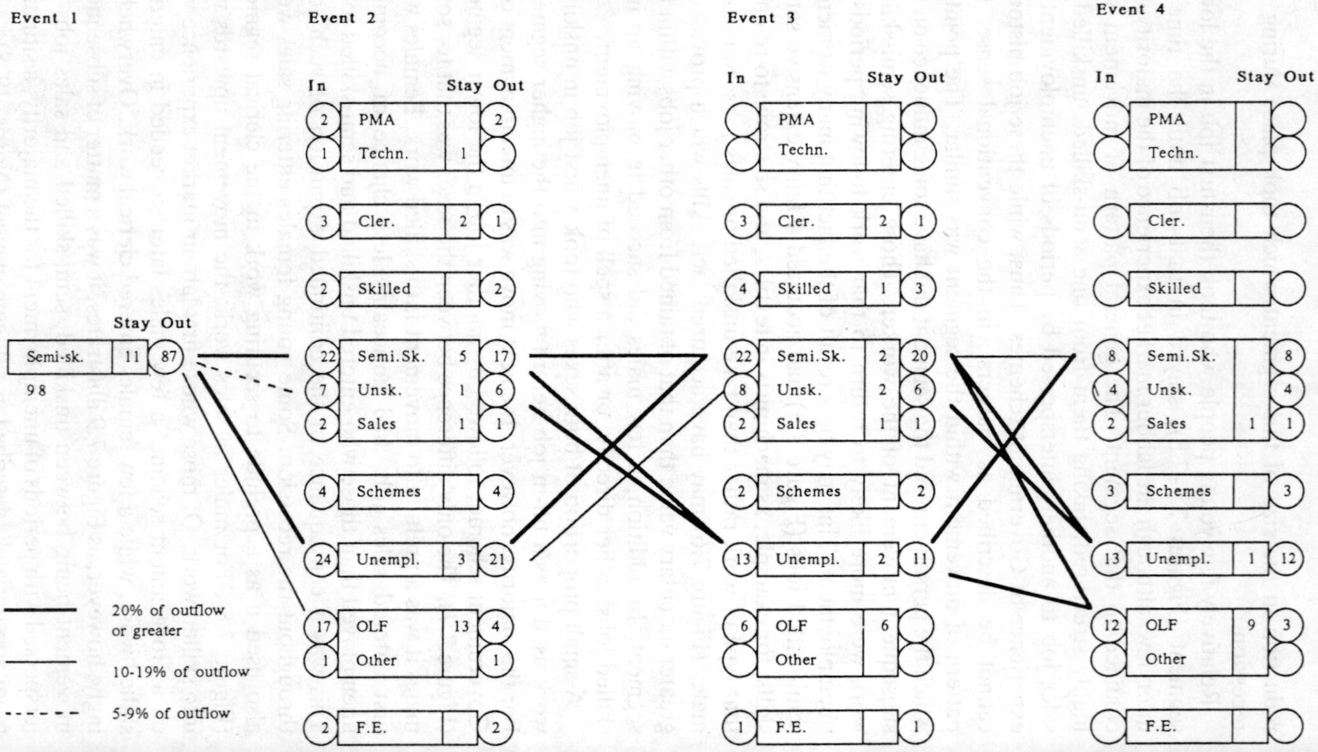

Event 1

	Stay	Out
Semi-sk. (98)	11	87

Event 2

In		Stay	Out
2	PMA		2
1	Techn.	1	
3	Cler.	2	1
2	Skilled		2
22	Semi.Sk.	5	17
7	Unsk.	1	6
2	Sales	1	1
4	Schemes		4
24	Unempl.	3	21
17	OLF	13	4
1	Other		1
2	F.E.		2

Event 3

In		Stay	Out
	PMA		
	Techn.		
3	Cler.	2	1
4	Skilled	1	3
22	Semi.Sk.	2	20
8	Unsk.	2	6
2	Sales	1	1
2	Schemes		2
13	Unempl.	2	11
6	OLF	6	
	Other		
1	F.E.		1

Event 4

In		Stay	Out
	PMA		
	Techn.		
	Cler.		
	Skilled		
8	Semi.Sk.		8
4	Unsk.		4
2	Sales	1	1
3	Schemes		3
13	Unempl.	1	12
12	OLF	9	3
	Other		
	F.E.		

——— 20% of outflow or greater

——— 10-19% of outflow

- - - - - 5-9% of outflow

FIGURE 7.6 *Patterns of job movement – males entering semi-skilled jobs as their first event*

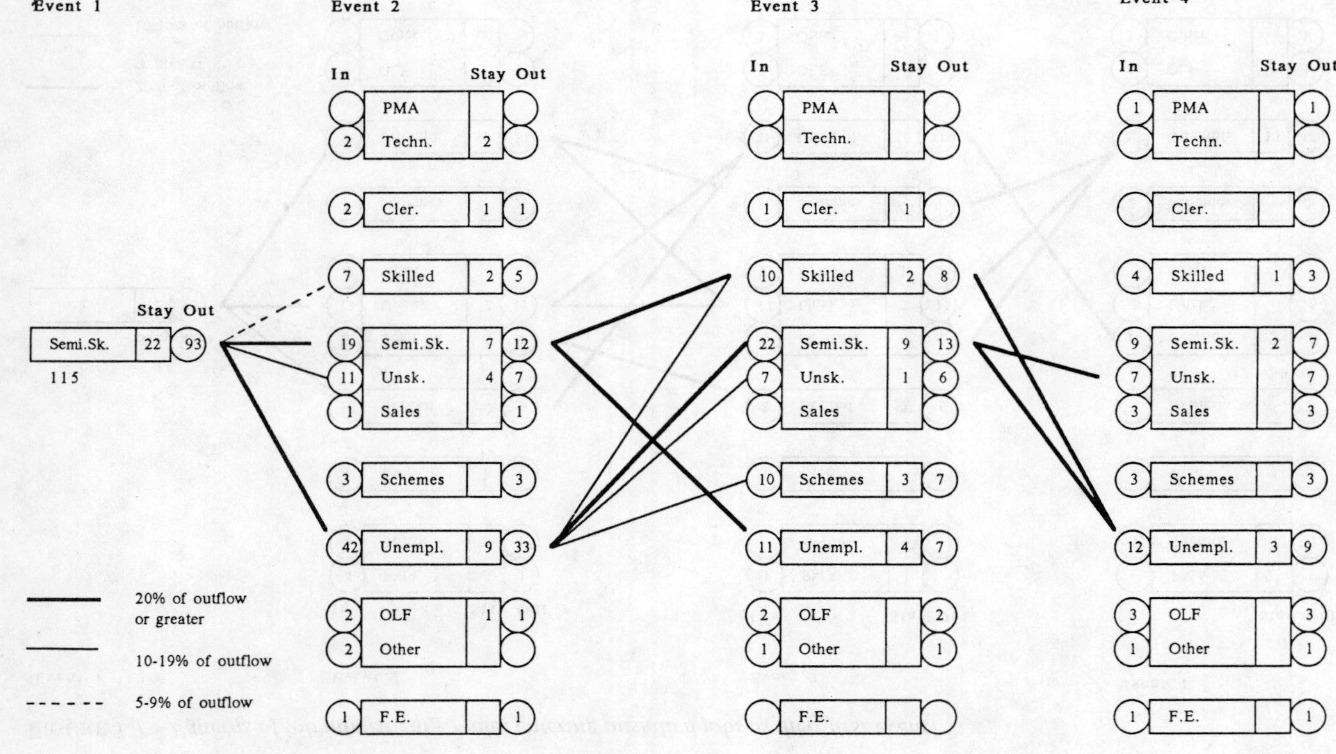

FIGURE 7.7 *Patterns of job movement – males entering unskilled jobs as their first event*

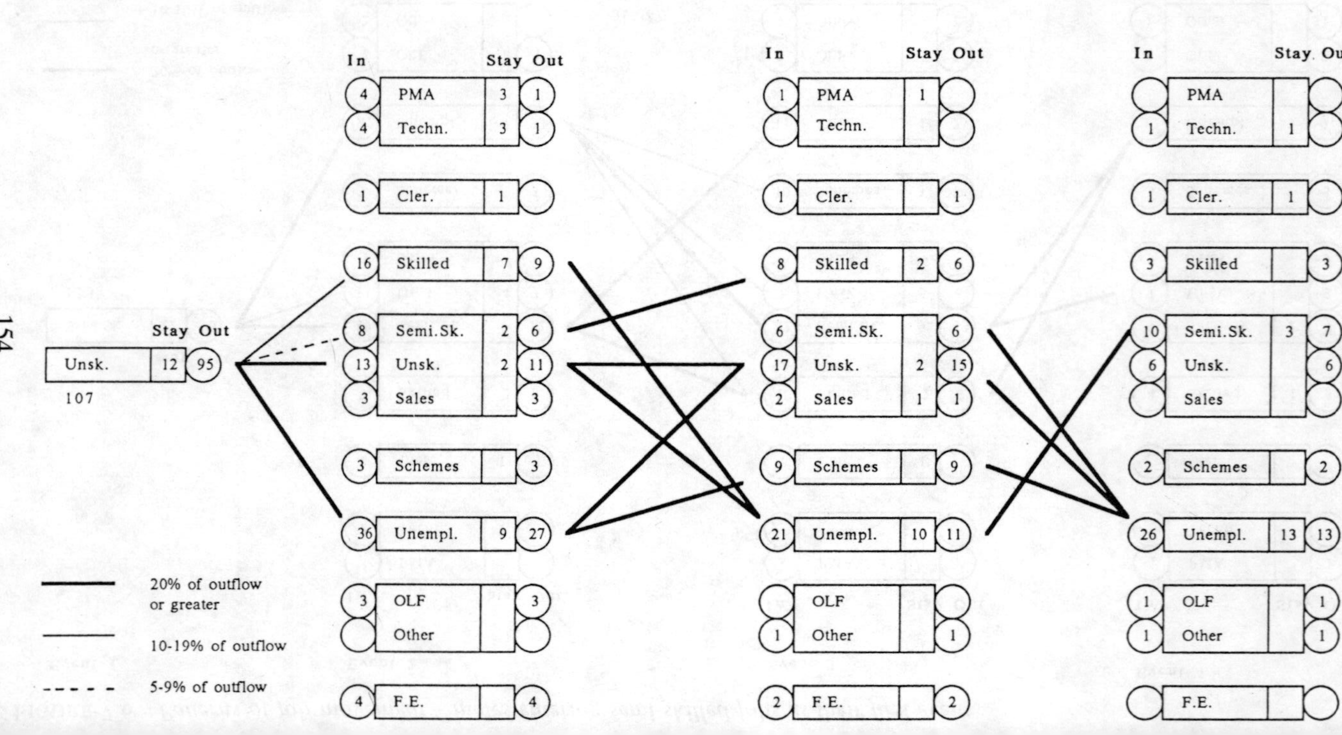

FIGURE 7.8 *Patterns of job movement – females entering sales job as their first event*

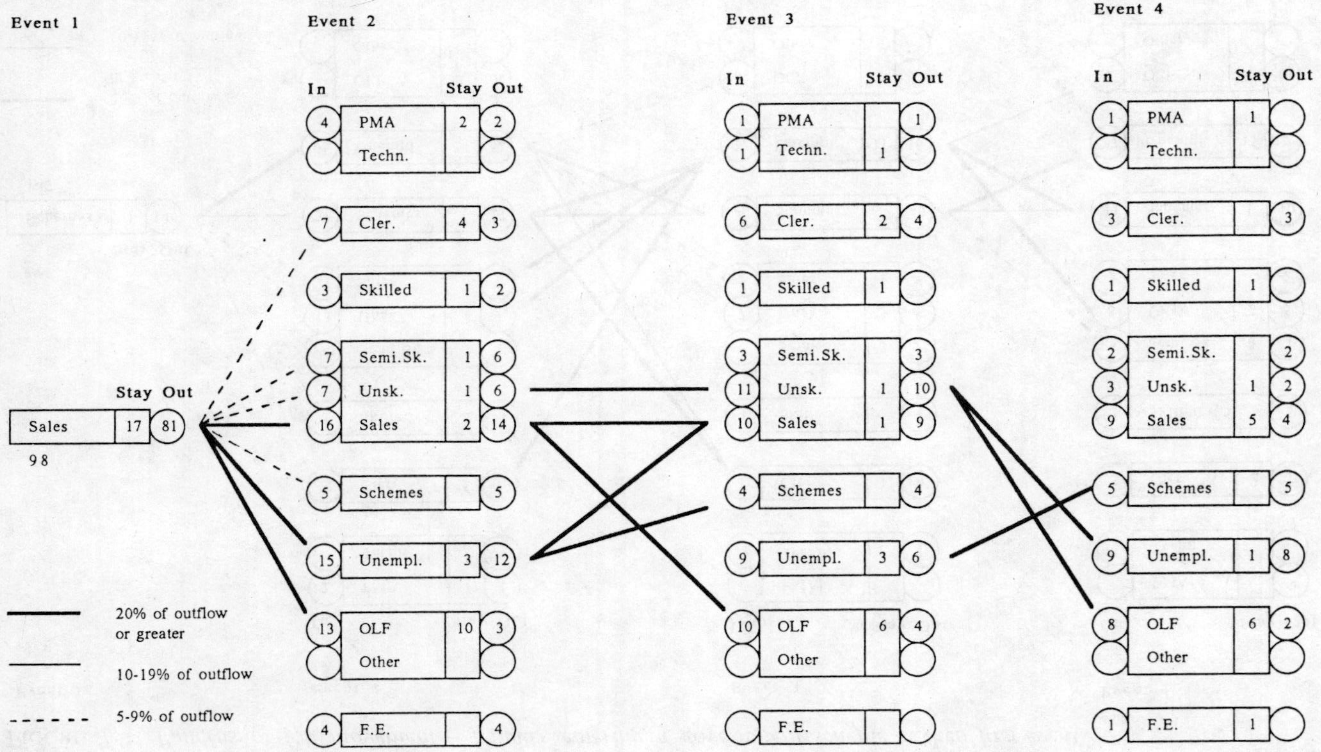

Event 1

	Stay	Out
Sales	17	81

98

Event 2

In		Stay	Out
4	PMA	2	2
	Techn.		
7	Cler.	4	3
3	Skilled	1	2
7	Semi.Sk.	1	6
7	Unsk.	1	6
16	Sales	2	14
5	Schemes		5
15	Unempl.	3	12
13	OLF	10	3
	Other		
4	F.E.		4

Event 3

In		Stay	Out
1	PMA		1
1	Techn.	1	
6	Cler.	2	4
1	Skilled	1	
3	Semi.Sk.		3
11	Unsk.	1	10
10	Sales	1	9
4	Schemes		4
9	Unempl.	3	6
10	OLF	6	4
	Other		
	F.E.		

Event 4

In		Stay	Out
1	PMA	1	
	Techn.		
3	Cler.		3
1	Skilled	1	
2	Semi.Sk.		2
3	Unsk.	1	2
9	Sales	5	4
5	Schemes		5
9	Unempl.	1	8
8	OLF	6	2
	Other		
1	F.E.	1	

—— 20% of outflow or greater

—— 10-19% of outflow

- - - - - 5-9% of outflow

FIGURE 7.9 *Patterns of job movement – females entering a government scheme as their first event*

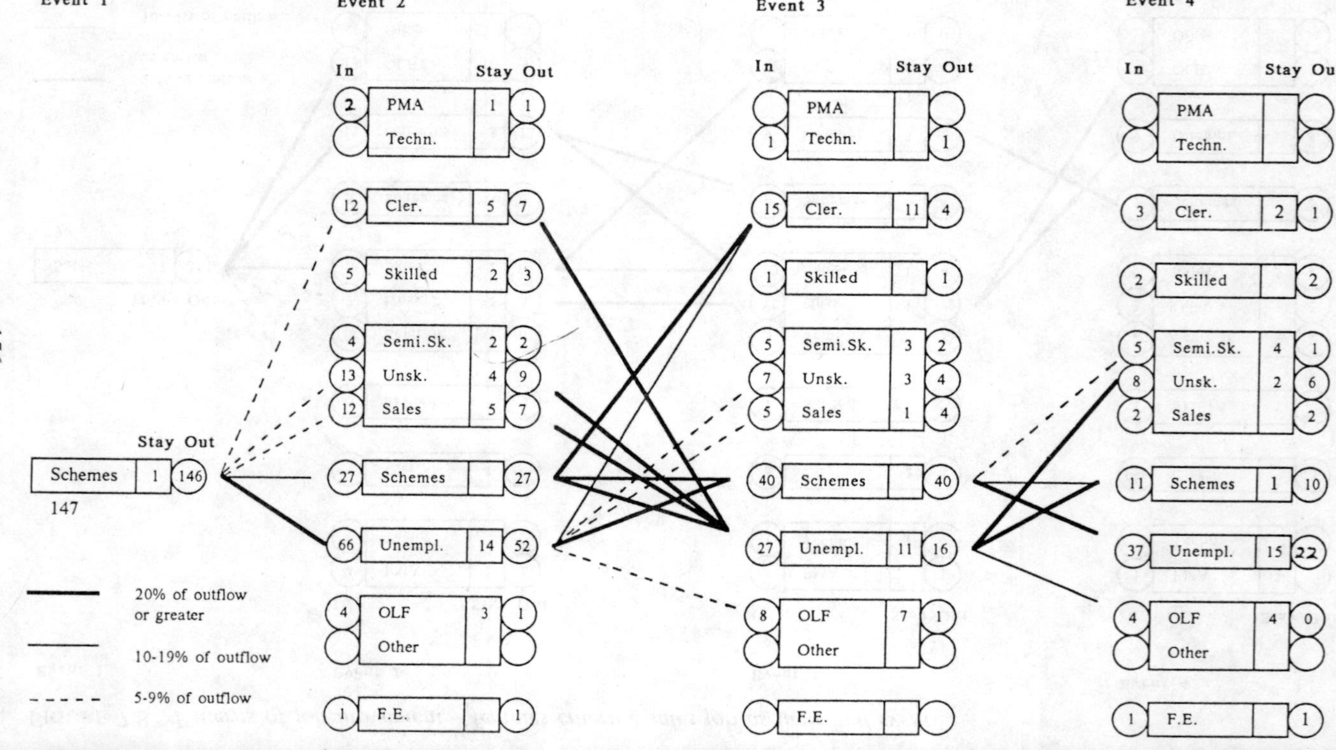

TABLE 7.4: *How long did it take you to learn this (first) job? (percentage of those providing definitive response – total sample)*

		less than one month	1–6mths	6mths to 1yr	1yr or more	still learning	
		%	%	%	%	%	
Professional							
Technician	Males	8	8	2	28	54	n = 129
Managerial	Females	14	11	8	17	49	n = 63
Clerical	Males	22	15	7	9	46	n = 44
	Females	31	26	15	9	20	n = 203
Sales	Males	61	11	7	4	18	n = 28
	Females	67	18	4	6	6	n = 114
Skilled	Males	9	9	7	30	44	n = 165
	Females	14	14	5	30	38	n = 37
Semi-skilled	Males	51	20	8	8	14	n = 133
	Females	50	33	5	2	11	n = 131
Unskilled	Males	77	8	2	2	12	n = 60
	Females	81	10	0	2	7	n = 59

Labour Market Segmentation and Training

As one of the distinguishing features of the labour market segments is the level of skill associated with them, then it was inevitable that there were substantial differences between the young adults' experiences of training.

Our findings confirmed the well-known fact that while those in the higher occupational orders or segments receive formal training over a long period of time, those in the lower segments receive little or no formal training. They also show something of the magnitude of these differences (Table 7.4). When asked, 'How long did it take you to learn this job?' approximately half of the 18–24-year-olds in the higher segment were still learning. Of those in unskilled work over 75 per cent had learnt their jobs in less than a month, with some reporting that it took them less than a day. This provides a crude measure of the demands which jobs in these different segments make on the cognitive and motor skills of young adults. Once again there were marked gender differences, with a greater proportion of males having longer learning times. However, after controlling for skill level the gender differences almost disappeared. There was a tendency for a slightly larger proportion of males to report being in jobs with shorter learning times, but clearly the reason for the lower level of training experienced by females lay primarily in the higher proportion of them entering the unskilled segments.

The segment of the labour market entered also determines the way in which young adults learn their job. Those who did receive training in the lowest segment obtained it either through induction courses or, more frequently, through on-the-job training. For those in the skilled and white-collar segments, training centres and day-release provision played a more prominent role in their training, with day-release being more readily available for males. It may well be that the more theoretical training associated with day-release courses is a preparation for the future promotion of males.

These differences in the forms of training were reflected in other ways in which young adults learnt the skills relevant to their jobs. Workers in the lower segment obtained their skills primarily from a combination of watching people and being taught while doing the job, whereas in the higher segments these processes were invariably supplemented by making things, job talks, visits to other departments and reading. In all cases the person who was most significant in imparting knowledge about the job was either the foreman/ supervisor or a workmate. Only in those segments where formal training was extensive did a significant proportion of young adults identify the training officer as the person who taught them most about their job.

Overall, the results portray a picture of massive differences in the time taken to learn the jobs which comprise the various segments, ranging from a day or even less in the lower segment to years in the higher segments. Over 75 per cent of those young adults who entered the labour market before YOP was introduced reported receiving some training, although the form of that training was primarily conditioned by the segment they entered.

A further aspect of training which is of crucial significance to the youth labour market, concerns what is frequently referred to as its front-end loaded character. That is, given the institutional provision of training, most of it is delivered when a young person first enters the labour market. This situation is created by the age limits on entry to many of the occupations which provide formal training (for example, apprenticeship), which make it difficult for those over 17 or 18 years of age to enter them.[5] As we have seen these institutional arrangements constitute one of the pressures which segment the labour market by age. One result of this is that those who move jobs stand less chance of subsequently obtaining a formal training, or indeed, any training. While approximately 40 per cent of males and 18 per cent of females in our sample received formal training for their first job, the corresponding figures for those entering their third or last job were less than 10 per cent for both sexes. Clearly, formal training provision structures the labour market for males to a much greater extent than it does the labour market for females. The consequences of not obtaining training on first entering the labour market may, therefore, be more serious for males than for females. One reason for this is that for many occupations which have traditionally been the preserve of females. notably in clerical work, much of the training is provided within the education system. Yet, although a smaller proportion of females obtain access to formal employment based training programmes, it appears from our sample that those programmes which are available to them are less age-specific, as the proportion of female respondents who undertook them while in their second and third or last job, did not fall as dramatically as it did for the males.

All this suggests that it is the institutional provision of training which plays a major role in segmenting the labour market for youths. What formal training exists is largely directed at males, and because access to it is at an early age, this acts as an important constraint on young people's labour market behaviour. The firm's investment in the employee's training provides one of the main mechanisms which generate the formation of segments. Having provided funds and resources for the training of the employee, the firm has a vested interest in maintaining the worker's commitment if that investment is to pay off. Where the firm is subject to external pressures, such as those from Industrial Training Boards or, to a lesser extent, from the Training Agency (formerly MSC) to provide a strong component of transferable skills in the training, then the conditions are established for the development of an institutionally regulated occupational labour market, such as those found in engineering and construction. However, it is not essential that such institutional arrangements exist for an occupational labour market to become established. There are industries where firms use comparable technology and where skills are also transferable, as in the case of female machinists in the knitwear and footwear trade. Where these industries are well represented in the local labour market, this also provides the basis for an occupational labour market within which trained females can move, but to which outsiders cannot gain access because they lack the necessary skills. If no such external pressures from Training Boards, professional organisations or the technological basis of the industry exist, then firms tend to limit their investment to job specific training. Often this will lock the employee into the firm's internal labour market.

From the young adults' standpoint, training provides one of the main mechanisms through which they become confined to a labour market segment, as their time is invested in the acquisition of skills which are specific to a particular job or segment. This investment can then only pay off if the worker continues in that particular job or one that is similar, which usually entails any movement being restricted to a job within the same segment. This is especially so in the skilled, clerical and higher segments, where the learning times are longer and where the workers' investment in training is greater. We found this to be true for respondents in the clerical and skilled segments and for males in the highest segment, where approximately 50 per cent of those who entered such jobs in their second or longest job reported using some of the same skills they had acquired in their first job. A lower figure of 38 per cent for females in the highest segment reflected the fact that many young women entered it after a period in a less skilled fill-in job.

In the lower segment just over 25 per cent of those entering jobs (apart from females in sales jobs) reported using the same skills they had acquired in their last job. This reflects the fact that there are few skills to be learnt in such jobs. Here the investment in skills cannot explain the reproduction of the labour market segments. It is the negative pressures that are important in explaining the persistence of this pattern of job movement. Young adults move within the segment not to capitalise on returns from their skills, but because, having left or been forced to leave a job, there are few other opportunities available to them. This is not to say that some may not have positive reasons for moving jobs within the segment, for example, because they want to work inside or outside, or to avoid working with an unpleasant supervisor or workmates (Blackburn and Mann, 1979). However, a large precentage who moved into their second and subsequent jobs from unemployment or a Government scheme took it because it was the only one available. The point is that the direction which many of the moves take is conditioned by negative features such as the lack of other opportunities, rather than by any desire on the part of the people concerned to maximise returns on investments they had made in previous training or more generally from their past work experience. This highlights the fact that the mechanisms which serve to maintain and reproduce the higher segments stem in part from the attempts by those who have entered them to capitalise on the advantages they have already received and to close them to outsiders. For those in the lower segments the pressures tend to be more 'external' to the individual in that young adults continue to move within the lower segment, not because of any personal ambition to continue in such jobs, but rather because they cannot get out of them. It is the very success of those in the higher segments in closing access to such jobs that conditions the behaviour and experience of those in the lower segments.

Attitudes to Work

Other research (Roberts, 1984, and Cockburn, 1987) has found that when young people are asked about the factors they consider important when judging jobs, they produce very different answers to those given when they are asked to name the reasons for entering their own particular job. That is, young people have a clear set of values and priorities which they use to evaluate jobs, but when faced with the constraints of reality, such criteria are often abandoned as the local labour market rarely affords much in the way of choice for working-class youngsters. Our results support these findings. They show young adults to be concerned with such factors as good pay, secure work, friendly workmates, a chance to make a career, interesting work and the chance to acquire a skill. Yet when we look at the reasons they gave for taking their jobs, well over half the total sample claimed that it was the 'only one available', suggesting that they had, in reality, little choice. A much smaller percentage gave 'interesting job' or 'good prospects' as the reason. The discrepancy between the responses to the two questions suggests that once in the labour market, the young person's job 'choices' are primarily a function of what is available. However, when we examine the results by the type of job entered and compare the responses of those entering different segments, interesting contrasts emerge.

Those entering the highest segment were least constrained by the lack of opportunities, with approximately 35 per cent giving 'only job available' as a reason. For them the reasons most frequently cited were 'interesting job' (over 50 per cent), 'to gain experience' (30 per cent) and 'good prospects' (almost 40 per cent). These were all reasons which suggest that the young adults were actually choosing between alternatives. By contrast, in the lower segment over 70 per cent gave 'only one available' as the reason, with only two other reasons, 'money' and 'interesting job' figuring at all prominently in their replies, and even then the proportions citing these reasons were very small.

Among those entering the clerical and skilled segments the results pointed to a greater degree of constraint, than among those in the highest segment, with between 50 and 60 per cent taking the job because it was the 'only one available'. However, a much higher proportion of this group cited 'good prospects' and 'interesting work' as reasons for taking the job, and made reference to greater variety of reasons than did those in the lowest segment.

There were also some significant differences between males and females within each segment. In the lowest segment males in sales and semi-skilled work were more likely to cite 'interesting work' than were their female counterparts, with males in sales also being more likely to show concern with 'prospects' and 'gaining experience'. That this group also had better chances of promotion than females also suggests that they were more likely to be entering career jobs. The only point of difference in the skilled segment was the greater proportion of males who gave 'good prospects' and 'security' as reasons. In the clerical segment, more females were constrained by the fact that it was the 'only job available' while a smaller proportion gave 'good prospects' and 'security' as reasons, suggesting again that females were entering the jobs with fewer promotion chances. Similarly, in the highest segment a lower proportion of females took the job because it was 'interesting' or had 'good prospects'.

The same contrasts between the segments was found when we examined the reasons given by respondents for taking their second and third or last jobs. However, within each segment, the pattern of response between the sexes shifted, as a higher proportion of females in almost all occupations cited 'interesting job' as their reason for taking their jobs, while in the clerical and higher segment females were more likely than males to cite 'security' and 'career' as a reason. This may be a result of the movement of many females into these segments after having had a fill-in job, or it could be that females become more concerned with questions of job interest and career prospects once they have experience of work.

Once again, the results point to a situation in which young people entering the higher segments are faced with a greater degree of choice, both at the point of entry and once they are in the segment, while the movement of those in the lower segment is primarily a product of constraints within the labour market. These provide powerful pressures which condition both the attitudes and behaviour of young adults.

The Effects of the Recession

By examining the status of young adults two years after the minimum school leaving age, we were able to obtain an estimate of the impact of the recession on the pattern of entry to the various segments (see Tables 7.5 and 7.6). The tables highlight major differences between the experience of males and females. In particular, they illustrate the dramatic impact of the recession in reducing the proportion of skilled and unskilled jobs available for males as the recession made itself felt on the 1979/80 and 1980/81 school leavers. Associated with this was an equally dramatic rise in the level of unemployment. By contrast the females appeared to fare better with a fall in the proportions entering clerical and sales jobs but with unemployment rising to 30 per cent of the 1980/81 leavers as compared with 45 per cent of the male leavers. However, this masks the distinctive feature of the females' experience, namely the growth in the proportion who moved out of the labour force as the effects of the recession were felt.

TABLE 7.5: *Status of young adults two years after the minimal school leaving age – females (percentage)*

Age at interview:	18	19	20	21	22	23	24
Year of leaving school:	80/1	79/80	78/9	77/8	76/7	75/6	74/5
Prof. and managerial	1	3	4	6	6	6	4
Technician	2		2	2	1		2
Clerical	13	29	17	21	18	24	21
Skilled manual	6	5	7	6	6	14	10
Semi-skilled	9	9	8	9	12	13	15
Unskilled	12	8	5	6	13	10	6
Sales	6	14	10	13	12	11	13
Schemes	2	6	4	2		1	
Unemployed	30	15	13	15	13	6	13
Out of labour force	13	10	15	6	9	4	4
Further education	6	4	15	14	6	10	12
Other & self-employed	1	2		1	4	1	
N =	91	115	136	101	78	71	68

TABLE 7.6: *Status of young adults two years after the minimal school leaving age – males (percentage)*

Age at interview: Year of leaving school:	18 80/1	19 79/80	20 78/9	21 77/8	22 76/7	23 75/6	24 74/5
Prof. and managerial	1	3	4	4	4	11	2
Technician	5	8	7	8	6	5	8
Clerical	2	2	9	3	3	8	2
Skilled manual	14	27	35	29	35	39	44
Semi-skilled	11	17	16	15	21	15	15
Unskilled	3	7	8	13	8	11	13
Sales	4	3		1	5	5	2
Schemes	10	4	6	4	1	2	2
Unemployed	45	23	13	18	13	5	4
Out of labour force	1		1		1		2
Further education	4	6	2	5	3		6
Other & self-employed	1	2	1	1	1		
N =	105	121	107	104	80	62	48

Upward Drift

Table 7.7 compares the distribution of the first status of school-leavers with that of their status at the time of interviews. It demonstrates what we have termed the phenomenon of the 'upward drift', namely an increase in the numbers of young adults in the higher status occupations and a decrease in their numbers in lower status occupations which occurs as a result of some of those in paid employment either sustaining or improving their position over time. Of course this conceals the substantial downward mobility discussed above, as it excludes those who become unemployed. For those in paid employment, however, there is an overall improvement in status.

This 'upward drift' was the net result of trends, so that over time there was a substantial inflow of young adults of both sexes into the segments comprising professional, managerial, technical and clerical work. There was a net outflow from all the occupations in the skilled and lower segments, with substantial numbers leaving the latter. It should be stated that the findings which generated this notion of the 'upward drift' may be partly attributable to our methodology, in that many of those entering the higher segments as their second or third event did so after staying on in Further or Higher Education to obtain more qualifications. However, this is not a sufficient explanation

TABLE 7.7: *Number of young adults in their first status on leaving school (starters) and their last status (finishers) – all events*

FEMALES Status	Starters	Finishers
Prof/Man/Admin	30	76
Technical	5	12
Clerical	135	158
Skilled	64	51
Semi-skilled	99	62
Unskilled	88	76
Sales	98	63
Schemes	147	36
Unemployed	0*	133
Out of labour force	35	177

* For an explanation of the absence of unemployment as a category for starters see Footnote 2

because there are labour market processes at work which would also produce such results. The most general of these has been identified as 'a movement between first occupation and subsequent occupation which shifts the population into better paying, more prestigious occupations across conventional boundaries' (Stewart, Prandy and Blackburn, 1980, p. 199). This general movement was revealed through the study of occupational mobility among males in Britain, the United States and Australia. The authors go on to report: 'There are, in fact, few starting occupations in our white-collar sample. Apart from the professions, four specific jobs cover most people who start their working life in the white-collar area: shop assistant, clerk, draughtsman and laboratory assistant. These are all occupations with heavy net losses between first job and current job, and in the case of clerks, we have seen that current holders of the job are not the same as those who started in it' (p. 199).

Our findings would support Stewart *et al.*, for young people are not recruited into certain more senior white and blue-collar jobs until they have the requisite experience. This is sometimes formalised in terms of specific age requirements which mean that youths have to spend a period of time either in Further or Higher Education or in fill-in jobs in the labour market. This was the case with girls who wished to enter nursing. In other instances, employers recruiting for management trainees in retail or leisure organisations looked for previous work experience in sales or similar jobs. Thus, part of this upward drift was a product of the exclusion of school-leavers from the more senior jobs. It was also due to the fact that some jobs, by virtue of the internal labour market to which they provided access, virtually assured young people of promotion. Accordingly, some moved from semi-skilled worker to supervisor or manager as a result of internal promotion.

Another factor contributing to the 'upward drift' was the process of the decline of the unskilled and semi-skilled jobs which accelerated during the recession, and which reduced the number of jobs in the lower segment. The number of clerical jobs was also declining, but the proportions of females occupying them increased. In addition, while sales jobs were expanding in number, there was a decline in the proportion of young adults in them.

Another possible explanation was that the movement of females out of the labour force was significantly greater among those located in the lower segment thereby skewing the distribution of respondents remaining in the labour market in favour of the middle and upper segments. But even if this was important we are still left with the fact that a similar pattern of 'upward drift' was observed among males, few of whom left the labour market. All this suggests that the upward drift is a product of the specific characteristics of the youth labour market.

The general tendency for the average employment status of young adults to increase over time was disrupted by the experience of unemployment. Table 7.8 details the occupational distribution of all those who had a job and then experienced an unemployment spell of more than three months. It shows their status before and after the unemployment spell and at the date of the interview, and suggests that the degree of disruption which a long spell of unemployment caused depended on the segment which the young adult had just left. For those who first entered jobs in the higher segment, a subsequent spell of unemployment (both short-term, less than three months and long-term, more than three months) did not appear to disrupt their career progress to the same extent as it did for those in the other segments. These, after all, are the occupations which continued to expand throughout the recession. It was the careers of those in the middle segments, notably female clerical workers and male skilled manual workers, which were most disrupted by unemployment. Following a period of unemployment only a minority of each group regained entry to the segment either immediately or by the time of the interview.

TABLE 7.8: *The effect of spells of unemployment of 3 months or greater on job histories*

	FEMALES			MALES		
	Before	After	Last Status	Before	After	Last Status
Prof./Man/Admin	3	4	5	1	5	7
Tech.	1	1		5		2
Self-Employed	1	1			4	4
Clerical	13	7	9	2	6	6
Skilled	6	3	1	22	15	18
Semi-skilled	11	17	9	20	18	25
Unskilled	18	20	17	14	12	9
Sales	8	8	1	6	7	8
Unknown	1	1		1	2	
Scheme	23	14	6	21	22	19
Unemployed	0*	28	50	0*	38	70
OLF	6	15	26	4	3	0
FE	0	1	0	0	1	0
No reply	0	0	0	1	0	1

* For an explanation of the absence of unemployment as a 'before' category see Note 2 at end of chapter.

For those in the lower segment, unemployment was a normal part of their experience of work. The data show that similar proportions re-entered semi-skilled, unskilled and sales jobs after unemployment. However, some of those entering jobs in this segment were undoubtedly people who were downwardly mobile from the middle segments, causing some of those who had started with jobs in the lower segment to be displaced and consigned to the ranks of the long-term unemployed. In general, for those in the lower segment, the recession had lengthened the time spent unemployed and shortened their experience of paid employment. In addition, 10.5 per cent of the sample had been excluded from this analysis because they had been unemployed since leaving school and had no experience of full-time work.

In summary, it appears that the recession and the structural changes associated with it had relatively little disruptive effect on the ability of those in the higher segments to participate in the 'upward drift'. In contrast, unemployment had disrupted the career paths of those in the middle and lower segments, and they were carrying the cost of the recession.

Age Segmentation

The previous section was concerned with analysing the vertical movement in the labour market. Here we move on to consider movement which takes place as a result of age discrimination. This sometimes takes the form of indirect age discrimination, for example, through the specification of minimum educational qualifications such as 'A' levels, which cannot normally be obtained until a person is 18 years of age. It can also take a more direct form, when employers either specify a minimum age for applicants or specify other age-related criteria such as family responsibilities as important for recruits. We refer to those jobs from which young people are excluded on grounds of age, as adult jobs. We sought to identify these jobs by asking respondents the question 'Are/were there any reasons why young people (16–18) would not be recruited for this job?' If young people were excluded, these were labelled 'adult jobs'. Those jobs for which youths either had sheltered access (e.g., apprenticeships) or for which they competed with adults, were labelled 'youth jobs'. The following analysis makes no differentiation between male and female respondents, and is based on an admittedly crude measure.

It could be expected that in the first job after leaving school very few young people would be working in jobs from which other young people were excluded. Of those who had been in full-time employment at some time only 10 per cent took first jobs which were classified as 'adult' jobs. By the time of the third or most recent job, this proportion had risen to 39 per cent. These figures indicate something of the nature of the transition from the youth to adult labour markets. If the segmentation is based purely on age discrimination, then by the process of aging individuals automatically transfer from one labour market to the other. The increase in the proportions in 'adult jobs', between the first and the third jobs, indicates that this transition took place.

There are important differences in the location of youth and adult jobs. It is well established that compared to the overall population, youths tend to be employed in smaller establishments. We had suspected that this might be because adults were excluded from a large proportion of these jobs, but this does not appear to have been the case. The results did not demonstrate any great differences in the proportions in youth and adult jobs between firms of different size bands. 38 per cent of youth jobs and 34 per cent of adult jobs were located in small firms. Therefore it could be that youths are concentrated in smaller firms because of a reluctance by adults to compete for what are usually relatively low-paid jobs.

The industrial distribution of jobs entered by members of the sample was skewed in a way which reflected the concentration of young people in certain sectors, as noted in Chapter 2. Respondents were heavily represented in the Distributive Trades, Miscellaneous Services and, to a lesser extent, Professional and Scientific Services, Clothing and Footwear and Public Administration. There were, however, a number of striking differences between the industrial distribution of youth jobs and adult jobs. The latter were less well-represented in Distributive Trades or Clothing and Footwear, but much more heavily concentrated in Miscellaneous Services (25 per cent) and Professional and Scientific Services (18 per cent). Conversely, fewer of the youth jobs were to be found in Professional and Scientific Services (7 per cent) and more in Distributive Trades (21 per cent). There was also a relatively lower percentage of youth jobs in Miscellaneous Services (13 per cent) *vis-à-vis* adult jobs.

In terms of their occupational distribution, some 25 per cent of adult jobs were in the top three classifications (Professional, Administrator and Manager), compared to only 5 per cent of youth jobs. Also, adult jobs were more concentrated in the unskilled categories than youth jobs: 19 per cent compared with 13 per cent. Some of these will have been jobs entailing heavy lifting or dangerous work which were considered to be too physically demanding for 16-year-olds. Of youth jobs, 43 per cent were concentrated in skilled and semi-skilled work, compared to 22 per cent of adult jobs.

Youth jobs also tended to differ from adult jobs in terms of their characteristics. For example, they were less likely to involve shift working. Of adult jobs, 29 per cent had shift working compared to 11 per cent of youth jobs. This was obviously partly due to the legislation in operation at the time, by which employers were required to obtain a special licence to enable young people below the age of 18 to work shifts. Another difference was in the amount of responsibility demanded. Of adult jobs, 43 per cent were felt to involve some degree of responsibility, while only 17 per cent of youth jobs did so. What was more surprising was the relatively high proportion of the adult jobs (22 per cent) in which respondents were undertaking formalised training akin to apprenticeships. For youth jobs this was only marginally higher at 25 per cent. This appears to confirm as the analysis of career paths suggests, that there is an alternative route to skilled status for those who fail to secure an apprenticeship on leaving school, although the numbers involved are small. For example, shift working in the hosiery trade prevents anyone under the age of 18 from being recruited as an apprentice mechanic. Another route to skilled status is through semi-skilled jobs in engineering, where this experience is used as a basis for entry into an apprenticeship later in the young person's career.

Relatively little has been written about the transition from the youth to the adult labour market. It is thought that as people mature in years they become eligible for jobs from which they were previously excluded. Thus, the range of jobs open to a 21–24-year-old is much greater than that open to a 16- or 17-year-old, *ceteris paribus*. In this sense the transition will be made automatically as a result of the aging process. This was found to be the case. Of the jobs held by 18-year-olds 94 per cent were youth jobs, whilst only 6 per cent were adult jobs. At the other end of the age scale, 53 per cent of jobs held by 24-year-olds were adult jobs. As the age increases, so does the proportion of that age group with jobs which can be classified as being in the adult labour market.

Another aspect of the transition process is the direction and size of the flows between the youth and adult labour markets. Thus far it has been implicitly assumed that the flow is uni-directional, that is, from the youth to the adult labour market. This was confirmed by our data.

For the first change, from first job to second job, 76.6 per cent of the young adults stayed in the same job category; that is, moved from one youth job to another, or from one adult job to another; 21 per cent moved in the predicted direction, from a youth job to an adult job; whilst only a small minority moved from adult jobs to youth jobs. The movement from second job to third job followed a similar pattern.

These results establish the significance of age segmentation and its influence in structuring the movement of young adults within the labour market. They also show how the distribution of youth and adult jobs differs between industries and occupations in a way which cannot be readily predicted from the overall distribution of youths and adults in the labour market. Also of considerable importance in distinguishing such jobs is the degree of responsibility attached to them and their location in the productive system. Consequently, for a majority of school and college-leavers, their early years in the labour market will be characterised by a transition from youth jobs to adult jobs. Unfortunately, our data did not enable us to explore gender differences in this transition. This is an important omission as by their early twenties, many of the young females will have left the labour market and so may not have made the transition into adult jobs.

Age and Family Formation

As young people mature in years and make the transition from youth to adult jobs, many are simultaneously involved in the transition from the family of origin to the family of procreation. It is this process which is crucial in explaining the movement of females out of the labour market. However, for those of both sexes who remain in the labour market it also has important implications for their behaviour and experience.

We have already seen how the reasons for taking jobs were conditioned by the type of segment entered and that in taking the first job 'money' was infrequently mentioned. However, as they aged and moved jobs, respondents cited 'more money' more frequently as the reason for taking jobs. With two exceptions, a higher proportion of every occupational group cited 'more money' as the reason for taking their second or longest job than was the case for the first job. The first exception was among unskilled workers, whose jobs tended to be low paid and the second was among male skilled workers, many of whom would still be more concerned with securing training. For the sample as a whole, the 24-year-olds were almost twice as likely as the 18-year-olds to mention 'more money' as the reason for taking the second job. Given the pressures faced by young people on first entering paid employment to secure the right type of work, the level of income they receive is not necessarily a major consideration. Indeed, any level of income is likely to be greater than that obtained from part-time work while at school or from pocket money. However, once a foothold in the jobs market has been obtained the young adults adjust their values, and as they leave home, get married or live with a partner and start a family, so the pressure on them to maximise their income increases.

Changes in domestic circumstances also impinge upon labour market experiences. To take the most obvious example, childbirth increases the tendency for females to leave the labour force, and is usually associated with two other life events; leaving home and getting married or living with a partner. Even here, the sequence and timing of events may be mediated by the factors of social class and labour market experience. Thus, those in the white-collar segments tend to space out the events of leaving home, getting married or co-habitation and childbirth, while for those in the blue-collar segments the three are more likely to be conterminous (Jones, 1987).

Marriage itself has little effect on labour market behaviour. Some females do leave the labour force but these are in a minority and the time spent out of the labour force tends to be short. When combined with other events, such as leaving home and having a child, then it does cause females to weaken their attachment to the labour force. Once out of the labour force very few of our sample had returned by the time of interview, but those who did found it difficult to re-enter their previous occupations and were obliged to take jobs at a lower skill level.[6] This often meant taking an unskilled job. As for males, it was difficult to establish with any degree of confidence what the effect of these life events were, relatively few had experienced such events – only 11 per cent were married. Our results do suggest that those males who had left home, got married or were living with a partner or had children, showed greater occupational stability after a life event occurred. If this should prove to be the case generally, then it gives support to the contentions of employers who claim that it is the absence of domestic responsibilities which causes young employees in the lower segment to be 'unreliable and irresponsible'. This is one reason which is regularly given for excluding them from such a large part of the labour market. From the point of view of the young adults, the absence of such 'responsibilities' provides them with the freedom to move between relatively unskilled, undemanding and often boring jobs.

CONCLUSION

The aim of this chapter has been to establish the distinctive features of the various segments which make up the youth labour market and their relationship with the adult labour market. As the youth labour market contains areas where youths and adults compete for the same jobs their relationship is of necessity very close. Yet the youth labour market is distinctive in that it consists of occupations which provide ports of entry into the general labour market. As Stewart, Prandy and Blackburn (1980) have pointed out some of the occupations which young people enter are conterminous with professions. Medicine, law, teaching and the other professions provide their own ports of entry. These lead into a hierarchical structure within their respective occupations, and this exerts a powerful influence over the movement of the individuals in those occupations. The same is true for those who enter apprenticeships, although the career ladder is shorter, consisting of fewer steps. Their results, and those discussed here, suggest that occupations such as clerk and salesman and the ports of entry available to youths within them are of a different order. Over the lifetime of an individual there is a very high level of movement out of these jobs as their incumbents are merely using them as a starting point on a career which will lead into administration, the professions or management. At the bottom of the labour market there is no such internal hierarchy, at least not for the majority of those who enter. Nevertheless, there are only a limited number of ports of entry even into this segment. Those who take jobs in this segment experience an equally structured pattern of movement incorporating periods in and out of Government schemes, semi-skilled and unskilled jobs and unemployment.

This is the same pattern that Harris (1987) found among working-class adults in South Wales during the recession, which they referred to as 'the chequered pattern', hailing it as a new experience for the working class. We are less inclined to see this as a radical departure from the past. Norris (1978) identified it as sub-employment in the 1970s. Our results suggest that such a pattern, which was restricted to sections of the unskilled working class in the past three decades, has now become the standard pattern of work experience for a substantial proportion of the working class in the 1980s.

Our research findings also point to the internal organisation of the occupations entered by females being significantly different than that of the occupations entered by males, in spite of the fact that there is some degree of overlap between the segments. The most important of these differences, apart from the level of income, appears to be the promotion chances associated with most jobs in the female segments. In sales and semi-skilled manual occupations, where promotion chances for males are few, those for females are even more restricted. Similarly, clerical work usually offers a career ladder for males but seldom offers the same opportunities for females. This is a crucial difference, for in the light of our tentative results from females returning to work and those from the Women in Employment survey, it is clear that most married females move out of these non-career jobs into a period out of the labour market. In their subsequent attempts to re-enter the labour market they can, at best, expect to regain entry to their previous segment, often on a part-time basis, while many have to take jobs in a lower segment.

The pattern of upward drift we have identified is thus primarily a function of the male labour market. Young females can and do participate in the early phase of this process, but their future is more likely to involve a move out of the labour market rather than further upward movement, either within or between segments.

Any movement between segments, tends to be highly structured by the same forces which lead to the closure of each of the constituent segments. We have identified paths of both upward and downward mobility as well as those occupations which can act as a clearing-house in this process.

It is also evident that some segments offer those who enter them much greater scope for individual decision-making, both in the exercise of their work task and in the direction and timing of job movements. In occupations offering a hierarchically structured career, the individual can expect to obtain promotion by moving jobs. In this process individuals may therefore see themselves as having a significant degree of control over their work histories. But the very mechanisms which ensure that opportunities for upward movement within an occupation are confined to those on the first rung of career ladders, exclude those from the lower segments gaining access to jobs further up the career ladder. Those who begin their working lives in the lower segments have few promotion chances. Their only means of exercising control over their work histories is to move into other dead-end jobs. In fact, their movement is more frequently precipitated by factors totally outside their control – their job is temporary or casual or the company makes them redundant. It is in this sense that their pattern of movement is subject to greater control by 'external' pressures.

The differences between the experiences of young adults in the higher and lower segments has been reinforced by the effects of the recession. As we have seen, throughout the recession, there was a growth in the numbers employed in those occupations which comprised the higher segments. Once young people had acquired the educational qualifications and personal attributes necessary for entry, then even spells of unemployment did not appear to have detrimental effects on their longer-term life chances and their ability to participate in the upward drift. This was not the case for those in the middle and lower segments. Their careers were severely disrupted by the recession. In particular, males in the skilled manual segment experienced spells of unemployment from which they did not appear to have recovered their former status. The effect of the recession on those in the lower segment was to lengthen the spells of unemployment they 'normally' encountered. Thus, 10 per cent of the sample had never experienced full-time paid employment. Those seeking entry to the labour market at the height of the recession were faced with a situation where many of the job opportunities in the middle and lower segments had gone altogether.

Once into work, the processes of aging and family formation, combined with the requirements of employers for 'responsible' workers, enable the majority of young people to make the transition to the adult labour market. This is not necessarily a part of the 'upward drift' we referred to, as many of the adult jobs are located in the lower segment. It occurs because a greater range of jobs opens up for youths at the end of the first phase of their experience of the labour market.

NOTES

1. Here we are using the concept of career in the sense in which Slocum (1966) uses it, namely as an orderly sequence of development involving progressively more responsible roles within an occupation. We are fully aware of the danger of generalising this notion beyond the confines of certain middle-class occupations (Stewart, Prandy and Blackburn, 1980), and for this reason use the more neutral term 'labour market histories' to refer to job movement which is patterned but does not incorporate the idea of progression. For recent discussions of the concept of career see Stewart, Prandy and Blackburn (1980) and Dex (1985). Harris (1987) makes the important point that especially in periods of recession we are studying not work histories – a sequence of jobs – but labour market histories – jobs interspersed with periods of unemployment.
2. This decision has led to certain anomalies in the presentation of the data. Thus in Tables 7.1, 7.7 and 7.8 it appears that no young people were unemployed on leaving school, which was clearly not the case. At this point in the analysis we are concerned to establish the pattern of movement. However, in retrospect the decision to adopt this coding practice has not proved fully satisfactory.
3. Factors such as the number of spells of unemployment and the length of time spent in a job are often conceptualised as individual characteristics (Borus, 1984). Schervish (1983) has already shown how certain structural characteristics, such as class position, economic sectors and periods of the business cycle, affect the vulnerability of individuals to unemployment. He concedes that personal characteristics such as race, age and education are all significant in determining the vulnerability of individuals to unem-

ployment, but argues that over and above these individual characteristics structural characteristics have an independent effect. From our point of view we would not wish to conceptualise factors such as race and age as 'individual' as opposed to structural. As we show later in the chapter, age and indeed race, take on their social significance because of broader structural constraints over which the individual has little control. In this sense the source of their social significance is just as firmly rooted in structural characteristics as in the economic sector of the firm in which they find employment.

4. The exceptions we refer to here are sales jobs for which males are recruited, with the prospect of promotion, and those jobs in the larger organisations in Retail, Hotel and Catering, which form part of an internal labour market (these are discussed in Chapter 6).
5. In addition to our work, the significance of age restrictions in determining the entry pattern of youths into employment has been documented in Raffe's work on the Scottish School Leaver Surveys. However, recent work by Payne (1986) suggests that there are still a number of opportunities for 17-year-olds to obtain apprenticeships.
6. The same pattern is found in the Women and Employment Survey (Martin and Roberts, 1984, and Dex, 1987).

8 Local Labour Markets

In examining the way in which employers structure the demand for youth labour we have concentrated on showing how the labour market is segmented and how the restructuring of the labour market has had a differential impact on the various segments. However, the size and composition of the various labour market segments vary from one locality to another. Because youths are restricted in their job search to the local labour market, this means that there are dramatic differences between local labour markets in the chances of youths securing employment, in the type of employment available and in their subsequent experience of the labour market.

As we have seen, the demand for labour and for specific types of labour is largely a function of the demand for particular types of products or services. Many of the service industries, such as health care, distribution, and hotels and catering, tend to be relatively uniformly distributed across the country. This creates a corresponding uniformity across local labour markets in the demand for the labour associated with them. In the case of other service industries, such as finance and business services, and the manufacturing industries, their location tends to be more geographically specific. As different types of manufacturing industries have tended to cluster in certain geographical areas they have also created pools of labour whose skills are industry specific. Examples of these are shipbuilding in Sunderland, hosiery in Leicester, and chemicals and aerospace in St Albans. Given the long-term decline of some of these industries in Britain over the last three decades, and especially the way in which the recession accelerated that process, this causes an imbalance at the local level. The local labour force, with its industry specific skills and local community ties, remains relatively immobile while capital is relocated. Over time the population tends to move from areas of high unemployment to areas of low unemployment but the speed with which manufacturing industry reduced capacity during the early 1980s was far faster than the time necessary to re-locate labour.

The result of these differences in the spatial distribution of industry is substantial variations in both the overall demand for labour and in the type of labour recruited by employers. It is these differences in the industry mix of the locality which are the main factors in determining the size and composition of the labour market segments at the local level. Thus, in those towns and cities in the North, such as Newcastle and Sunderland, in which heavy engineering and shipbuilding industries have been located, there has traditionally been relatively little demand for professional, managerial and technical labour but a large demand for skilled manual labour. This has led to the growth, over time, of a large skilled manual segment and a lower segment of unskilled and semi-skilled labourers. In the northern ports such as Hull and Liverpool, the demand was for more unskilled and semi-skilled labour rather than for skilled labour. By contrast, in parts of the South, such as Crawley and St Albans, the establishment of more modern industries, such as aerospace, chemicals, and electrical and electronic engineering, has generated a demand for a higher proportion of professional, managerial and technician non-manual workers and fewer unskilled, semi-skilled and skilled workers. As a result the relative size of the various segments which make up the local labour market varies substantially from one area to another.

It is the combined effect of these two factors, the relative size of the various segments which comprise the local labour market, and the discrepancy which can occur between the ensuing demand for labour at the local level and its supply, which we refer to as the local labour market effect. There are also suggestions from our evidence that these factors may generate distinctive cultures within the local communities which create significant differences in attitude between the populations of the respective local labour markets. While we are not yet in a position to explore the component parts of this local labour market effect, our results do suggest that it is of crucial significance in the analysis of labour markets.

These local variations are of particular significance for 16-year-old school-leavers, because the majority enter the lower segments. The higher segments tend to be national in character. When employers recruit to these jobs they expect employees to be geographically mobile in order to further their careers. To obtain the higher educational qualifications necessary for entry recruits have often made the break from their family of origin on entering university or polytechnic. Many of the jobs in this segment are linked to internal labour markets which operate on a national basis. For example, mobility is a prerequisite in the recruitment of graduates to the Civil Service, and the management of manufacturing subsidiaries for the large conglomerates, as well as in retail, hotels and finance.

For recruitment at the lower levels, employers do not expect the same degree of mobility. When closing a plant in one part of the country and opening one in another, some of the employers we interviewed did not expect or encourage their manual workers to move. It was more economical for the company to pay the costs of redundancy and recruit afresh in the new location. Indeed, in one instance the decision to close a plant and relocate had been influenced by a desire to get rid of the labour force attached to one plant, because of its attitudes, and to recruit and train a new labour force in a 'green field site'. This policy of recruiting locally is possible because, as we have seen, the learning times for jobs in the lower segments are relatively short and the skills are specific to the organisation. The total costs of relocating labour are greater than the cost of local recruitment and training. Thus, when firms are either rationalising existing operations or investing in new plant, considerations regarding the 'attitude of labour' or the strength of worker organisation, can become particularly significant.

Those youths who leave school at 16 are more closely tied to the local labour market for a number of reasons. On leaving school as an unskilled worker or trainee, the level of income they can command is low, and even in times of full employment is not usually sufficient to enable them to maintain their existence independent of their family of origin, at least not in their first year in the labour market. In addition, their family and peer group ties are strong. This further inhibits their ability to either set up an independent household or move away from the local labour market. At this age their income from waged work is only sufficient to enable them to participate in teenage culture if the family continues to subsidise their housing and maintenance costs. Moreover, with the introduction of Government schemes which have reduced the wage level of youths, this dependence on the family of origin has increased in recent years. In addition, their methods of job search are often informal, and, especially in times of high unemployment, youths rely on social networks for information on job vacancies (Ashton and Maguire, 1986). This contrasts with the more formal methods, such as national press advertising, which are used for recruitment to the higher segments. For all these reasons, the life chances of youths tend to be more dependent than those of other age groups on the structure of opportunities in the local labour market.

VARIATIONS IN THE STRUCTURE OF LOCAL LABOUR MARKETS

In all four localities we chose to study, namely Leicester, Stafford, Sunderland and St Albans, the same two industrial orders, Distribution and Professional & Scientific Services dominated service sector employment. Where the local economies differed was in the size of their service sectors and the type of industry on which the manufacturing sector is based. Sunderland had experienced high levels of unemployment throughout the 1970s, caused by the decline of its traditional industries of shipbuilding, marine engineering and mining. In this respect it is typical of many towns in the North, such as Bradford, which had previously relied on labour-intensive industries which were now in chronic decline and whose class structure is characterised by a large manual working class. In 1978, 61 per cent of employed males were in manual work, and a higher proportion of females were in manual work than in the other three areas. However, the majority of females still found employment in the service sector.

The contrast with St Albans is marked. St Albans was chosen because it had a history of low unemployment, a large service sector, and a manufacturing base composed of modern, high-technology, capital intensive industries. In this respect it is typical of many of the towns in the South, such as Reading, Newbury and Crawley, which have benefited most from the economic growth which followed the recession. Its manufacturing industry is composed primarily of vehicles (aerospace), chemicals and instrument engineering, but manufacturing industry provides for a much smaller proportion of total employment than is the case in Sunderland, with manual workers representing only 31 per cent of all male workers in St Albans. Among female workers, those in manufacturing represent a smaller proportion of total female employment than is the case in Sunderland. The class structure of St Albans, like that of many towns in the South, is dominated by the middle class.

Leicester and Stafford lie between these two extremes, although there are significant differences between them. Leicester has a larger manufacturing base than Stafford and hence a large working class. Stafford has a large service sector and a higher proportion of white-collar workers than Leicester, although at the time of our research they had similar levels of unemployment which approximated the national average. However, in spite of their differences, all four local labour markets have experienced a decline in the size of the manufac-

TABLE 8.1: *Percentage of young adults (18–24-year-olds) entering each occupation*

Skill level	Leicester F	Leicester M	St Albans F	St Albans M	Stafford F	Stafford M	Sunderland F	Sunderland M
Professional, Managerial, Technical	9	20	12	32	9	16	8	12
Clerical	26	8	37	11	31	8	23	5
Skilled Manual	7	30	6	21	7	30	5	23
Semi-skilled Manual	35	22	13	17	13	22	13	16
Unskilled Manual	6	8	10	11	9	12	10	11
Sales	8	5	20	6	21	4	15	3
Other (never had a job)	9	8	2	3	11	8	26	31
n =	209	241	231	219	245	205	225	211

turing sector and a growth in the service sector over the last two decades.

One of the most immediate effects of these differences in the industry mix of the locality is on the relative size and composition of the labour market segments. This can be seen in Table 8.1 which shows the distribution of the first job entered by our sample of school and college leavers in the four localities.

The major contrast is between St Albans and Sunderland. The St Albans labour market for males was dominated by the segment composed of the professional, managerial and technician jobs, which accounted for 32 per cent of the young males' first jobs. In Sunderland this segment was much smaller and accounted for only 12 per cent of young adults' first jobs. The clerical segment in St Albans also provided a higher proportion of young males' first jobs than was the case in Sunderland. The proportions entering manual employment were very similar in both localities but this was because of the high level of unemployment in Sunderland. Of the jobs in the lower segment only in sales was a higher proportion employed in St Albans. The distinctive feature of Sunderland was the high proportion who had never experienced full-time paid employment. Thus, of available jobs in Sunderland, skilled manual jobs remained the single largest category.

In general the differences between the female segments in the two labour markets were not as pronounced as those for males. There were more opportunities for females in professional, managerial and administration jobs in St Albans than there were in Sunderland, as well as many more opportunities in clerical work. The numbers entering skilled manual work were the same in both localities. More females entered sales jobs in St Albans, whereas a high proportion of the female sample in Sunderland had failed to obtain any full-time paid employment at the time of interview.

There was a greater similarity in the relative size of the male segments in Leicester and Stafford, with the skilled manual segments providing the largest proportion of jobs for those first entering the labour market. The main difference between the two was in the female labour market. Stafford had a higher proportion of young females entering clerical work, but the major contrast was in the relative size of the lower segment. In Leicester 35 per cent of all first jobs were to be found in semi-skilled manual work. The corresponding figure in Stafford was 13 per cent. Thus, where a young person lived played a large part in determining the type of job opportunities that were available to them.

Another major contrast between the local labour markets was in the total number of jobs available *vis-à-vis* the supply of young people coming on to the labour market at any one point in time. In Sunderland 59 per cent of males and 44 per cent of females who had not left the labour force were unemployed at the time of the interview, compared with 22 per cent of males and 13 per cent of females in St Albans. This imbalance between demand and supply was so great in Sunderland that 31 per cent of males and 26 per cent of females had never experienced full-time paid employment compared with figures of 3 per cent for males and 2 per cent for females in St Albans.

UNEMPLOYMENT

At the local level the existence of mass unemployment has a profound effect on the relationships which normally hold between the characteristics of individuals and their chances of securing a job. Previous research has indicated that having a part-time job whilst at school and having achieved educational qualifications such as '0' and 'A' levels, should decrease the young person's chances of becoming unemployed (Main and Raffe, 1983; Payne and Payne, 1985). Other findings have suggested that those who experienced unemployment in their early years in the labour market would be more likely to be unemployed at the time of interview (Lynch, 1987). When subjected to logit analysis, our data confirmed that these relationships held for the sample as a whole.[1] In addition, the influence of social class, defined by the occupation of the head of the household, was found to have a significant effect on the probability of securing employment. At the aggregate level, all the relationships we would expect from earlier research findings held up.

However, when the relationships between these characteristics and the probability of being unemployed were examined at the local level there was less support for some of the findings of earlier research. In the case of males, the individual characteristics affected the probability of unemployment in the way previous research results suggested they should. Having a health problem increased the probability of unemployment in all areas except Sunderland. Having experienced part-time work while at school decreased the probability of unemployment in all areas although it was not statistically significant. Similarly, the longer the period of unemployment the less likely was the prospect of the individual securing future employment.

For females this consistency was not found in all areas. Having a part-time job decreased the probability of being unemployed. A lengthy period of previous unemployment increased the probability of being unemployed at the time of the interview in Sunderland and Stafford and was statistically significant. In Leicester and St Albans, however, a previous spell of unemployment did not increase the chance of being unemployed at the time of interview.

Generally, the sample exhibited an expected pattern of there being a relationship between the likelihood of experiencing unemployment and social class, as defined by the occupation of the 'head of household'. The exception was in Sunderland, where respondents from middle-class households had the same likelihood of experiencing unemployment as those from working-class backgrounds.

The most important finding at the local level referred to the relationship between educational qualifications, social class and the probability of being unemployed. Here our results did not support those from earlier research. Only in St Albans did all the variables operate in the way predicted from the analysis of the total sample. Thus, those with '0' or 'A'-level passes were considerably less likely to experience unemployment than those with no educational qualifications. The results were similar for both sexes in St Albans, so that the greater the educational achievement of the individual the less was their chance of becoming unemployed. In Leicester the relationships were different in important respects, as holding an '0'-level pass did not significantly reduce the young male's chances of being unemployed although it did for young females. In Sunderland, however, the relationships which had been found to exist among the sample as a whole no longer held. There, neither educational qualifications nor a middle-class background decreased the young person's chances of being unemployed. Clearly, relationships which hold at the level of aggregate data become weaker or non-existent at the local level.

The traditional relationship between educational qualifications and employment chances had collapsed in Sunderland. The sheer scale of the unemployment problem meant that it extended into all social classes, so that the unemployed were no longer distinguishable by their lack of qualifications or skills. Other criteria had become far more important in determining access to jobs.[2] In common with other areas of high unemployment, employers tended to rely to a great extent on informal channels of recruitment, notably word of mouth referrals through members of the existing workforce. Therefore, having access to the networks through which the information about the availability of jobs was transmitted was crucial in determining who got a job.[3]

Our previous research had shown that even in areas of high unemployment, employers, when hiring, tend to discriminate against those with lengthy spells of unemployment, as they are considered to constitute an unnecessary risk when labour is plentiful.

Thus, in Sunderland, those who had previous experience of unemployment would be highly likely to endure further spells of unemployment. The wealth of job opportunities in St Albans, where employers often found it difficult to recruit and retain labour, afforded respondents the comparative luxury of being able to resign from a job in the certain knowledge that they would only be unemployed for a very short time before securing a job which suited them. A period of unemployment would be short-lived and would not impair their chances of future work. Those seeking clerical and professional jobs were able to choose to 'stick out' for an appropriate job, rather than 'snatching' at the first job which came along.

The collapse of the demand for labour in Sunderland resulted in social class background being less valid as a determinant of employment status. With so few jobs available, social class background and all the advantages in terms of cultural capital and educational achievement which a middle-class background convey, failed to open the appropriate doors in the labour market. Whereas respondents from middle-class backgrounds in St Albans were able to obtain entry to white-collar jobs, often in the higher levels of the occupational hierarchy, their counterparts in Sunderland were often compelled to seek unskilled or semi-skilled manual jobs, or face lengthy spells of unemployment. This meant that across labour markets, notably between Sunderland and St Albans, comparisons could not be made. For example, the chances of young people obtaining white-collar jobs were better for those from the working class in St Albans, than for those from middle-class backgrounds in Sunderland.

The situation in Sunderland gave credence to the views of many young adults there, that educational qualifications were a waste of time and effort. After all, 33 per cent of those unemployed at the time of interview had '0' or 'A' level qualifications. In addition, the unemployed were slightly better qualified, educationally, than those in jobs in the lowest segment. Our respondents could point to brothers, sisters and friends who had good educational qualifications but were out of work. Consequently, many of them could see little point in working for educational qualifications which appeared to make no difference to their employment chances. From their perspective, there is an obvious rationality in the decision to reject educational achievement as a means of securing access to jobs, especially if they live in those communities where the long-term unemployed are concentrated, and which are cut off from the information networks used by employers.

Notwithstanding these observations about perceptions of the limited usefulness of educational qualifications, those who succeeded in entering jobs in the higher segments in Sunderland possessed the same type of qualifications as those entering similar jobs in St Albans, Leicester and Stafford. This suggests that employers were using the same educational criteria when recruiting into the higher segments in all four areas.

Further light can be shed on the relationship between educational qualifications and employment by comparing responses from Sunderland and St Albans. Having established that employers use educational qualifications in different ways in their selection procedures, according to the segment for which they are recruiting, and that these segments differ in the extent to which workers within them are likely to experience unemployment, it follows that the degree to which educational qualifications are demanded by employers will be related to the relative size of the various segments. Put simply, if most vacancies are for jobs in the higher segments the demand for educational qualifications will be greater and so they will play a more significant role in the allocation of youths within the labour market. This was the case in St Albans. If, for the sake of comparison, we exclude those who had failed to obtain a full-time job at the time of interview, then in St Albans 44 per cent of first jobs held by males were in the two highest segments compared with 25 per cent of first jobs in Sunderland. For females the corresponding figures were 50 per cent and 41 per cent respectively. Thus, the proportion of jobs for which educational qualifications were required and which exhibited higher levels of job security, was much greater in St Albans than in Sunderland, especially for males. From the point of view of the young adult, educational qualifications would be demanded much more frequently in St Albans than in Sunderland.

For males in Leicester and Stafford the failure of '0' levels to generate greater job security may have been due to the impact of the recession on apprenticeships and technician jobs which often require '0' levels for entry. While such qualifications would have improved the young person's chance of securing an apprenticeship or technician job, the collapse of manufacturing industry in these localities meant that many were made redundant. Hence, at the time of interview, possession of '0' levels would not necessarily have increased the probability of securing employment.

Another way in which local labour markets affected the experience of unemployment was in influencing the total length of time an individual spent unemployed. This was particularly so for those who entered the lower segment where, as we have seen, their experience of the labour market consisted of spells in paid employment, and/or Government schemes, interspersed with periods of unemployment. Thus, of those who were successful in obtaining jobs in Sunderland, 36 per cent of the males who entered semi-skilled or unskilled jobs in the lower segment subsequently experienced spells of unemployment in excess of 12 months. In St Albans the corresponding figure was 12 per cent. Within each segment the average length of time spent unemployed was greater in Sunderland than in St Albans. In Sunderland, if a person lost a job it took them longer to re-enter work, because of the greater intensity of the competition for jobs.

JOB MOVEMENT

Background

The findings of research on the transition from school to work in the 1960s and 1970s suggested that, for the vast majority of young people, entry to the labour market was effected smoothly (Ashton and Field, 1976). Although there was a tendency for some school-leavers to 'job-hop', before settling down in a job, this did not seriously affect the smoothness of the transition. The research was usually targeted on 16–18-year-olds, and was typically conducted on national samples, or in specific local areas. The results showed that it was not unusual for young people to have four or five jobs, with only short spells in each, in their early years in the labour market. Recent analysis of data from a study in Leicester in the mid-1960s revealed that 18 per cent of the sample had had three or more jobs in their first two years in the labour market.

Since these studies were conducted important changes have taken place in the institutional arrangements which structure the transition. The raising of the school-leaving age in the 1960s and the introduction of first YOP and later YTS, have delayed the entry into full-time paid employment by creating a new transitional status of trainee. In addition, in our sample, each successive age group, as they entered the labour market, faced a progressively increasing level of youth unemployment. For many their first experience was no longer paid employment but a place on a Government scheme. Our respondents' behaviour in the labour market, as well as their attitudes, indicate some of the consequences of these changes. Rather than moving between jobs before finding a suitable one, those who were successful in finding work tended to stay longer in the first job they entered. For others, the transition to work had been replaced by long spells of unemployment, creating anxiety and uncertainty about their future prospects. As a result, once they found jobs our respondents tended to stay in them. Even at the time of interview 45 per cent of the total sample were still in their first job. Some did move jobs; for example, of the 18-year-olds, 2 per cent had four or more jobs, and of the total sample 5 per cent had more than five jobs, but these represented only a small minority of the total sample.

These results suggest that the recession has had a major impact on the behaviour of young people by transforming the social conditions under which the transition was made. Ideas derived from earlier work, of young people leaving school, and then 'job-hopping' or experiencing a moratorium period during which they experiment with different types of jobs before settling down are no longer valid, certainly for young adults in the more depressed regions. In a time of recession the degree of 'choice' available to most school-leavers was negligible, and, in some areas, almost non-existent.

While the recession reduced the scope for moving between jobs, and of avoiding jobs with unpleasant conditions, it did not have such a significant impact on the rate at which young adults left their jobs. Just under one-quarter of the sample had left their first job within six months, a quit rate that was actually slightly higher than those reported amongst young adults in the 1960s and 1970s. At first sight this may appear somewhat contradictory but in fact it was a result of the same set of circumstances which produced the low rate of job change. Firstly, while one effect of the recession on young adults was to encourage them to hang on to their first jobs, this was counteracted by the redundancies and closures which forced others out of work. Secondly, some of the jobs were only casual or short term and so those who entered them found themselves unemployed again after a short period in work. The net result was a relatively high quit rate.

Local Labour Market Differences

Given that local labour markets have a profound effect on the process of job entry and unemployment, it is not at all surprising that they should also affect the pattern and frequency of job movement. One area where local labour markets had an effect was on the number of jobs held by those who had been employed. In Sunderland just 13 per cent of females and 11 per cent of males had had more than two jobs, compared with 32 per cent of females and 26 per cent of males in St Albans. Moreover, when we consider that most job changes took place among those who entered the lower segments and that this segment was larger in Sunderland, the contrast is even more marked. Of the 23- and 24-year-olds, who had spent between five and eight years in the labour market, 51 per cent who had had jobs in Sunderland were still in their first job compared with 34 per cent in St Albans and 21 per cent in Leicester.

These results suggest that once respondents in Sunderland had secured a job, they tended to remain in it. Despite this, the proportion of young males leaving jobs within six months was higher in Sunderland than in the other areas – 30 per cent left their first job within six months, compared to 21 per cent in St Albans and 16 per cent in Leicester. This was due to the effects of firms closing down, so that those who left tended to do so involuntarily. When occupations were held constant, and the areas compared, it was found that males who had entered skilled and semi-skilled manual jobs in Sunderland had the highest quit rate. In contrast, fewer females in Sunderland left their jobs within six months, primarily as a result of the high level of stability among clerical workers.

Another aspect of job movement concerns the extent to which job moves are confined to the same segment of the labour market. Although there was expected to be a similar pattern across all the local areas, the results showed interesting differences. In Sunderland job movement tended to be confined to moves into other jobs within the segment first entered. Just over 50 per cent of all moves, for both sexes, from first job to second job, were contained within the same segment. In St Albans the figure for females was 38 per cent, with most moves being between segments. The same pattern was observed in the direction of movement from second job to third job. Moreover, a higher proportion of moves in St Albans were upward. For example, 33 per cent of the males who moved between their first and second jobs improved their status by moving into a higher segment, compared with only 22 per cent of males in Sunderland. These results suggest that in areas of more buoyant labour demand, the pressures of segmentation are reduced. As the number of jobs increases, employers anxious to secure staff pay less attention to qualifications and previous experience, thereby opening up new opportunities for some job-seekers. In the depressed areas, the converse is the case. Faced with a surplus of labour, employers can be more selective and are more likely to insist on applicants having qualifications and appropriate experience, thereby reducing the opportunities for individuals to move out of the segment they first entered. Alternatively, it may be that because more of the available jobs in Sunderland were concentrated in the lower segment, moves tended to be within that segment.

One final aspect of job movement concerns that which takes place within the organisation. Respondents were asked if they had done the same job throughout their employment. As Table 8.2 shows, there were wide variations in responses between labour market segments. Overall, the results revealed considerable internal movement, especially among those who entered jobs in the higher segments. Young adults in professional, managerial and technician jobs

TABLE 8.2: *Percentage in each skill level reporting job movement with same employer (first job)*

	Prof/ Tech/ Man.		Clerical		Sales		Skilled		Semi-skilled		Unskilled	
	M	F	M	F	M	F	M	F	M	F	M	F
Leicester	23	28	5	16	0	6	14	8	10	16	0	0
St Albans	41	37	25	27	25	9	13	23	19	10	0	0
Stafford	21	18	19	5	0	4	8	6	14	6	0	5
Sunderland	17	11	30	35	0	9	6	8	12	10	9	17

moved most frequently within their organisation. In the lower segment, movement within the organisation was confined almost exclusively to those in semi-skilled jobs.

The results also show interesting local labour market variations. The St Albans sample had the largest overall percentage who moved within their firms. In particular, those who entered the uppermost segment in St Albans exhibited the highest rate of movement. This may have been caused by a higher rate of job turnover associated with the buoyant labour market in St Albans, creating more opportunities for internal movement. Alternatively, it may be that the more technologically advanced industries in that area had more elaborate internal labour markets which offered more prospects of job movement. In contrast, those in the higher and clerical segments in Sunderland had the lowest percentage of moves. However, there was no simple one-to-one correspondence between the level of unemployment in the local labour market and job movement within the organisation for there was greater internal movement in the clerical segment in Sunderland, for both males and females than in any other segment of any of the four labour markets. What local labour markets did, was to influence the chance of obtaining a job. Once it was obtained the chance of internal movement was strongly influenced by the labour market segment within which the job was located.

In summary, these findings suggest that local labour markets had an all-pervasive influence on job movement. In areas of low unemployment young adults had a greater range of choice. They found it easier to obtain their first job, and, once in it, had more opportunity of changing to another should they wish. In addition, when they moved they were more likely to be upwardly mobile and to move outside the segment they originally entered. In the areas of high unemployment, by contrast, entry to full-time paid work was delayed, and once a job was obtained there was less likelihood of a move to another. What job movement there was tended to be horizontal within the same segment. Unless young adults were successful in entering a firm with an elaborate internal labour market, they were less likely to move within the firm. Those who lost their jobs could face a long wait on the dole before obtaining another. Thus, differences in local labour market characteristics have an all-pervasive influence, not just on the point of entry to jobs, but throughout the 'career' of the young adult. Unless the young adults entered an organisation that could offer prospects of internal movement, the harsh labour market conditions depressed the options available at every point in their work history.

Training

So far we have focused primarily on the way in which differences in the industry mix of the local economy generate different opportunity structures and levels of employment, which in turn affect the pattern of job movement. In general terms our analysis suggests that the level of unemployment in the local economy explains many but not all of the differences in the pattern of job movement. With regard to the young adults' experience of training, the state of the local economy had no clearly discernable effect, although it did affect the young adults' attitudes towards training.

It was to be expected that the more technologically advanced industries to be found in St Albans would provide greater training opportunities because they provided a higher proportion of those jobs in the highest segments of the labour market for which a long formal period of training is required. Sunderland, by contrast, had a higher proportion of its total jobs in the lower segment for which less training is required. However, when controlling for these differences by holding sex and the type of occupation entered constant, interesting findings emerged. The proportion of males obtaining formal training in the highest segment was the same in all four areas. However, in the case of females entering the clerical segment, in St Albans 20 per cent had a formal training compared to 13 per cent in Leicester, 10 per cent in Sunderland, and only 5 per cent in Stafford. In the lowest segment there were also major variations in the proportion obtaining a formal training among those in semi-skilled work.

Thus, while only 2 per cent of males in Stafford had a formal training, the corresponding figure in St Albans was 16 per cent. In the case of females, the local labour market differences were even greater with 36 per cent of those in Leicester having had a formal training compared to none in Stafford and Sunderland and 3 per cent in St Albans.

Our discussions with employers suggested that the uniformity of training provision in the higher segments is a product of the national organisation of these occupations. For example, the professions expect the same training content to be replicated across the country. In the middle and lower segments, training is organised on a more local basis and its provision is determined largely by the characteristics of the production process of the local industries. Thus, the more extensive provision of specified training programmes followed by semi-skilled female workers in Leicester is a consequence of the dominance of the hosiery and footwear industries in the local labour market. Employers in these industries typically provide a period of 'formal' training, whereas the training for semi-skilled jobs in the other three labour markets is usually acquired on the job. These results suggest that most training provision is very local in character.

Just how far these differences are a result of local employers' attitudes, as opposed to constraints on employers from the requirements of the production process or product market, is open to question. However, the weight of evidence suggests that we should seek the explanation in the characteristics of each industry's production process and products rather than in the 'attitudes' of employers. To argue this is not to deny any role to local labour markets. As we have seen, the concentration of specific industries in a given locality generates over time a pool of labour trained in that industry. The very existence of such a pool means that some employers can opt out of training and recruit in the external market for trained labour, without incurring the costs of training. For employers in the same industry who are located in areas where they are the sole representative of that industry, there is no choice. In the absence of a pool of trained labour the employer has to undertake training if the production process requires a fairly high level of skills.

ATTITUDES TO WORK AND TRAINING

Attitudes to Training

Given the differences we have identified between the young adults' experience of work, unemployment and training, it would be surprising if these were not reflected in their attitudes to work and training. What we found was that each of the local labour markets appeared to have its own specific culture which was reflected in the young adults' attitudes. These did not appear to be merely a product of the level of unemployment in the locality but were influenced by the type of work available locally and the institutional provision of education and training. The industry mix which characterises the locality seems to provide a set of social and economic conditions which not only structures the range of opportunities in the local labour market but also influences the worker's experience of mobility, training and the work situation. These in turn provide a set of shared experiences which generate and sustain attitudes and values which are distinctive of the locality. This we refer to as the local labour market culture, for it transcends the differences we have already identified as characteristic of the various labour market segments.

One of the ways in which these local labour market cultures manifested themselves was in the respondents' attitudes towards education and training. In St Albans the respondents had a more positive attitude to education and training and this was evident in their educational achievement. Although one of the most important influences on educational achievement is social class, the effect of social class varied across the localities. Thus, in St Albans, 53 per cent of those from lower-working-class backgrounds had '0' or 'A'-level passes, in Sunderland it was 37 per cent, while in Leicester the figure fell to 26 per cent. These differences in educational achievement are not a result of the level of unemployment as Leicester has had a much higher level of employment than Sunderland throughout the last four decades.

Strong area differences were recorded in respondents' attitudes to education and whether they had any regrets about leaving school. A higher proportion of respondents from St Albans and Stafford expressed regrets about leaving school than was the case with those from Leicester and Sunderland. These same area differences were reflected in participation rates in Further Education. Whilst the most significant factor associated with the variation in participation rates was the segment of the labour market entered, there were still area differences. For example, of the females entering semi-skilled and unskilled work, 44 per cent of those in St Albans had experienced either part-time or full-time Further Education, compared with 14 per cent in Sunderland. We suggest that the more positive attitude and behaviour towards education that is found in St Albans, and to a lesser extent in Stafford, may be a result of the larger professional, technical, managerial, and clerical segments that are found there and for which educational qualifications are necessary to enter. We would stress that these are not the only factors, for research has shown that schools (Halsey, Heath and Ridge, 1980) and educational systems (McPherson and Willms, 1987), have an independent effect on the level of achievement. In towns such as St Albans the demands for educational qualifications in the local labour market may be merely reinforcing attitudes and values which are more widely held throughout the community than in towns such as Leicester or Sunderland. From the young adults' perspective, if they leave school in a town such as St Albans and enter a labour market in which a high proportion of jobs require educational qualifications then they are more likely to regret not achieving them than in Sunderland and Leicester where many of the jobs do not require educational qualifications for entry.

Local area differences were found in the respondents' attitudes to training; 62 per cent of males in St Albans and 51 per cent of females thought more training or qualifications would have improved their job prospects, compared with figures of 31 per cent for males and 34 per cent for females in Sunderland. When asked if they had thought of trying to obtain additional skills, or if there was any training they would like now, the respondents in St Albans expressed more positive answers. Even among those who had had one or more spells of unemployment, 49 per cent of males and 30 per cent of females in St Albans had considered undertaking a training course while unemployed, as against 26 per cent of males and 21 per cent of females in Sunderland. As with their attitudes towards educational qualifications, we suspect that what was important in determining attitudes towards training was the likelihood of training paying off in the labour market in terms of a better job. If there was a chance of this happening, then training was seen as useful and positive. If experience had taught them that this is not the case, then further courses and certificates were seen as pointless or irrelevant.

Attitudes to Work

In response to questions about why they had taken their first and subsequent jobs, the reason most frequently cited was 'only one available'. However, while over three-quarters of respondents cited this reason in Sunderland, the proportion citing it in St Albans was just over a half. The St Albans respondents showed more concern with finding interesting work and securing good prospects. Again this reflects the greater degree of choice and the prevalence of more career opportunities in St Albans. However, when asked which were the three most important factors to be considered in choosing work, the results were more uniform across the areas, with respondents in all areas ranking factors such as good pay, interesting work and secure work as the most important. These results suggest that although there is an element of uniformity in the factors which young people regard as being important in their thinking about work, in practice local labour market conditions exert a powerful influence in determining their behaviour and attitudes towards work.

Local labour market conditions also exerted a significant influence on young person's evaluations of school and their job histories. When asked if there were any ways in which they could have been better prepared for work while at school, the St Albans respondents were the most critical, with 64 per cent of males and 56 per cent of females suggesting that provision could be improved, compared with 39 per cent of males and 37 per cent of females in Sunderland. These results suggest that where there were more opportunities and, hence, decisions to be made, and where the young adults were better educated, they were more critical. Where there were few choices to be made they were more fatalistic. In Sunderland the young people appeared to appreciate that there was little the schools could do about the situation. This same fatalism was reflected in the replies of respondents in Sunderland to a question which asked whether they would choose the same job if they were to start their working life over again. In spite of the fact that over 75 per cent of the respondents in Sunderland had taken their first job because it was the only one available, 54 per cent of males and 58 per cent of females reported that they would choose the same job again. These figures were comparable to those found in the other three areas. Given the restricted opportunities in Sunderland at the time of the interview the results suggest that the respondents there were evaluating their achievements in the context of a depressed economy and lowering their aspirations accordingly.

THE EXCLUDED

The discussion so far has been concerned with those who had some experience of full-time paid employment. In fact 10 per cent of the total sample had never experienced full-time paid employment. Again, however, respondents in this latter group were not evenly distributed across the local labour markets, being concentrated in Sunderland, where they amounted to 31 per cent of males and 26 per cent of females. In Leicester it was 8 per cent of males and 9 per cent of females, while in St Albans it was 3 per cent of males and 2 per cent of females. Yet even within the four towns, our results indicated that the long-term unemployed were concentrated in certain limited geographical areas, usually on council estates and/or inner-city areas. In the areas of Sunderland covered in our interviews, the long-term unemployed were concentrated in two large council estates, in Leicester and Stafford they were concentrated in one estate, and in St Albans it was a single street. Apart from in St Albans, we found whole communities where the vast majority of people were without work. The size of the communities were a function of the level of unemployment in the locality. Within these communities it was often the case that members of the family had not experienced paid employment for a considerable period of time. The young adults there were starting to raise families without ever knowing the experience of paid employment.

In these circumstances the use of structured interview schedules based on the assumption that the respondents were involved in paid employment or even concerned about it were of limited use in the collection of data. For this reason, and in order to obtain a better understanding of the position and experience of the long-term unemployed, unstructured, in-depth interviews were conducted with a small sub-sample of 20 long-term unemployed respondents in Sunderland. Analysis of this data suggested that while these communities were a creation of high levels of unemployment, once they were established, a number of social mechanisms came into operation which served to perpetuate them. Many of the young adults who had failed to obtain a full-time paid job were from families of the long-term unemployed. Our results indicated that their level of educational achievement was below that of young people from the lower working class, and consequently they were more likely to leave school without any educational qualifications. When they entered the labour market their handicaps were increased as they were far less likely to enter employment than those from a lower-working-class background; 49 per cent of males from families where the father was unemployed had failed to find work, compared with 29 per cent of males from the lower working class. These results, together with those of Payne (1987), suggest that there is a degree of social inheritance of unemployment.

One of the mechanisms which would explain this social inheritance and hence the perpetuation of these communities through time is the operation of local labour market information networks. As the level of unemployment rises, employers cease to use formal publicly available channels to advertise jobs. This is because such large numbers apply for any vacancies that are publicly advertised and the cost of handling and processing them becomes prohibitive. As a result they prefer to recruit by word of mouth. As whole families and communities become unemployed, the number of people who are in work, and so in a position to transmit information about vacancies, shrinks. Eventually the unemployed who form these communities become detached from the job information networks and hence excluded from the possibility of applying for what few jobs might become available. Should they hear about a job, there are other hurdles to surmount. From the point of view of employers in these areas, anyone with more than six months' unemployment tends to be regarded as a bad employment risk and as such is discriminated against. This completes the circle and ensures the exclusion of this group from the labour market.

Within these communities the main source of income has to be state benefits. Reliance on such benefits generates tension and fear in the community as the consequences of being reported for an incorrect declaration of personal circumstances constitutes a serious threat to the family income. Because of reliance on state benefits, poverty and deprivation are widespread and dominate the daily experience of such groups. Financial deprivation appears to be the greatest problem which they confront. This creates pressures for finding ways of supplementing income, often through petty theft and 'fiddle' jobs. Financial impoverishment restricts the range of activities family members or individuals can engage in as they do not have the financial resources to support social activities. Their basic needs for food are serviced by local stores selling stale bread and groceries which are past their sell-by dates. Clothes are obtained either from jumble sales or, if new, from acquaintances who supply them with no questions asked. Lack of finance also restricts their mobility and makes them prisoners of their own communities. Neither can they afford holidays or even trips outside the town.[4]

Apart from the problems of poverty, findings from our in-depth interviews suggest that the management of time is one of the other main problems which confront the long-term unemployed. In the larger survey, boredom was one of the most frequently cited problems encountered by the unemployed. In the absence of work, paid or unpaid, which imposes a structure on daily activities, other structures have to be devised. For some this meant watching videos, or hanging around the town or street corners, while for others time was filled by developing their interest in music and community affairs. For almost all the long-term unemployed, work, in the form of full-time paid employment, was not part of their everyday consciousness. They had come to terms with the fact that it was not available locally and that time spent looking for it was wasted. In order to avoid the despondency of constantly searching for something that was not available and the implied threat of personal failure, attention was directed to other matters. They no longer thought much about work.

These results point to the creation in Sunderland, and perhaps to a lesser extent in Stafford and Leicester, of what some have referred to as an 'underclass' (Roberts *et al*, 1986), which by virtue of its exclusion from the labour market is denied the opportunity of participating in the material and psychological benefits of contemporary society.[5]

The contrast with St Albans is dramatic. There the difference between the middle and working classes is being reduced, at least when measured in terms of the educational achievement of children and their access to jobs. The educational achievement of those from families in which the parents were unemployed was little different from that of the lower working class. The mechanisms through which long-term unemployment and the deprivations associated with it were transmitted from one generation to the next had not been established on a large scale. We suspect that most of the young adults in St Albans who were unemployed at the time of interview were still moving into and out of jobs, and as such differed little from those in the lowest occupational segment, where unemployment was a relatively frequent experience. Few had fallen into the ranks of the long-term unemployed. In St Albans there were no communities of unemployed people cut off from the information networks which provided access to jobs. Jobs were available to those coming out of school so that the mechanisms which function to reproduce the exclusion of large groups from the labour market in places like Sunderland did not operate.

CONCLUSION

Hitherto much of the work by sociologists and economists on the relationship between education and the labour market has been based either on aggregate national data or more in-depth studies of single local labour markets. What our results show is that it can be very misleading to either generalise down from national data bases to the local level, or, alternatively, to generalise up from the study of one local area to the level of the society as a whole. What we have shown is that with respect to job movement, training provision and attitudes towards work and training, labour markets develop distinctive 'cultures' which appear to exert an independent influence on the life chances of youths. Spatial location can be of crucial importance in determining life chances, certainly for those who do not proceed into Higher Education and thence into the national labour market.

This is not to argue that the traditional relationships between social class, educational attainment and occupational achievement, as documented by Halsey, Heath and Ridge (1980) and Gray, McPherson and Raffe (1983) did not hold in these areas. Apart from the period when the labour market collapsed in Sunderland, as it did in other Northern towns, these relationships continue to hold. What we are arguing is that it is the relationship between the educational system and the labour market which differs across local labour markets. In St Albans the need for qualifications in the labour market creates pressure on those in education to maximise their attainments. In Sunderland the large proportion of youths who cannot find work, combined with the high proportion of jobs for which qualifications are not necessary, reduces the pressure on working-class youth to achieve. At the local level, just as much as at the national level, the institutional links between the educational system and the local labour market exert an independent influence on the behaviour of youth.

NOTES

1. The only exception to this was females with 'A' levels. Our results suggested that having an 'A' level lowered the probability of employment when compared to those holding 'O' levels. This may have been because those with 'A' levels only had low grades, as the normal step for those with good 'A' levels is into Higher Education.
2. This phenomenon has also been noted by Harris (1987), who found that the relationships predicted on the basis of human capital theory, for example between skill levels of individuals and ability to obtain employment, such that those with greater skill are more likely to obtain employment than those with few skills, fail to hold in periods of acute recession.
3. Informal networks have been found to be important in a number of different contexts. See for example, Manwaring and Wood (1984), Bresnen *et al*. (1985) and Harris (1987).
4. For a more detailed ethnographic account of the problems facing the young unemployed in communities such as this see Coffield *et al*. (1986). The Wolverhampton Youth Review (1985) documents the effects of financial deprivation on the activities of young people.
5. We have deliberately avoided using the term 'underclass' because of the connotations of individual failure associated with its use in the USA.

9 The Youth Labour Market and Social Policy

In this final chapter we address two major policy issues. The first is the problem of youth unemployment which has been characteristic of many of the economies of the West throughout the 1980s. Our analysis suggests that in spite of the projected decline in the number of youths entering the labour market it is premature to regard the problem as having been solved in Britain. While the degree of mass school-leaver unemployment has been reduced, the problem of youth unemployment has been transformed into the systematic exclusion of large groups of young adults from effective participation in the labour force. This is a problem which requires a very different policy response. The second issue we tackle is that of training. The introduction of large-scale training programmes has been one of the weapons used to 'solve' the problem of school-leaver unemployment. Yet our analysis suggests that by hurriedly imposing a national training scheme the Government has unintentionally reinforced a national system of training which is inappropriate for an advanced industrial society. What it has done is to fossilise a system of training which was developed for labour-intensive industries, but which is at variance with the underlying structural changes that we have identified.

THE TRANSFORMATION OF THE UNEMPLOYMENT PROBLEM

Redundant Youth

In the previous chapters we have argued that the structural changes taking place in the economy are increasing the demand for more highly-qualified labour and reducing that for unqualified school-leavers. The market for unskilled or poorly-qualified youth is shrinking. We have also argued that although school-leavers and youths remain excluded from large parts of the labour market, there are areas where they compete directly with adults and others where they have sheltered access. Because of this, any change in the level of demand will have immediate effects on the recruitment of youths. For these reasons we would agree with Raffe (1986) that the youth and adult labour markets are linked, and that the most realistic way to reduce youth unemployment substantially is through measures that reduce unemployment among all age groups.

There are a number of ways in which the level of demand can be increased. One is to use the resources of the state to lower inflation, increase business confidence and reduce the power of groups, such as trades unions, to affect employers' decisions and correct 'inefficiencies in the labour market'. Proponents of this view would point to the success of such a policy in creating economic growth in Britain since 1981 and reducing unemployment, although many would doubt the extent of such success. The problem of school-leaver unemployment was, however, 'cured' by much more direct Government intervention. An alternative way of increasing demand would be to use the power of the state to manage the exchange rate and stimulate those industries in which the society was felt to have a competitive advantage, while at the same time pursuing an active labour market policy to retrain the unemployed. Such a policy was tried successfully in Sweden, preventing the emergence of mass unemployment of either school-leavers or youths. Clearly, no matter which path they take, governments possess the resources to affect the general level of demand.

The problem of youth unemployment is also susceptible to demographic changes in the supply of school-leavers. The number of 16–19-year-olds in Britain peaked in 1983 at 3.7 million and will fall to 2.6 million by 1994. A fall of this magnitude will, of course, inevitably reduce the problem, assuming that there is no further collapse in labour demand. Thus, it is argued that a combination of increasing labour demand and falling numbers of teenagers will eradicate the problem of youth unemployment.

There are a number of problems with this argument. Firstly, from the demand side, the assumption that a high level of unemployment is a cyclical phenomenon which can be cured purely by economic growth is increasingly being questioned in the light of the experience of advanced societies over the last two decades. A growing weight of evidence (Therborn, 1986; Ashton, 1986) suggests that unemployment has become disassociated from economic growth. Indeed, Britain has experienced a period of economic recovery which, by mid-1988 with manufacturing output approaching the levels of 1979, still maintained a level of unemployment which (even according to official figures) was one million higher than that of 1979. As Therborn has argued, some societies were able to sustain low levels of unemployment throughout the crisis of the 1980s, whilst others experienced much higher levels.

Secondly, the view that a combination of improved economic demand and a reduced supply of youths will resolve the problem of youth unemployment rests on either of two mistaken assumptions. One is that labour is homogeneous and that different types of labour are interchangeable. If this were the case then a combination of increased demand for labour and reduced supply would lower unemployment levels. The other assumption is that the youth and adult labour markets are totally separate in which case the bulge caused by youth unemployment would move into the adult market, increasing adult unemployment while the smaller numbers entering the youth labour market would reduce youth unemployment. As we have shown, the youth/adult separation is neither complete nor stable. Indeed, our research has revealed both markets to be highly segmented and subject to long-term processes of change, thereby rendering such 'solutions' problematic. Certainly, the fall in the number of teenagers is itself no guarantee that the problem of youth unemployment will be resolved. It ignores the effects of the long-term processes of change which we have identified as confining unqualified school-leavers to certain segments of the labour market where they are at constant risk of becoming excluded. Since our research began in the late 1970s, there has been a progressive transformation of the lower segments of the labour market as they have become dominated by insecure, short-term, casual, temporary and part-time jobs. As a result, the problem of unemployment is itself becoming transformed and incorporated into the everyday experience of a large section of the working class.

The restructuring which has occurred throughout the recession has also had a major impact on the patterns of segmentation within the youth labour market. The emergence of global markets and the enhanced competition associated with them, the relocation of the labour-intensive industries, and the effects of new technology have combined to destroy many of the full-time skilled and semi-skilled manual jobs which formed the basis of the old working class. Even those firms which have survived the recession have transformed many of the jobs which remain in the manufacturing sector. The adoption of new labour management strategies has produced not only a more flexible multi-skilled labour force, but also an increasing proportion of casual, self-employed, part-time and temporary workers. The emergence of large numbers of these short-term unskilled jobs has led to drastic alterations to the working conditions of a large part of the new working class. In the course of this restructuring the market for the labour of the less qualified school-leaver has shrunk.

In the service sector, where employment has grown, the increasing dominance of large corporations and the enhanced competition between commercial institutions has meant that many of the new jobs being created are predominantly part-time. This is certainly the case in the lower segments of the labour market, where the bulk of 16-year-old school-leavers compete for jobs. Moreover, whereas many of the full-time jobs that have been lost were filled by males, the new part-time jobs are the preserve of females. Young females do not necessarily benefit from this situation, as they must struggle to maintain their hold on jobs in this part of the labour market in the face of intense competition from married women.

In the place of the traditional working class, based on full-time male manual labour, we have seen the growth of a new working class, based on short-term, temporary and casual labour, part-time jobs and self-employment, with the paid labour of females occupying a more central role. The formation of this new section of the working class has taken place during a period when there has been a permanent shortfall in the demand for labour. The result has been that those who have failed to obtain these new jobs have fallen into a condition of permanent unemployment. Together, these conditions have created the basis for the exclusion of a large group from effective participation in the labour market. Many young people seeking to enter the lower segments of the labour market experience periods of unemployment, interspersed with short-term tenancy of jobs.

The problem has been exacerbated by the concentration of the more rapidly growing high-technology industries, as well as the head offices of the major companies, in the South East. Thus, a high proportion of the jobs which have been created in the companies themselves or in the services which support their headquarters, are in highly-skilled occupations, such as scientists, professionals and managers. By contrast, the North has seen the decline of the older labour-intensive industries and the associated jobs which provided the backbone of the traditional working class. Moreover, in the absence of company headquarters and their support services, not only have these regions lost traditional jobs, but the service sector employment which has emerged there has tended to have consisted of more unskilled part-time jobs. The result has been the exclusion of large numbers from the labour market and the concentration of unemployment in these regions and the inner cities. The fact that this phenomenon has occurred in other European societies and continues to exist in the USA, suggests that it is a structural feature of most advanced industrial societies.

Those youths who enter the lower segments of the labour market in the more affluent areas also experience movement between Government schemes, unemployment and short-term jobs. However, the spells of unemployment tend to be relatively short when compared with those in the more deprived areas. These young people also run less risk of being permanently excluded from the labour market. In the more deprived areas, the spells of unemployment become longer and the chances of obtaining even short-term employment become remote. A pattern of labour market experience which in the affluent areas can be described as one of sub-employment, becomes one of chronic sub-employment. In some unemployment blackspots, paid employment in full-time, permanent jobs has become the exception rather than the rule. Many youths become permanently excluded from the labour market on leaving school or completing YTS.

This exclusion of large numbers of youths is likely to continue in deprived areas in the absence of a major change in Government policy. Given the continuance of the underlying trends we have identified, some of the more highly-skilled professional, managerial, administrative and scientific jobs need to be redistributed to those deprived areas. The absence of such jobs, and the shortfall in the number of less skilled jobs, will combine to create an imbalance in the demand and supply of labour. In spite of attempts such as TVEI to reform the curriculum, continuing high levels of unemployment will reduce the incentive for youths to acquire qualifications and the labour market will continue to be characterised by a large annual influx of unqualified youth. Although the predicted fall of one-third in the number of youths coming on to the labour market will ease the situation it is unlikely to resolve it.

Long-Term Youth Unemployment and the Exclusion of Young Adults from the Labour Market

If it is accepted that under existing labour market conditions the problem of sub-employment and unemployment among young adults is likely to remain prominent, the adequacy of existing policy measures must be questioned. The initial response to rising levels of youth unemployment was the introduction of a series of Government schemes which were later to form the basis of the YTS programme. In one sense these measures can be said to have solved the problem of 16- and 17-year-old unemployment by taking large numbers of youths off the unemployment register. Similar programmes in other EEC countries have achieved the same results. In localities where there is a buoyant demand for labour they have been successful in easing the transition to work. Where there is a major imbalance in the relationship between the demand and supply of labour they have been far less successful.

Like the problem of youth unemployment, that of the exclusion of young adults from the labour markets, rather than being a specifically British problem, has arisen in many advanced industrial societies. In some local labour markets, the end result of these various national programmes has been the production of successive cohorts of 'trainees' who subsequently face either long-term unemployment or spells of unemployment interspersed with short-term casual, temporary or part-time employment.

The solution to the problem of these 'excluded' young people rests in part, as we have argued earlier, on an increase in the general demand for labour. However, this will provide only part of the answer, as, once established, the mechanisms which serve to reproduce this group can operate independently of an increase in economic growth or political initiatives which may generate additional jobs. As the experience in the USA in the 1960s has shown, economic growth can continue to produce jobs and improve the standard of living of the majority of the population, while at the same time, the conditions and life chances of minorities can actually deteriorate. This has been true of Britain in the 1980s, and it will clearly take more than the generation of additional jobs, whether through economic growth or political action, to resolve the problem.

What is needed are policies aimed at negating the mechanisms which serve to reproduce this group through time. These would have to be wide-ranging. For example, to counter the regional imbalance in the rate of job creation and in the type of job created requires political measures designed to both enhance the rate of job creation and encourage the siting of company headquarters in the North. This could lead to a relocation of the other business support services which can help generate the emergence of the professional, technical and administrative jobs that are lacking there. The Government could take the lead by relocating some of its own departments to the regions, following the examples of the MSC in Sheffield and the Driving Vehicle Licence Centre in Swansea.

At the local level, policies should be established to combat the exclusion of many youths from the labour market. Assuming the success of policies aimed at creating more highly skilled, well-paid jobs in the local labour market, this would require the upgrading of the skills of the existing labour force. Although the YTS has been partially successful in achieving this, the internal stratification of the scheme, which is discussed below, prevents it from being the most appropriate policy response to this problem. At the moment many of the youths who are a product of these processes of exclusion would be in no position to compete for jobs requiring qualifications, even if they became available. This was evident from research carried out by Roberts *et al.* (1986), focusing on youths in Liverpool and Cheltenham. If the greater availability of jobs is forthcoming, action should be taken to counter the mechanisms which lead to the reproduction of this group of disaffected long-term unemployed by enabling those who are not in paid employment to participate fully in the local community.

The question of upgrading skills will be discussed in the next section. As far as policies to prevent the continued emergence of large numbers of excluded youth is concerned, a number of initiatives may be considered. Firstly, although it would clearly be regarded as sacrilege by the Thatcher Government, raising the level of income of the long-term unemployed would reduce the extent to which they are precluded from participating in mainstream social and economic life. To achieve this may require not merely increasing the level of existing benefits but changing the form in which they are delivered. For example, a system of minimum income entitlement would have the advantage of reducing the anxiety and tension which the present means-tested administration of welfare benefits introduces into the communities of long-term unemployed. It would help remove the fear felt by many families of state agencies withdrawing all or part of their income.

Interventions are also required to help generate a more effective use of time on the part of the unemployed. After financial deprivation, boredom and the difficulty of handling time is the most frequently reported problem among the long-term unemployed (Ashton and Maguire, 1986). This could be countered by the provision of activities which would enhance the personal skills necessary for human development. At the moment, YTS, besides offering skills training and a possible means of entry to the labour market, provides a structure to the lives of many 16–18-year-olds, who, particularly in areas of high unemployment, would be unemployed. Much of this structure is concerned with work activities which render the individual young person 'acceptable' to society and their local community. A similar function is performed by job clubs and adult training schemes for the long-term unemployed. However, in some areas of high unemployment the long-term unemployed tend to be concentrated in certain estates. Young people from these communities tend to enter lower status schemes offering little in the form of specific skills and few opportunities to develop manipulative and cognitive skills. While in theory YTS offers the promise of providing a significant improvement in these skills, the fact that it is delivered primarily through employers who require labour for relatively unskilled jobs suggests that this promise is unlikely to be realised. Some YTS schemes are for occupations for which, traditionally, less than one month's training is required. Moreover, if such schemes do not lead to jobs, the level of motivation they generate is low. What they do achieve is to structure time, by providing a set of daily activities which are often seen as 'better than the dole'. They may not, however, develop broader skills and the self-confidence necessary to participate effectively in contemporary society. For this to happen, more imaginative programmes, which can challenge and stretch the capabilities of young people are required, far more than the tasks associated with the jobs which make up the lower segment of the labour market.

An appropriate programme of activities could take different forms. One way would be to provide grants for specific projects which were devised, controlled and executed by the young people themselves. We have seen evidence of this operating successfully in Sunderland, where some unemployed young people have acquired funds to develop printing businesses, housing cooperatives and pop groups. In a more formal and bureaucratic manner, grants are already available. The Enterprise Allowance Scheme assists those setting up their own business, although the applicant is also required to make a substantial financial contribution. Such grants should be available not only for projects which are business oriented but also for those which offer the prospect of developing the human potentiality of young people. Existing programmes such as Employment Training provide little more than a set of routine activities, and, as they are administered and controlled by official agencies, young people have few chances to direct and control their own activities. The type of projects we advocate here would enable youths and young adults to acquire the skills involved in administration, coping with bureaucratic official agencies, negotiating contracts, and managing finance, as well as the manipulative and cognitive skills required for specific work tasks. The range of skills developed would be far more complex than those delivered through the lower status YTS and Employment Training. They would enable the youths who participated in the projects to create their own employment or move into full-time permanent work if and when it became available in the local labour market. For such schemes to be effective a more decentralised form of administration needs to be provided, with the local community having a greater say in determining the range of activities which would be eligible for support.

This proposal assumes that the young unemployed already have the considerable intellectual and social skills necessary to take on and engage themselves in self-directed activities, whereas it could be argued that many of the young people from deprived working-class backgrounds lack the necessary confidence and skills. In order to help this group develop their capabilities a different form of provision may be required. This could involve the sort of structured learning experiences which were pioneered in some areas under the Youth Opportunities Programme. The youths participating in these courses were able to define the objectives of the course, which could range from anything from guitar-making to urban survival skills. The learning stemmed from the process of working through the objectives of the course. It is essential to their success that such courses should centre on the learning needs of the individual or group involved and not on the requirements of employers or on what professional groups, such as teachers, define as appropriate material for young adults. Such courses have already proved their worth in developing the confidence and abilities of young people who had been dismissed as 'failures', or had rejected the conventional system of education. It also appears to be very important that the courses are geared to practical problems and the skills delivered are those which can be utilised on a day-to-day basis. Once again they would enable young people to move into jobs as and when they become available or to move on to the types of projects discussed above. Both forms of provision would also equip young adults with the skills necessary for organising their own community forms of action. There would be no reason to impose age limits on entry to the schemes. The idea is to provide a set of continuous learning experiences through which individuals and groups could negotiate their own way. Instead of being centrally co-ordinated and planned, grants could be administered through the local community and courses provided by local education authorities. If demand in the local economy picked up and provided 'real' jobs, many of the courses and projects would cease as demand for them lapsed. If, subsequently, the young adults were to experience spells of unemployment, they would at least have been provided with a wider and more varied set of skills on which to draw than those available to youths moving through some of the lower status YTS schemes.

An alternative strategy would be to redistribute jobs more equally, using positive discrimination to ensure that the long-term unemployed had access to spells of employment. This policy would be easier to implement in the public sector, as private sector employers would require subsidies as an incentive to take on labour which could be regarded as superfluous to the needs of the organisation. However, given the lack of skills which characterises many of the long-term unemployed, they would be likely to be restricted to jobs in the lower segment. Thus, even with this policy, the unemployed would in all probability only have access to casual or temporary unskilled jobs which provide them with little more than a marginal increase in income and a more structured set of daily activities. Moreover, workers already in insecure jobs would be displaced to let in the unemployed. The most insecure and least well equipped would pay the cost of helping the long-term unemployed. Unlike our earlier proposals, it would not lead to the acquisition of new skills across a range of areas (social, cognitive and manipulative), which serve to enhance the confidence and autonomy of the individuals and groups involved. Neither would it enhance the personal and collective abilities of the people concerned to substantially improve their life chances, should more opportunities become available as a result of economic growth or political action.

Labour Market Policy

The creation of groups of people who are excluded from effective economic participation has resulted from recent changes in the labour market. The alleviation of this problem is, therefore, partly dependent on interventions into the workings of the labour market.

Our analysis points to two areas where this could happen. Firstly, there is a need to dismantle some of the barriers which inhibit movement between labour market segments. If some groups are confined to the lowest segment, in a position of sub-employment, with poor-quality jobs being interspersed with periods of unemployment, then there will always be a risk of the formation of an 'underclass' of long-term unemployed people in periods of high unemployment. This is a complex task as the barriers to movement were originally erected to counter the uncertainties of labour market forces.[1] Thus, to remove them would mean providing greater security in the labour market while simultaneously changing the conditions under which training is provided for the more prestigious jobs. It would require the dismantling of the system of front-end loaded training which is characteristic of British society, and the provision of access to training through forms of continuous education. This would enable movement to occur at any point in an adult's career. One way in which this is already achieved is through the construction of internal labour markets, which can provide an element of security while affording individuals the opportunity to enhance their range of skills. As we have seen, evidence suggests that this is already occurring in parts of the service sector, where firms are introducing internal labour markets into organisations previously dominated by unskilled and casual jobs in hotels, catering and retail. Young entrants to these jobs have the possibility of moving beyond the confines of the lower occupational segments, into supervisory and managerial jobs. The introduction of such changes is not an easy task and even if it is achieved there is no guarantee that internal labour markets and their associated career ladders would not reproduce discrimination on the basis of gender and race. For example, many males already have access to promotion opportunities within their organisations. Therefore, attempts to extend internal labour markets would need to be mindful of the danger of encourgaing or condoning discrimination. There are clearly complex issues involved. We merely wish to emphasise the necessity of changing the structure of training and the relationships between jobs within organisations, if movement between segments is to be enhanced.

The second related area where action is required is to improve the quality, in terms of tenure and conditions, of new jobs, many of which are unskilled, casual and part-time. Again, this is a longstanding and complex issue, although its importance has grown in the light of the underlying processes of change which are transforming the labour market. For while professional, managerial and technical jobs represent one area of growth, the other has been in casual, fixed-term or part-time unskilled jobs, which can form part of the structure of sub-employment. They tend to provide a low, often variable and uncertain source of income and offer few opportunities for the development of skills. High rates of labour turnover are associated with them, so that they afford very insecure footholds in the labour market. The transformation of such jobs in the context of the competitive product markets within which employers operate, is a difficult task. However, a combination of legislation, unionisation and action by employers has succeeded in restructuring similar casual, low-paid jobs in the past.

THE TRAINING PROBLEM

Absent Youth

The restructuring of the labour market which we have documented has coincided with political attempts to restructure the educational system. At the level of secondary education these have involved cuts in educational expenditure linked to falling school rolls, and attempts to introduce a stronger vocational element into schools and colleges through the Technical and Vocational Education Initiative and the Certificate in Pre-Vocational Education. In Higher Education, financial cuts have been imposed on the basis of the same rationale and similar attempts have been made to shift the balance of the academic curriculum from the arts to science and technology and to orientate the curriculum more towards business culture by introducing enterprise skills.

It is against this background that we consider the policy implications for education and training of the trends which have been restructuring the labour market. Two are particularly important. One is the decreasing demand for youth labour and the deskilled, casual, short-term and part-time basis of many of the jobs that are left for the less qualified 16-year-old leavers. The other is the increasing demand for more highly qualified youth, which persisted throughout the recession and has continued since then. This was evident from our analysis of the occupational structure, which revealed that in spite of the dramatic fall in levels of employment which took place over the years 1979–84 the professional, managerial, administrative and scientific occupations continued to grow. It was also reflected in the evidence from our interviews, where some of the largest employers in the manufacturing sector reported persistent shortages of scientific and professional staff throughout the recession. Similarly, among service sector employers, there has been a demand in Commerce for well-qualified personnel, while in Retail and Hotel and Catering the large corporations now require new professional staff as a result of their rationalisation of the labour process. Roberts *et al.* (1986) reported similar findings from their interviews with employers. Also, the Engineering Industry Training Board found that, in spite of a loss of one-third of the labour force over the period 1978–85, the demand for professional engineers, scientists and technologists in Engineering increased by 46.5 per cent. As further confirmation, our analysis of young adults' labour market experiences demonstrated how those in the higher segments were relatively unaffected by the recession.[2]

At the end of previous recessions it has been usual for employers to report skill shortages which resulted from a failure to train (see Chapter 5). However, the shortage of highly skilled labour is more than just a cyclical phenomenon. It is part of a process which preceded the recession and is common in other industrial societies, being associated with the introduction of new technology, the expansion of large corporations, and the growth in demand for business and financial services. It should be stressed that the demand for more highly qualified manpower is primarily a result of fundamental changes in the type of work that people do, rather than being a product of qualification inflation. It is not due to employers increasing the level of qualification without there being any change in job content. Those occupations which have traditionally demanded higher educational qualifications are the ones which have expanded, rather than the quasi-professions. This is not to deny that the process of qualification inflation has not had a part to play, but it is one which is more prominent in the middle-level occupations, where representative bodies are striving to upgrade their status, than in the more established professions.

The 'Problem' of Training in Britain

One consequence of the process of the expansion of jobs which require higher educational qualifications for entry has been that 16-year-olds have found access to this expanding segment being increasingly denied to them. As a result the proportion of

16-year-olds entering the segment has continued to decline. Meanwhile the demand for the labour of less qualified school-leavers collapsed. In 1978, 85 per cent of 16-year-old school-leavers entered employment, whereas by 1987 this had fallen to 31 per cent, with 50 per cent on YTS and 19 per cent unemployed. This pattern has continued since, indicating that as Britain has emerged from the recession, an over-supply of less qualified youths has persisted. While the reduction in the numbers of 16–19-year-olds entering the labour market will ease the situation, it will not, for reasons we cite below, eradicate the problem of over-supply in deprived areas.

The effect of YTS has certainly not been inconsequential. It now represents the majority experience of those 16-year-olds who leave school and thereby provides a 'surrogate labour market' (Lee *et al.*, 1987). However, it has played only a minor role in affecting the distribution of job opportunities available. As a result of being implemented through employers rather than through the educational system or directly by the MSC, it has been powerfully influenced by existing labour market structures (Turbin, 1987). YTS has not been particularly successful in opening up many of the jobs from which young people have traditionally been excluded. Our results suggest that its main contribution has been in keeping the doors open to young females in the less skilled service sector occupations. However, because of its focus on the preparation of young people for semi-skilled and unskilled jobs in the lower segments, it continues to train young people for jobs in a shrinking part of the labour market.

This brings us to one of the main contradictions highlighted by this research, namely the continuing over-supply of less qualified youth, which coexists with a shortage of qualified labour. Both trends are likely to continue into the foreseeable future, thereby exacerbating the situation.

The Origins of the Problem

The origins of this problem partly emanated from the tendency for British youth to leave the education system at an early age. Compared with other advanced industrial societies, Britain has one of the highest, if not the highest, proportions of 16-year-olds entering the labour market. Only around 45 per cent remain in education, compared with 95 per cent in Japan and 80 to 90 per cent in Canada. There are two main reasons for this. The first concerns the attitude of young people towards education. Since the establishment of state education in Britain, certain sections of the working class have offered collective resistance (Gardner, 1984). Evidence of manifestations of this resistance can be found in the work of Willis (1977) and Corrigan (1979). Brown (1987) has recently shown that the majority of working-class youth, rather than resisting education, have an instrumental orientation, looking to conformity at school to lead to the attainment of basic educational qualifications, and access to a 'good' job at 16. This is in marked contrast to the situation in Canada, where most working-class youth choose to continue in education at least until the age of 18, and where there is no evidence of the collective resistance to education (Ashton, 1988). As Gaskell (1985) has shown, Canadian youth are no less instrumental, but their instrumentality leads them to stay within the educational system until they are 18 years old.

The second reason, which is not unconnected to the first, relates to the institutional links between education and the labour market and, especially, the organisation of training. Historically, training has been organised around the apprenticeship system, which, as shown in Chapter 4, gave the British system of training its front-end loaded character. The training which was provided on first entering the labour market was deemed sufficient to last the individual for the rest of his or her working life. Employers' recruitment practices have been largely geared to taking 16- or 17-year-olds, and so most applicants over that age have effectively missed out. This has put pressure on 16- and 17-year-olds in Britain to leave school at this early age if they are to obtain 'a good job'. Staying on at school can damage many young people's employment chances, as it causes the school-leaver to be caught between segments and therefore to fall into the lower segment.

In Canada, where employers do not recruit for apprenticeships in manufacturing industry below the age of 20, and then usually after the person has spent some time working for the company, there is no such pressure to leave school early. Young females who are trained for office skills in the educational system tend to leave earlier than males who stay on in school. In Britain the converse is true. Males tend to leave at 16 to compete for the prestigious apprenticeships in Engineering and Construction, while those females who do not enter hairdressing tend to stay on an extra year to obtain office and business skills. The constrast between the recruitment and training practices in the two societies serves to highlight the fact that it is the way in which recruitment and training are linked to the educational system which perpetuates early leaving in Britain.

Historically, the recruitment of youths straight from school into apprenticeships or operative jobs proved to be an adequate method of acquiring a labour force for what were essentially labour-intensive industries, in which the rate of technological change was slow. The perpetuation of this system at a time when there is a growing demand for more highly qualified labour to service a technologically advanced industrial base can only inhibit the development of the growth sectors of the economy.

Policy Responses

This problem has so far gone unrecognised, because education and training are seen as separate fields of activity and academic enquiry in Britain. In responding to calls for a better qualified labour force, policy measures have shown little understanding of the way in which the relationship between education and training is institutionalised. The Great Debate focused on the 'failure' of the educational system to meet the requirements of employers, and the need for a more vocationally oriented curriculum. More recently there have been calls for higher standards of education. Three main solutions have been essayed. To meet the needs of employers and provide greater vocational relevance, work experience in schools was introduced, followed by TVEI and CPVE. The core curriculum is intended to raise educational standards, while YTS has been introduced to improve the standard of training.

Studies of initiatives such as TVEI suggest that, although there are some positive effects, they do not fundamentally change young people's orientation towards school (Bell and Howieson, 1988). For some it has made school a more pleasant experience and the curriculum more relevant to their personal circumstances. However, the same high proportion of 16-year-olds are still leaving school in order to try for the jobs which are available. No matter how interesting or relevant the curriculum might be, if you want a 'good' job you still have to leave at 16 or risk losing out in the competition for the best jobs. Those who wish to enter Higher Education opt for the more academic curriculum, while for those who choose to stay on in Further Education, but are unable to obtain 'A' levels, the range of jobs available is reduced.

For many young people, their limited educational achievement through such programmes makes no significant improvement to their prospects on the labour market (Raffe, 1988). The reason for this is that employers recruiting for jobs in the lower segment pay little attention to formal qualifications. As many of the jobs on offer have a learning time of less than a month, employers are much more concerned with personal attributes than with job specific skills. Given the persistence of existing training and recruitment practices, the introduction of the core curriculum seems unlikely to produce any fundamental change in young people's orientation to school or to lead to a major shift in the size of the proportion who choose to carry on into Further and Higher Education.

In the same way that the education debate has placed the blame on the schools and colleges, the debate on training has focused on the failure of employers. Compared to other industrial societies, Britain in seen to be falling behind in the amount of resources devoted to training, primarily because of employers' failure to invest in it. This situation was exacerbated by the abolition of some of the industrial training boards.

Against this background, YTS became a most significant policy innovation. As an MSC training measure, YTS suffered from the fact that it had its origins in YOP, which was essentially an unemployment measure, and that when it was launched the Government insisted that it had to provide a solution to the problem of school-leaver unemployment (Turbin, 1987). In so far as it keeps young people off the streets for two years, this objective has been achieved, but at a high cost to its objectives as a training measure (Raffe, 1987a). To 'solve' the problem of school-leaver unemployment YTS had to be directed at the less-well-qualified. Moreover, given the resources available, it could only provide the kind of minimal training required for jobs in the lower segment. There was no way in which it could cover the costs of apprenticeship training. All that could be achieved here was to incorporate the first two years of the training period into the scheme. While YTS is an official training scheme, in terms of the 'training problem' identified here, its main achievement has been to produce a more highly trained set of workers for a diminishing number of semi-skilled and unskilled jobs, rather than tackling the more fundamental problem of the lack of more highly qualified workers.

The introduction of YTS as an employer-based scheme was forced on the MSC by a Government intent on operating through the mechanism of the market and reducing the powers of local authorities which were thought to be slow to respond to changes in local labour markets. This resulted in YTS being incorporated into employers' existing selection and recruitment practices. A specified amount of off-the-job training is provided, but little has been done to encourage employers to reassess their practices, particularly in relation to the exclusion of young people from consideration for the majority of job opportunities. Furthermore, it has encouraged the continuance of existing practices which lead to the recruitment of youths at the age of 16, by subsidising them and providing those who leave school at this age with a guaranteed income. In this way one of the unintended consequences of the scheme has been to reinforce the very recruitment practices which play such a large part in encouraging youths to leave school early, thereby fossilising the relationship between the educational and training systems.

Both the educational and training reforms have done little to help solve the problem of an underqualified labour force. By treating education and training as separate, autonomous areas, there has been a failure to see that it is the way in which the two relate to each other which is at the heart of the problem.

In conclusion we would argue that it is time that the problem was reconceptualised. On a theoretical level this means focusing on the interdependence of education, training and industrial relations as specific configurations with their own properties. This is essential if social science is to advance our understanding of the problem. At the most elementary level, it is a precondition for avoiding the kind of mistakes identified above and for the development of more effective policy measures. If our focus is on the interdependence of education and training, we can then devise reforms which will act on the institutional links between the two spheres. Given the training problem we have identified above, this would require breaking the very close link between the age at which basic academic credentials are awarded and the point at which employers recruit people for the jobs in the middle levels of the occupational hierarchy which are the most attractive to 16-year-olds. It may mean changing the age at which the main public examinations are taken, as well as the age at which employers recruit for the more prestigious jobs. This could result in young people having more incentive to stay on at school and enhance their qualifications. They could be further encouraged to stay on by the use of financial incentives. First year YTS trainees may deride their £29.50 weekly allowance, but for some it could still constitute an incentive for leaving school. Together, these initiatives would greatly enlarge the pool of more-qualified labour, while at the same time opening up some of the jobs in the higher segments to working-class youth.

CONCLUSIONS

We embarked upon the research on which much of this book has been based, by asking whether the collapse in the demand for youth labour which occurred in the early 1980s was a product of cyclical or structural change. It rapidly became apparent that such a phrasing of the problem, in 'either/or' terms, was totally inadequte and that both types of change were occurring simultaneously. The labour market was responding to a number of separate sources of change, some of which were producing effects which were contradictory and these in turn were masked by a cyclical downturn. The development of global product markets had been set in train long before 1979, but during the period 1979–84 the impact on the British economy was accelerated by the policies of the Thatcher administration and the effects of the world recession. The result was mass unemployment, with managements seizing the chance to restructure the conditions of labour of those who remained in jobs. During this period the labour movement was caught unawares and had difficulty in producing a co-ordinated response. The consequences for the manufacturing sector were intensified by the introduction of new technology, as those companies which survived attempted to maintain their position in world markets. Similar processes were operating in the financial sector, although these markets were expanding. In large parts of the service sector different processes of change were under way in what were predominantly expanding markets. Yet while the process of the restructuring of the labour force was similar to that in other sectors, the outcome in terms of the type of job created was very different.

One consequence of this restructuring has been an increase in the living standards of many of those who are employed in permanent, full-time jobs. Another has been a reduction in the need for routine, unskilled manual labour to produce manufactured goods and to co-ordinate the flow of information in Banking and Finance. But in parts of the expanding service sector, the consequence has been an increase in the routine manual labour required. Taken together with the restructuring of the labour force in manufacturing and finance, this has produced a rapid growth in the proportion of peripheral or marginal workers. The whole process has been aided and abetted by political initiatives aimed at increasing the role of market forces and reducing the role of the state. The ultimate price of this has been the growth of a large group of sub-employed young adults and long-term unemployed adults, who have carried the costs of change and whose living standards and quality of life has fallen.

The exclusion of large groups from full-time participation in the labour market has its roots in the forms of industrial organisation and labour management relations which are characterised by firms locked into competing in international and national product markets. Although it is not a creation of political action *per se*, the actions of the state have contributed towards its emergence. We have attempted to show some of the ways in which these costs can be avoided or minimised if the political will to do so is present.

The same forces of change have been increasing the demand for more highly qualified labour. Moreover in an age of global markets, the educational level of the national labour force becomes ever more important in determining the location of new capital investment. Transnational companies are unlikely to locate their more advanced plants in societies where the educational level is low. Yet while the underlying trends are creating a demand for more highly qualified labour, the institutional links between the education system and employers' recruitment and training practices are inhibiting its supply. Thus, there is a conflict between the underlying trends in the economy and the institutional structures which regulate the socialisation of the population. Without the introduction of institutional change aimed at resolving this conflict, any economic growth that may be attainable in Britain will be hampered by problems of labour shortages occurring at the same time as the continuation of high levels of long-term unemployment.

NOTES

1. For a discussion of the original function of labour market segments in restricting movement see Ashton (1986).
2. For further evidence of the growth of managerial, scientific and technical workers see Rajan and Pearson (1986), Goldthorpe and Payne (1986).

Bibliography

Ashton, D.N. (1986), *Unemployment under Capitalism: The Sociology of British and American Labour Markets* (Brighton: Wheatsheaf).

Ashton, D.N. (1988), 'Sources of Variation in Labour Market Segmentation: A Comparison of Youth Labour Markets in Canada and Britain', *Work, Employment & Society*, Vol. 2, No. 1, pp. 1–24.

Ashton, D.N. and Field, D. (1976), *Young Workers: The Transition from School to Work* (London: Hutchinson).

Ashton, D.N. and Maguire, M.J. (1980), 'The functions of academic and non-academic criteria in employers' selection strategies', *British Journal of Guidance and Counselling*, 8(2)

Ashton, D.N. and Maguire, M.J. (1983), 'The Vanishing Youth Labour Market' (London: Youthaid).

Ashton, D.N. and Maguire, M.J. (1984), 'Dual labour market theory and the organisation of local labour markets', *International Journal of Social Economics*, vol. II, No. 7, pp. 106–20.

Ashton, D.N., Maguire, M.J. and Garland, V. (1982), *Youth in the Labour Market*, Research Paper No. 34, Department of Employment, London

Ashton, D.N. and Maguire, M.J., with Bowden, D., Dellow, P., Kennedy, S., Stanley, G., Woodhead, G., and Jennings, B. (1986) *Young Adults in the Labour Market*, Research Paper No. 55, Department of Employment, London.

Atkinson, J. (1984), 'Manpower strategies for flexible organisations', *Personnel Management*, August.

Ballance, R. and Sinclair, S. (1983) *Collapse and Survival* (London: Allen & Unwin).

Becker, H.S. and Carper, J.W. (1956), 'The development of identification with an occupation', *American Journal of Sociology*, 61, pp. 289–98.

Bell, C. and Howieson, C. (1988), 'The status of vocational education and training: The case of TVEI', Mimeo. Centre for Educational Sociology/ Department of Education, University of Edinburgh.

Bendix, R. (1963), *Work and Authority in Industry* (New York: Harper & Row).

Blackburn, R.M. (1987), 'The Economics of unemployment: A sociological interpretation', University of Cambridge, Department of Applied Economics, Mimeo.

Blackburn, R.M. and Mann, M. (1979), *The Working Class in the Labour Market* (London: Macmillan).

Blau, P.M. and Duncan, O.D. (1967) *The American Occupational Structure* (New York: Wiley).

Borus, M.E. (1984), *Youth and the Labor Market*, UpJohn, W.C., Institute for Employment Research, Kalamazoo, Michigan.

Breen, R. (1984), 'Status attainment or job attainment? The effects of sex and class on youth unemployment', *British Journal of Sociology*, Vol. 35, pp. 363–86.

Bresnen, M., Wray, K., Bryman, A., Beardsworth, A.D., Ford, J.R. & Keil, E.T. (1985), 'The Flexibility of Recruitment in the Construction Industry: Formalisation or Re-casualisation', *Sociology*, Vol. 19, No. 1, pp. 108–24.

Brown, P. (1987), *Schooling Ordinary Kids: Class Cultures and Unemployment* (London: Tavistock).

Brown, P. and Ashton, D.N. (eds) (1987), *Education, Unemployment and the Labour Market* (Lewes: Falmer).

Cairnes, J.E. (1874), *Some Leading Principles of Political Economy Newly Expanded* (London: Macmillan).

Chandler, A.D. (1977), *The Visible Hand: The Managerial Revolution in American Business* (Mass.: Cambridge).

Chaney, J. (1981), *Social Networks and Job Information: The Situation of Women Who Return to Work*, EOC/SSRC Joint Panel on Equal Opportunities.

Cockburn, C. (1987), *Two Track Training: Sex Inequalities and the YTS* (London: Macmillan).

Coffield, F., Borrill, C. and Marshall, S. (1986), *Growing Up at the Margins* (Milton Keynes: Open University Press).

Corrigan, P. (1979), *Schooling The Smash Street Kids* (London: Macmillan).

Cross, M. (1985), *Towards the Flexible Craftsman* (London: Technical Change Centre).

Dale, A. (1987), 'Occupational inequality, gender and the life cycle,' *Work, Employment and Society*, Vol. 1, No. 3, pp. 326–51.

Dex, S. (1985), *The Sexual Divisions of Work* (Brighton: Harvester).

Dex, S. (1987), *Women's Occupational Mobility: A Lifetime Perspective* (London: Macmillan).

Elias, N. (1956), 'Problems of involvement and detachment', *British Journal of Sociology*, Vol. 7, No. 3, pp. 226–52.

Finn, D. (1983), 'The Youth Training Scheme's a New "Deal"?', *Youth and Policy*, pp. 16–24.

Finn, D. (1987), *Training Without Jobs: New Deals and Broken Promises* (London: Macmillan).

Freedman, M. (1976), *Labor Markets: Segments and Shelters* (New York: Allanheld, Osman).

Freeman, R.B. and Wise, D.A. (eds) (1982), *The Youth Labor Market Problem: Its Nature, Causes and Consequences* (London: Chicago University Press).

Frith, S. (1980), 'Education, training and the labour process', in Cole, M. and Skelton, R. (eds), *Blind Alley: Youth in a Crisis of Capital* (Ormskirk: Hesketh).

Furlong, A.J. (1987), 'Coming to terms with the declining demand for youth labour', Brown, P. & Ashton, D.N. (eds) op. cit.

Furlong, A.J. (1987a), 'The Effects of Youth Unemployment on the Transition from School', PhD Thesis, University of Leicester.

Gardner, P. (1984), *The Lost Elementary Schools of Victorian England*, (London: Croom Helm).

Gaskell, J., (1985), 'Explorations in vocationalism: Through the eyes of high school students', in Mason, G., *Transitions to Work*, Institute for Social and Economic Research, Winnepeg, pp. 206–24.

Gill, C., (1985), *Work, Unemployment and the New Technology* (Cambridge: Polity Press).

Goldthorpe, J.H. and Payne, C. (1986), 'Trends in intergenerational class mobility in England and Wales 1972–1983', *Sociology*, Vol. 20, No. 1, pp. 1–24.

Gordon, D.M., Edwards, R. and Reich, M. (1982), *Segmented work, divided workers: The historical transformation of labour in the United States* (London: Cambridge University Press).

Gray, J., McPherson, A.F. & Raffe, D. (1983), *Reconstructions of Secondary Education: Theory, Myth and Practice Since the War*, (London: Routledge & Kegan Paul).

Griffin, C., (1985), *Typical Girls? Young Women from School to the Job Market* (London: Routledge & Kegan Paul).

Halsey, A.H., Heath, A.F., and Ridge, J.M. (1980), *Origins and Destinations: Family, Class and Education in Modern Britain*, (Oxford: Clarendon Press).

Harris, C.C., (1987), *Redundancy and Recession in South Wales* (Oxford: Blackwell).

Harvey, E.B. and Blakely, J.H. (1985) 'Education, social mobility and the challenge of technological change', in Mason, G. (ed), *Transitions to Work* (Manitoba: Institute for Social and Economic Research).

Heinz, W.L. (1987), 'The transition from school to work in crisis: Coping with threatening unemployment', *Journal of Adolescent Research 2*, pp. 127–41.

Jenkins, R. (1983), *Lads, Citizens and Ordinary Kids* (London: Routledge & Kegan Paul).

Jones, G. (1987), 'Leaving the parental home: An analysis of early housing careers', *Journal of Social Policy*, Vol. 16, No. 1, pp. 49–74.

Junankar, P. and Neale, A. (1987), 'Relative wages and the youth labour market', in Junankar, P. (ed), *From School to Unemployment: The Labour Market for Young People*, (London: Macmillan).

Labour Market Quarterly Report (1987), Sheffield: Manpower Services Commission.

Lash, S. and Urry, J. (1987), *The End of Organised Capitalism*, (Cambridge: Polity Press).

Lawson, T. (1981) 'Paternalism and labour market segmentation theory', in Wilkinson, F. (ed.) *The Dynamics of Labour Market Segmentation* (London: Academic Press).

Layard, R. (1982), 'Youth unemployment in Britain and the U.S. compared', in Freeman, R., and Wise, D. (eds) *The Youth Labour Market Problem* (Chicago: University of Chicago Press).

Lee, D.J., Marsden, D., Hardey, M., and Rickman, P. (1987), 'Youth training, life chances and orientations to work' in Brown, P. and Ashton, D.N. (eds), op. cit.

Lowe, G.S. (1987), *Women in the Administrative Revolution* (Cambridge: Polity Press).

Lynch, L. (1987), 'Individual differences in the youth labour market; a cross-section analysis of London youth', in Junankar, P. (ed.) *From School to Unemployment? The Labour Market for Young People* (London: Macmillan).

Lynch, L. and Richardson, R. (1982), 'Unemployment of young workers in Britain', *British Journal of Industrial Relations*, Vol. 20, pp. 363–72.

McPherson, A. and Willms, J.D. (1987), 'Equalisation and improvement: Some effects of comprehensive reorganisation in Scotland', *Sociology*, 21, pp. 509–39.

Maguire, M.J. and Ashton, D.N. (1981), 'Employers' perception and use of educational qualifications', *Educational Analysis*, 3(2).

Main, B. and Raffe, D. (1983), 'Determinants of employment and unemployment among school-leavers: Evidence from the 1979 survey of Scottish school leavers,' *Scottish Journal of Political Economy*, No. 30, pp. 1–17.

Makeham, P. (1980), *Youth Unemployment*, Research Paper No. 10, Department of Employment, London.

Manwaring, T. and Wood, S. (1984), 'Recruitment and recession', in Beardsworth *et al.* (eds), *Employers and Recruitment: Exploration in Labour Demand*. International Journal of Social Economics, Vol. 11, No. 7, pp. 49–63.

Marsden, D. (1986), *The End of Economic Man* (Brighton: Wheatsheaf).

Martin, J. and Roberts, C. (1984), *Women and Employment: A Lifetime Perspective*, Department of Employment/OPCS (London: HMSO).

Massey, D. and Meegan, R. (1982), *The Anatomy of Job Loss*, (London: Methuen).

Maurice, M., Sellier F. and Silvestre, J. (1986), *The Social Foundations of Industrial Power* (London: MIT Press).

NEDO (1986), *Changing Working Patterns: How Companies Achieve Flexibility to Meet New Needs* (London: NEDO).

Norris, G.M. (1978), 'Unemployment, Subemployment and Personal Characteristics' (a) The Inadequacies of Traditional Approaches to Unemployment, (b) Job Separation and Work Histories: the Alternative Approach, *Sociological Review*, 26, pp. 89–108 and pp. 327–34.

OECD (1985), *The Integration of Women into the Economy* (Paris: OECD)

Osterman, P. (1980), *Getting Started. The Youth Labour Market* (Cambridge, Mass./London: MIT Press).

Pahl, J.M. and Pahl, R.E. (1971), *Managers and Their Wives* (Harmondsworth: Penguin).

Payne, C. and Payne, J. (1985), 'Youth unemployment 1974–1981: the changing importance of age and qualifications', *Quarterly Journal of Social Affairs*, Vol. 1.

Payne, J., (1986), 'Unemployment, apprenticeships and training – Does it pay to stay on at school?' (Oxford: Department of Social and Administrative Studies).

Payne, J., (1987), 'Does unemployment run in families? Some findings from the General Household Survey', *Sociology*, Vol. 21, No. 2, pp. 199–214.

Pollert, A. (1987), 'The "Flexible Firm": A Model in Search of Reality or a Policy in Search of Practice?', Warwick Papers in Industrial Relations, University of Warwick.

Raffe, D. (1984) 'The Transition from School to Work and the Recession: Evidence from the Scottish School Leavers Surveys, 1977–1983', *British Journal of Sociology of Education*, Vol. 5, pp. 247–65.

Raffe, D. (1984a) The Effects of Industrial Change on School Leaver

Employment in Scotland: a Quasi-Shift-Share Analysis, (Edinburgh: Centre for Educational Sociology).

Raffe, D. (1986) 'Change and continuity in the youth labour market: A critical review of structural explanations of youth unemployment', in Allen, S., Watson, A., Purcell, K. and Wood, S. (eds), *The Experience of Unemployment* pp. 45–60 (London: Macmillan).

Raffe, D. (1987), 'Youth unemployment in the United Kingdom', in Brown, P. and Ashton, D.N. (eds) op.cit., pp. 218–47.

Raffe, D. (1987a), 'The context of YTS: An analysis of its strategy and development', *British Journal of Education and Work*, Vol. 1, No. 1, pp. 1–31.

Raffe, D. (1988), 'The Status of Vocational Education and Training 2: The Case of YTS', Mimeo. Centre for Educational Sociology, University of Edinburgh.

Rajan, A. (1984), *New Technology and Employment in Insurance*, Banking & Building Societies, IMS/Gower.

Rajan, A. (1987), *'Services – The Second Industrial Revolution?' Business and Jobs Outlook for UK Growth Industries* (London: Butterworth).

Rajan, A., and Pearson, R. (1986), *U.K. Occupation and Employment Trends to 1990* (London: Butterworth).

Reich, R. (1983), *The Next American Frontier* (New York: Time Books).

Roberts, K. (1984) *School Leavers and Their Prospects* (Milton Keynes: Open University Press).

Roberts, K., Dench, S. and Richardson, D. (1986), *The Changing Structure of Youth Labour Markets*, Research Paper No. 59 (London: Department of Employment).

Roberts, K., Dench, S. and Richardson, D. (1986a), 'Youth Employment in the 1980s', Mimeo, Department of Sociology, University of Liverpool.

Roberts, K., Dench, S. and Richardson, D. (1987), 'Youth Rates of Pay and Employment', in Brown, P. and Ashton, D.N. (eds) op. cit., pp. 198–217.

Rubery, J., Tarling, R. and Wilkinson, F. (1984), 'Labour market segmentation theory: An alternative framework for the analysis of the employment system', Department of Applied Economics, Cambridge. Paper presented at the British Sociological Association Conference, Bradford.

Sapsford, D. (1981), *Labour Market Economics* (London: Allen & Unwin).

Schervish, P.G. (1983), *The Structural Determinants of Unemployment* (New York/London: Academic Press).

Scott, J. (1979), *Corporations, Classes and Capitalism* (London: Hutchinson).

Sengenberger, S. (1988), 'From Segmentation to Flexibility', Discussion Paper No. 5 (Geneva: International Institute for Labour Studies).

Sinfield, A. (1981), *What Unemployment Means* (Oxford: Martin Robertson).

Singleman, (1983) 'The Process of Occupational Change in the United States, 1960–80'. Paper presented to SSRC, Labour Markets Workshop, Manchester.

Slocum, W.L. (1966), *Occupational Careers: A Sociological Perspective.*

Spilerman, S. (1977). 'Careers, labor market structure and socio-economic achievement', *American Journal of Sociology*, 83 (3), pp. 551–93.

Spilsbury, M. (1986), 'Individual Youth Unemployment and the Local Labour Market'. Working Paper 10, Labour Market Studies, University of Leicester.

Spilsbury, M., Maguire, M.J. and Ashton, D.N. (1986), 'The Distribution and Growth of the Self-Employed Using Data from the Labour Force Survey, 1979–84'. Working Paper 12, Labour Market Studies, University of Leicester.

Stern, E. and Turbin, J. (1986), 'Report of a One Year Pilot Study in Four Rural Areas' (London: Development Commission).

Stewart, A., Prandy, K. and Blackburn, R.M. (1980), *Social Stratification and Occupations* (London: Macmillan).

Taylor , M. and Thrift, N. (eds) (1982), *The Geography of Multinationals* (London: Croom Helm).

Therborn, G. (1986), *Why Some People Are More Unemployed Than Others* (London: Verso).

Trinder, C. (1986), *Young People's Employment in Retailing* (London: NEDO).

Turbin, J. (1987), 'State Intervention into the Labour Market for Youth: The Implementation of the Youth Training Scheme in Three Local Labour Markets', PhD Thesis, University of Leicester.

Wallace, C.D. (1987), *For Richer, For Poorer* (London: Tavistock).

Wallace, C.D. (1987a), From generation to generation: The effects of employment and unemployment upon the domestic life cycle of young adults', in Brown, P. and Ashton, D.N. (eds), op. cit. pp. 138–59.

Wells, W. (1983), *The Relative Pay and Employment of Young People*, Research Paper No. 42 (London: Department of Employment).

Westwood, S. (1984), *All Day Every Day* (London: Pluto Press).

Wilkinson, F. (ed.) (1981), *The Dynamics of Labour Market Segmentation* (London/San Francisco: Academic Press).

Willis, P. (1977), *Learning to Labour* (Farnborough: Saxon House).

Youth Review Team (1985) *The Social Conditions of Young People in Wolverhampton in 1984*, Wolverhampton Borough Council, Wolverhampton.

Index